LIBYA

ALISON PARGETER

LIBYA

THE RISE AND FALL OF QADDAFI

YALE UNIVERSITY PRESS
NEW HAVEN AND LONDON

To my children, Alex and Laila

For information about this and other Yale University Press publications, please contact:

U.S. Office: sales.press@yale.edu   yalebooks.com
Europe Office: sales@yaleup.co.uk   www.yalebooks.co.uk

Set in Janson MT by IDSUK (DataConnection) Ltd

Printed in Great Britain by TJ International Ltd, Padstow, Cornwall

Library of Congress Cataloging-in-Publication Data
Pargeter, Alison.
   Libya : the rise and fall of Qaddafi / Alison Pargeter.
      p. cm.
   Includes bibliographical references and index.
   ISBN 978-0-300-13932-7 (cloth : alk. paper)
   1. Qaddafi, Muammar.   2. Qaddafi, Muammar—Influence.
   3. Qaddafi, Muammar—Political and social views.   4. Presidents—Libya—
Biography.   5. Dictators—Libya—Biography.   6. Libya—Politics and
government—1969–   7. Political culture—Libya—History.
   8. Political persecution—Libya—History.   I. Title.
   DT236.Q26P27 2012
   961.204'2092—dc23
   [B]
                                                                                       2012014819
A catalogue record for this book is available from the British Library.

10 9 8 7 6 5 4 3 2 1
2016 2015 2014 2013 2012

Contents

List of Illustrations

Acknowledgements

I would like to thank a number of people who helped make this book possible. Firstly thanks go to my Libyan friends who have given me their help and support over many years, particularly given the difficulties of carrying out research on Libya under the Qaddafi regime. These include Ashur Shamis, Noman Ben Othman, Guma Al-Gumaty, Mohamed Abdelmalek, Alamin Belhaj, Giuma Bukleb, Hassan Al-Lamushe, Hassan Bergali, Amal Obeidi and Mohamed Zahi Mogherbi. I thank them all for their kindness and frankness, and the key insights they have provided. I would like to thank, too, Mohamed Belqassim Zwai and Abdel Ati Al-Obeidi for helping me to secure visas to Libya and for being such willing interviewees. Special thanks go to the late Mohamed Tarnish, the former head of the Libyan Human Rights Association, who sadly passed away in 2011 and who provided me with such valuable assistance during my time in Libya. I would like to thank, too, my editor at Yale, Phoebe Clapham, for her invaluable comments on the manuscript and for her enduring patience.

TUNISIA

Mediterranean Sea

12°   16°   20°   24°

Zuwara
Tripoli
Al-Zawia   Homs Zliten
Yifren   Tarhouna Misarata
Al-Gharyan
Nalut   Zintan   Bani Walid
Jebel Nafusa

Derna
Al-Baida   Tobruk
Benghazi
Jebel Akhdar

TRIPOLITANIA
Sirte
Zuetinah
Ajdabia
Ras Lanuf   Marsa Brega

Ghadames
30°   30°

Hun   Jalu

Sebha

FEZZAN   CYRENAICA
26°   26°
Murzuk

Ghat
Kufra

ALGERIA

E
G
Y
P
T

22°   22°

N I G E R   C H A D

0   100   200   300 Miles
0   300 km

⊗ Airport
⊘ Major port

12°   16°   20°   24°   SUDAN

Libya

Introduction

In February 2011, Libya's little-known eastern capital of Benghazi erupted in a popular uprising. Within a matter of days, the whole of the eastern region had fallen into rebel hands. After almost six months of intense fighting and an international military campaign led by NATO, Tripoli, the capital, also fell. By October, Colonel Muammar Qaddafi, the mercurial leader who had been at the helm of the country for over four decades was found hiding in a stinking sewage pipe, having narrowly escaped a NATO strike on his convoy. The dazed and dishevelled dictator was dragged from his hiding place and subjected to a brutal attack, before being summarily executed by the young rebels who had discovered him. In just eight months, Libyans had succeeded in doing what no one believed they could ever do: they had taken their fate into their own hands and overthrown what was one of the most repressive regimes, even by Middle Eastern standards.

This revolution did not occur in a vacuum. It was inspired and spurred on by the momentous events that were shaking the entire region. The Arab Spring, which started in neighbouring Tunisia and quickly spread to Egypt and beyond, provided Libyans with the extraordinary courage they needed to rise up and change the course of their own history. The reasons why Libyans took to the streets were not difficult to find. The resentments and grievances that had fuelled the revolutions in Tunisia and Egypt were just as present in Libya. Libyans wanted jobs, services and an end to the mafia-like state that had terrorized and humiliated them for decades. They also wanted a future. As one Libyan ruefully commented, 'Under Qaddafi, we Libyans didn't even dare to dream.'[1]

But Libyans had other, more specific reasons to rise up. For forty-two years, their leader, who had taken power in a military coup in 1969, had used Libya as a giant laboratory for his own personal philosophy. Qaddafi had subjected his people to a litany of bizarre whims and half-baked political and economic experiments, which had plunged the country into a permanent state of chaos. Libyans were forced to live their lives by the mantra of his famous *Green Book* – the treatise, published in the mid-1970s, that laid out his political, economic and social vision. This youthful and idealistic vision was based loosely on the principles of Socialism, Arabism and Islam, the three ideas that underpinned his revolution. Indeed, Qaddafi believed himself to be an intellectual, destined for higher things than the 'simple' business of ruling. He was a perpetual revolutionary, a man of action, for whom radical ideals took precedence over building a functioning and economically dynamic state.

Theoretically at least, Qaddafi placed the masses at the heart of his philosophy, arguing that the unique political system he had created – the Jamahiriyah, or 'State of the Masses' – was the very embodiment of 'people power'. In reality, however, Qaddafi created one of the most personalized and authoritarian systems anywhere in the Middle East. He filled every space, moulding the entire country around himself. He believed he *was* Libya – that his fate was inextricably intertwined with that of the land of sand and oil he had come to lead. As far as he was concerned, there was always only ever room for one man in the Jamahiriyah; Libyan society was to be faceless, totally consumed within his eccentric political philosophy.

Qaddafi also displayed an unbridled contempt for the Libyan population, lashing out at them whenever his madcap schemes went wrong, or when they failed to live up to his lofty ideals. To add insult to injury, while he ran one of the most repressive regimes in the region, Qaddafi always maintained that he was nothing more than a guide, a point of reference for his glorious revolution. It was for this reason that he insisted on being called the 'Leader of the Revolution' or just 'Brother Leader', and refuted any suggestion that he was head of state.

But Qaddafi's ambitions went beyond Libya. The Colonel sought to project his revolutionary ideology far and wide, believing his Jamahiriyah to be the pinnacle of human achievement. With his inflated sense of self-importance, the Colonel invested enormous efforts in trying to convince the rest of the world to adopt his unique system. He also sought to turn himself into a world leader, taking on the mantle of champion of the weak against the strong, of the oppressed against the oppressor. It was for this reason that the 'Brother Leader' took to supporting a mind-boggling array of national liberation movements, not only in the Middle East, but also in Africa, Europe and Latin America. The Colonel also gave his backing to a number of terrorist groups, seemingly going out of his way to befriend figures such as Carlos the Jackal (the Venezuelan who achieved notoriety for his 1975 raid on the OPEC headquarters in Vienna, which killed three people) and the infamous Palestinian fighter Abu Nidal, who once boasted: 'I am the evil spirit which moves around only at night causing ... nightmares.'[2]

This unstinting commitment to challenging imperialism wherever it reared its head put the Colonel on a direct collision course with the West, where, for many years, he came to be personified in the international media as a kind of super villain. Descriptions such as 'quixotic', and 'erratic' abounded − to say nothing of the less flattering 'Mad dog of the Middle East', as US President Ronald Reagan once dubbed him. With his overextended sense of flamboyance and showmanship, Qaddafi both repelled and fascinated simultaneously. Yet challenging the West was all part of the Colonel's revolutionary ideology. He had come to power on an anti-imperialist ticket, vowing to rid Libya of the vestiges of a monarchy that had been little more than a 'puppet of the colonialist powers'. As a young man who had come from nowhere, and whose revolution had not been born out of a national liberation struggle, anti-imperialism was a key source of legitimacy for this simple Bedouin from the desert. It also tied in with his unstinting Arab nationalism – a passion that, for all its bitter disappointments, was to endure.

It was this incessant need to challenge the dominant world order that landed the Colonel in very hot water. Not only was the country subjected to an attack by the US in 1986, but Libya was also placed under international sanctions in 1992 for its refusal to hand over the two suspects accused of being behind the bombing of Pan Am Flight 103 over Lockerbie in 1988. The embargo was to plunge the country into further isolation. It also placed greater pressure on the regime, which by this point was struggling against an increasing number of domestic challenges, not least of which was an Islamist insurgency. It was largely as a result of these pressures that Qaddafi decided to temper his ideology with *Realpolitik*. At the end of the 1990s, in a bid to find a way out of isolation, he began trying to restore Libya's tattered relations with the West – a process that started with the agreement in April 1999 to hand the Lockerbie suspects over for trial in The Hague and that culminated in the December 2003 announcement that Libya would abandon its weapons of mass destruction programmes.

So it was that Qaddafi turned his back on his old ways, ditching his support for terrorist groups and doing his best to demonstrate to the outside world that Libya really had changed. This former 'pariah' suddenly found himself with a new collection of friends, all hailing his courageous decision to re-join the international fold as they tripped over each other in the rush to take advantage of the new opportunities opening up in the country's revamped energy sector. The Colonel even hosted British prime minister Tony Blair, and Italian premier Silvio Berlusconi, in his trademark tent.

While no longer deemed a 'super villain', the reformed Qaddafi continued to capture the world's imagination, although more often than not, vilification gave way to ridicule. Rarely was there an article in the Western media that did not comment on the Colonel's appearance or his more idiosyncratic aspects. In August 2009, the US magazine *Vanity Fair* went so far as to run a special tongue-in-cheek piece entitled 'Dictator Chic: Colonel Qaddafi – A life in fashion'.[3] Yet, derision aside, Qaddafi had successfully turned his fortunes around and given his regime a whole new lease of life.

Many Libyans hoped that this return to the international fold would prompt the Colonel to shed some of his revolutionary philosophy and turn the country into something more akin to a conventional state. There were certainly high hopes that he would open up the country's tightly guarded economy. However, Libyans were to be sorely disappointed. While there were some moves towards economic reform, these were few and far between and did little to benefit the masses. The regime's unwillingness in this respect prompted no small degree of resentment among the Libyans, especially since, given its tiny population and vast energy reserves, the country should have been the jewel of North Africa. Indeed, Libyans often remarked bitterly that their country should have resembled Dubai.

Yet as one walked around Tripoli before the revolution, it was clear that this was no Dubai. Despite the fact that foreign investment was once again flooding into the energy sector, there was little real evidence on the ground that the lives of ordinary Libyans had improved much. It is true that, in the years before the February 2011 uprisings, Tripoli had begun to sport shiny new buildings, as well as smart cafés, five-star hotels and private businesses that sat rather incongruously alongside the fading public buildings, dilapidated houses and rubbish-strewn streets. However, this was little more than evidence of a new entrepreneurial elite that was bound tightly to the regime and that was benefiting from the new economic opportunities that rehabilitation had brought. For most Libyans, life had changed very little. The system was as dysfunctional as ever, and, as the rich got richer, most people still struggled to make ends meet.

To make matters worse, those who were benefiting most from the country's new wealth were Qaddafi's own children. His various offspring, who ran roughshod over the population, set about amassing huge personal fortunes in almost every sector. The fingers of one or other of them were in every pie – from energy to the security sector; from health to aviation and maritime transport; from communications to the construction sector. Some of Qaddafi's sons also gained a reputation for bad behaviour. Libyans – known for their social conservatism and traditional outlook – abhorred the stories that emerged in the international media of the Qaddafi boys cavorting with models and Western pop stars at lavish, alcohol-fuelled parties held in exotic locations. Qaddafi's failure to rein in his children was a serious cause of resentment.

Libyans were also angered at the fact that, despite the regime's repeated promises of reform, there was no serious effort to really open up on the political front. While Qaddafi's son Saif Al-Islam engaged in some reform initiatives related to governance and human rights, these were primarily propaganda efforts, carefully crafted to convince the rest of the world that Libya really was changing. Although there was some loosening, and although people were given space to criticize the formal institutions of state, Libyans were still frightened to speak out against the Leader, his family and the upper echelons of the regime. Grim-faced security agents still skulked around corners and uniformity was still the name of the game. It was not by chance that the doors, shutters and window frames of all publicly owned properties were still painted the standard shade of regulation green – the colour of Qaddafi's 1969 revolution.

Moreover, one could never forget who was boss. Garish giant portraits of Qaddafi in various poses still stared out from public buildings, street corners and public spaces. Revolutionary slogans, many of them taken from the *Green Book*, were hung all over Tripoli. The Brother Leader was everywhere, in one guise or another – something that contributed to the city's slightly surreal quality. In fact, the whole atmosphere remained utterly stultified. It was near impossible to get hold of copies of local newspapers, let alone the foreign press, and most of the city's bookshops were stocked with little more than dusty volumes spouting regime propaganda. Internet cafés had sprung up, offering some window to the outside world; but these were carefully monitored by the regime, so that their most common use (for those who could afford it) was for some online flirtation. Although the sanctions had been lifted, Tripoli still seemed somehow introverted and at one remove from the rest of the world.

If things in Tripoli were bad, they were even worse in Benghazi. The Leader, who was always suspicious of the east (not least because it was where the country's monarchy had sprung from), developed a particular antipathy towards the eastern regions, after they were the centre of an Islamist uprising in the mid-1990s. Benghazi was made to pay for its rebellious streak, and the city was put under siege. What followed was years of neglect, leading the city's inhabitants to feel as though they were being treated as second-class citizens. Prior to the 2011 uprisings, Benghazi already resembled a kind of post-conflict zone. Buildings in the desolate city centre were simply left to crumble, and some of its streets were littered with rubbish and piles of rubble. The main lake, where families went to picnic, had untreated human waste pumped straight into it, so that the surrounding air was heavy with the stench of sewage. The housing shortage was so acute that, in some of the poorest districts, entire extended families were crammed into falling-down apartment blocks, the countless satellite dishes on the roofs the only testimony to any connection with the outside world. It is hardly surprising that a surly resentment and suspicion could be read on the faces of some of Benghazi's inhabitants.

It is easy to understand, therefore, why the 2011 revolution began in the east. The region had long been restless, and the Arab Spring was simply the spark that ignited the fire. Yet even so, Libya's revolution still came as a surprise. Even the most seasoned of Libya-watchers were stunned that the Libyans were finally able to shake off the fear and to rise up en masse. But this sense of shock was in part testimony to the fact that Qaddafi and his repressive security apparatus had always seemed so all-encompassing. It was somehow inconceivable that the multi-layered security apparatus that Qaddafi had employed so effectively against the country's six million people for so many years would not be able to force the Libyans back into submission. In fact, this judgement was not too far off the mark. Had NATO not entered the conflict when it did, it is likely that the rebel forces would not have been able to dislodge Qaddafi from the west of the country and would not have prevented him from re-taking the east.

Yet this shock was also related to the fact that the Colonel had succeeded in creating such a cult of personality around himself, and had survived so many previous challenges, that he had taken on a quasi-immortal aspect. For many, Libya without Qaddafi was almost unthinkable. Thus Libya's revolution was all the more remarkable and brought an end not only to a regime, but to a dictator who presided over what was surely one of the strangest experiments in political history.

This book is an attempt to chart the rise and fall of Muammar Qaddafi and his regime. It traces the origins of the young idealist and his 1969 revolution and follows the Colonel through the early years of his rule, when he was at his most experimental. It looks at the 1980s, when Qaddafi carved out his reputation as an international pariah, and then chronicles the crises of the 1990s, when his revolutionary ardour came back to haunt him in the spectre of international sanctions, an Islamist rebellion and an increasingly restless population that had become utterly disengaged from his radical ideals. The book also tells how the regime pulled itself out of these crises and succeeded in securing its rehabilitation within the international community in 2003. It shows, too, how the opportunities provided by this rehabilitation were squandered in the period that led up to the 2011 uprisings, not least by members of Qaddafi's own family. And finally, it recounts the story of the 2011 revolution and looks at the challenges facing Libya's new leaders as they try to rebuild the country.

Drawing on my years of research on Libya, my visits to the country, the interviews I have carried out with Libyans from all walks of life and the conversations I have had with Libyan friends over countless cups of coffee, this book is an attempt to tell the story of a man and of a country. It is a bid to explain how a simple Bedouin from the desert came from nowhere and almost single-handedly put an entire nation at his service. It examines the tools he used to transform the country into the outward expression of his youthful ideals, and it explores how he ceaselessly adapted his revolution to ensure that everything stayed the same. It also explains why the events of 2011 unfolded in the way they did, showing how the brutality of the final struggle was a direct result of the extremity of four decades of Qaddafism. It explains, too, why Qaddafi's legacy will cast long shadows over Libya for many decades to come.

CHAPTER 1

Land of the Conquered

Writing in 1934, Italian colonial civil servant Angelo Piccioli described his first sighting of Tripoli as he approached by steam boat across the Mediterranean:

> Today as we came to this white town crowned with palms and girdled with serenity, as we gazed at Tripoli rising from the sea among the light mists of morning, our hearts were filled with a strange joy, confident and thoughtful … Bright, solemn and silent stood the ancient uncouth city; time here seems to have stopped, and the city keeps intact its Islamic, medieval soul. It looked as though it were suspended in an airy domain of its own, like a block of carved marble between the twin brilliance and immensity of sky and sea.[1]

Anyone making the same approach to Libya's capital city today would be greeted by a rather different sight. Modern-day Tripoli boasts a large and bustling industrial port, a perilously busy motorway that runs along the seafront, and a somewhat unprepossessing strip of reclaimed land that separates the city from the sea. Indeed, the view of the old city, rising up from the water, is marred by these testimonies to the progress of the Libyan revolution of 1969. Moreover, Tripoli has sprawled out far beyond its old city, and even beyond the colonnaded, tree-lined streets of its Italian-built centre. Tripoli's suburbs, some comprising street after street of well-to-do villas and others packed with concrete high-rise government housing projects, now extend so far that they are beginning to merge with other towns along the coast. The city centre also now boasts a hotch-potch of gleaming new office blocks and towering five-star hotels.

Yet beyond this evidence of the modern Libyan state, Tripoli's old city retains some of the characteristics Piccioli describes. Under the intense Mediterranean sun, its white buildings and minarets still rise up in sharp contrast to the piercing blue of the sea and the sky. There is an eerie quietness about the old town, or medina, at certain times of the day, when the burning heat forces its residents inside. Time really does seem to be standing still, particularly in the sand-covered alleyways and unspoilt *souqs* (enclosed markets) where men still beat copper by hand and where gold is still weighed out on old-fashioned scales.

Yet the medina, with its faded charm, has not escaped all the trappings of the modern world. Young men, with their rap music and smart training shoes, hunch up against the walls, staving off the boredom of having nothing to do. There is also the modern, Italian-style café, serving lattes and cappuccinos on its smart terrace, as well as a handful of touristic restaurants and hotels – reminders of the Qaddafi regime's last few concessions to the Western world. Prior to the 2011 revolution, some quarters of the old city were inhabited almost entirely by African immigrants, unable to afford the rents elsewhere in the capital. It was the sound of West African beats, rather than Arabic pop music, that belted out of barber-shop door-ways along the narrowest alleyways and the most run-down parts of the old city. Most of these immigrants, along with those from other parts of the Arab world, fled as soon as the 2011 conflict broke out, leaving Tripoli and its inhabitants to their fate.

Yet Libya is about more than Tripoli. It is a vast land covering 1.7 million square kilometres, most of which is desert. There are no rivers and it rains rarely and sporadically, making much of the land unsuitable for cultivation. Prior to the discovery of oil in the 1950s, pastoralists and nomads in much of the country eked out a living as best they could from the unyielding dry land. Before the country struck 'black gold', it was one of the poorest nations in the world. Because of the harsh landscape, Libya's main population centres are located on the coast, in two main clusters on the west and the east of the country. But these centres are separated by huge expanses of empty desert. There is no railway connecting the cities of the west and the cities of the east, and not even a motorway joins these two main population centres; unless time is no object, the only way to travel between the two is by air.

This lack of connectivity between the two centres reflects one of the defining characteristics that have shaped the country. Libya has always been a land of three distinct parts, each with its own partic- ular identity. There is Tripolitania in the west, which includes Tripoli and other towns such as Al-Zawia, Misarata and Tajoura; Cyrenaica in the east, which comprises the regional capital of Benghazi, as well as smaller towns such as Derna, Al-Baida and Tobruq; and the largely desert area of the Fezzan in the south, whose main town is Sebha.

That these three regions continue to have their own sense of identity is hardly surprising. Libya only came together as a country in the 1950s, at the time of independence from colonial rule. Even that coming together was an accident of history. Libya was a child born of the machinations of the victorious Allied powers, as they readjusted to the new realities of the post-Second World War world. Yet even after the country united under a single flag, it still struggled to overcome regional differences. While these divisions have less-ened in recent decades, largely as a result of rapid urbanization and the modernization that accompanied it, they have not disappeared altogether. Libya's history has, then, always been a story of regions.

The east, known for its tightly preserved tribal structures, has always had its face half turned towards Egypt, in part because many eastern Libyan tribes extend across the border into the deserts of its neighbour. Despite Benghazi's being a port, the city – and the east more generally – has remained somehow closed off from the outside world, and its inhabitants have a reputation for being more tradi-tional and socially conservative than their western counterparts. This may be something of a fallacy, as urbanization touched the east as much as it did the west. However, the remnants of tribalism, and the traditions that go with it, are still more deeply ingrained in the east. Tripolitania, meanwhile, has its face turned firmly towards the Mediterranean, and its encounters with the various peoples that have come from there, either as conquerors or as traders, seem to have left a legacy of a more open people. Tripolitanians or *Tarabulseen*, as they are known in Arabic, are proud of what they consider to be their more worldly take on life; the city is certainly more cosmo-politan than its eastern counterpart, which sometimes feels as though it is a place that time forgot.

The Fezzan, on the other hand, is Libya's overlooked region. It is so sparsely populated and so far from the main cities of the coast that it somehow never generates the same interest as its northern coun-terparts. Yet Fezzan is the Libya of the desert, of caravans and of the Tuareg and the Toubu – nomadic peoples whose tribes straddle the borders with Mali and Niger, and with Chad, respectively.

Yet in spite of themselves, these three regions came together to form the history of what we know today as Libya, a term first used by the Ancient Greeks to denote all of North Africa west of Egypt. It is, first and foremost, a history of invasion: a story of successive civilizations forcing themselves on this arid, empty land of Berbers – the indigenous inhabitants of North Africa. Invasion has been such a feature of Libya's experience that in one of his memoirs Qaddafi recounts how, when he was growing up, men feared the sea, refusing to settle near it, because of the conquerors it might bring on its waves.[2]

Yet what these conquerors had in common was that they nearly all struggled to impose themselves beyond the coastal areas, failing to tame the tribal hinterlands whose tough inhabitants refused to submit to the will of successive colonial administrations. In many ways, this failure only reinforced the sense of regionalism already created by geographical boundaries. It was also accentuated by the fact that, at many points in Libya's history, one set of colonizers ruled over the west of the country, while another controlled the east.

All of these factors meant that, when Qaddafi came to power in 1969, Libya had still not managed to develop any real sense of unity or nationhood; this left him an almost empty playing field upon which to impose his own unorthodox brand of nationhood.

Early conquerors

Libya is a country that wears its history on its sleeve. Not only can visitors to the country amble along colonnaded, Italian-built streets, but they can also marvel at ancient Greek temples, breathtaking Roman archaeological sites and exquisite Ottoman mosques and houses. Indeed, the country boasts some of the most magnificent archaeological remains anywhere in the Mediterranean. Many of these relics are the legacy of the Ancient Greeks, who, fleeing drought in their native Thera (Santorini), conquered eastern Libya in 630 BC. The Greeks founded Cyrene – from which the name Cyrenaica is derived – a place that became one of the most renowned intellectual and artistic centres of its day.

For all their power, the Greeks were never able to expand down into the deserts of the Fezzan that were controlled by the famed Garamantes – a tribe of either Berber or Tuareg origin. Greek historian Herodotus describes the Garamantes in his famous *Histories*: 'to the south of this region ... that is teeming with wild animals, are the Garamantes, who shun all human intercourse and contact'.[3] Herodotus also tells of his encounters with other Libyan nomadic tribes and of their curious practices. Many of these tribes used to cauterize the veins on the top of their children's heads with hot grease, which they extracted from sheep's wool. This was done to prevent the children from coming to harm from the 'down flow of phlegm from the head'.[4] If the children went into convulsions during this procedure, they would be cured by having goat's urine sprinkled on them. Such practices led Herodotus to describe the Libyans as 'the healthiest people in the known world'.[5]

The Greeks were followed by the Romans, whose main settlements were at Leptis Magna, Sabratha and Oea – the three towns from which Tripoli takes its name (from the Ancient Greek *tri polis*, literally 'three cities'). These settlements became thriving Roman centres, which supplied wheat, barley and olive oil to Rome. Although they were unable to conquer the Garamantes in the south, in 74 BC the Romans did extend their empire from Tripolitania into Cyrenaica, uniting the two regions politically for the first time. However, this union was short-lived and the two areas separated again when the Roman Empire split in two, with Tripolitania being run from Rome and Cyrenaica coming under the control of the Byzantine Empire.

The Romans were eventually pushed out of Libya by the Vandals, a Germanic tribe that arrived in AD 429 and that wreaked havoc on the local landscape, until it was usurped by the equally unpopular Byzantines around a hundred years later. However, like the Greeks, the Romans left behind some remarkable archaeological sites that remain astonishingly intact to this very day. Walking around the magnificent amphitheatres, bath houses and mosaics of Leptis Magna and Sabratha, set against the sparkling backdrop of the Mediterranean Sea, it is easy to imagine oneself back in the bustle of a prosperous Roman centre. The Roman presence can also be felt in Tripoli, where the imposing Marcus Aurelius Arch still stands proud, and where ancient Roman columns have been built into some of the dwellings in the old medina.

Yet while these wonders of the ancient world enthral the handful of tourists who make it to the country, many Libyans today feel little connection to them. It is as if, by their non-Islamic heritage, these testimonies to Libya's past are not really part of the country's history or soul. They are viewed as part of the European world and something that is alien to the country's identity. A former tourism minister, Ammar Mabrouk Al-Lateef, used to describe the Roman remains as 'Christian tourism', and one piece of graffiti carved into the amphitheatre at the stunning Sabratha site goes so far as to proclaim: 'See what befell the idol-worshippers!'

The Romans failed, then, to leave any really lasting impression on the native population, and it was the Arab forces, which came in two waves in the seventh and the eleventh centuries, that were to completely alter the complexion of what we now call Libya. These forces, the first group of which crossed into Cyrenaica from Arabia in 642, were a hardy lot. Made up mainly of poor, illiterate Bedouins, they made their way westward, meeting with little resistance until they reached Tripolitania. It was here that they came up against the fierce Berber tribes of the mountains. One of the best-known Berber resisters during this period was the queen and prophetess, Dahlia, who is still lauded by the Berbers today for having fought so hard to repel the Arabs. Legend has it that the imposing Dahlia sent her tribe to destroy local towns, cut down trees and burn down woods to ensure that there were no spoils for the Arab armies to loot and no cities for them to take over. However, Dahlia ultimately proved no match for the new conquerors, who took Tripolitania and who even went on to triumph over Gerama, the Garamantes capital in the south, in 663.

Yet it was not only physically that the Arabs succeeded where earlier invaders had failed. These new conquerors brought Islam with them – something that was to have a lasting effect on the whole of North Africa. The indigenous Berbers absorbed this new faith with surprising willingness and speed. That is not to say that there was no resistance to the invaders themselves: although the vast majority of local inhabitants readily converted to Islam, many were still resentful of the Arab newcomers and their bid to subjugate the locals. The Arabs insisted, for example, on still taking *jiziya* (a tax paid by non-Muslims living in an Islamic state) from those Berbers who had converted to Islam – on the grounds that their new faith was not heartfelt!

In the eleventh century, a second, much larger wave of Arab conquerors arrived and spread across Libya, altering the ethnic complexion of all three regions. These new arrivals, who were from the Bani Salim and Bani Hilal tribes, had originated in Najd in the Arabian Peninsula, but had settled in Egypt until they were forced out following a famine. This was no small-scale affair: thousands of tribesmen, accompanied by their families and flocks, flooded into the sparsely populated Cyrenaica and beyond. The Bani Hilal moved primarily into Tripolitania, while the Bani Salim settled in the east. These tribes, and the Bani Hilal in particular, behaved like most invading forces: they seized land and water resources for themselves and turned many Berbers (as well as Arab tribes from the earlier invasion) into their clients and vassals.[6] They also mixed and inter-married with the Berbers, resulting in the almost total Arabization of what we now call Libya. This was particularly the case in the east, which is one of the most ethnically and religiously homogeneous regions in North Africa today.

It is not clear exactly why these Arab invaders succeeded where others failed. However, the lack of resistance may well have been related to the shared Bedouin culture and lifestyle, and to the fact that both Berber and Arabs practised nomadism as a means of social organization.[7] What is clear, however, is that, despite the stream of foreign occupiers with their different cultures and religions, it was the Arabs who were able to put a truly lasting stamp on the local population. Arab identity remains strongest for Libyans today and in spite of repeated attempts by Colonel Qaddafi at the end of the 1990s to foster a sense of African identity among the Libyan population, Libyans remain resolutely proud of their Arab and Islamic heritage.

The Ottomans

The next group of conquerors who were to have a lasting presence were the Ottomans, who seized the port of Tripoli in 1551, and whose rule was to endure until the early twentieth century.[8] Yet while their presence may have been lengthy, like most of their predecessors the Ottomans were never able to fully subjugate the whole of the territory. Successive Ottoman rulers struggled to bring the recalcitrant tribes of the hinterland, especially those in the east, under their control. This was particularly true during the first two hundred years of Ottoman rule, when Tripoli was governed by a Turkish *bey*, who answered directly to his masters in Constantinople. During this time, Ottoman control was restricted mostly to the coastal towns, and there were only 'occasional and half-hearted forays into the hinterland to collect taxes'.[9]

Constantinople's attitude towards its territories at this time was to give them ample freedom to conduct their own affairs. This somewhat laissez-faire approach meant that there was no major objection on the sultan's part when, in 1711, an upstart Ottoman military officer, Ali Pasha Qaramanli, seized control of Tripoli and established his own dynasty. Yet for all their efforts, the Qaramanlis were not much better at bringing the unruly tribes under their control. Although they succeeded in extending their rule eastwards, beyond Tripolitania and into Cyrenaica, aside from in the coastal cities, where urban dwellers were forced to pay taxes, they had little real impact on the locals or on the Bedouin tribal structures that still held firm. They also failed, for a long period, to make any real inroads into the Fezzan, where an independent trading state called Awlad Mohamed had been founded by a Sharifan (one who claims descent from the Prophet) who came from Fes in Morocco.

The Qaramanli period was a turbulent one and was characterized by bloodshed. This bloodletting was not only prompted by the dynasty's bid to bring the rebellious tribes under its control, but was also a result of its own internal squabbles, as various family members vied for power. When Ali Pasha Qaramanli fell ill, for example, one of his sons was so intent on taking over that he killed his brother in cold blood in his mother's quarters. This episode led to civil war in Tripolitania.

By the 1830s, the twists and turns of the Qaramanli dynasty were becoming too much for Constantinople. The continued instability was all the more worrying for the Imperial Palace, which was also fretting about European expansion in North Africa. As a result, Sultan Mahmoud II decided it was time to reassert authority over Tripoli and moved to establish direct rule over the territory once again. Given what was at stake, this time around the Ottomans were determined to subjugate the entire population. They launched three major campaigns to extend their control over Tripolitania, Cyrenaica and Fezzan. Yet despite these efforts and the tiny population size,[10] it still took them more than twenty years of bloody conflict against rebellious tribes to bring western Libya and the Fezzan under their rule. Cyrenaica meanwhile remained largely out of reach.

The Ottoman failure to penetrate Cyrenaica was due in part to a formidable presence that had developed in the eastern regions. This was the famed Sanussiya – a Sunni Sufist religious order that shaped the evolution of the east of the country in the most profound of ways. This order was first founded in Mecca in the early nineteenth century by the scholar Sayed Mohamed Ali Al-Sanussi, known as the Grand Sanussi, who originated from Mostaganem in present-day Algeria. After Al-Sanussi was forced out of the Hijaz (in the west of what is now Saudi Arabia), he settled in Cyrenaica, establishing his first religious *zawiya* (lodge) in the eastern coastal city of Al-Baida in 1843.

The Sanussiya followed a strict religious doctrine that sought to reform and purify Islam. They rejected the more folkloric types of the faith that were popular at the time, looking down on the 'vulgar' use of processions, music and piercings of the flesh that were some-times used by other orders to get closer to God.[11] Such carryings on were not uncommon at that time. Piccioli vividly describes a ghoulish scene he witnessed in the *zawiya* of Saint Sidi Husain Hamza, where, to the accompaniment of fierce rhythms beaten out on drums and tambourines, an old cripple, intoxicated with devo-tion, proceeded to cut himself in the stomach with a dagger several times before seemingly slitting his throat. Piccioli also recounts how 'Other fanatics were rocking themselves; some were swallowing keys, others live scorpions, others bits of broken glass. The whole of that gloomy arcade was filled with the same fever of blood and pain.'[12] It was exactly these kinds of grisly and theatrical practices that the Sanussiya shunned, preferring a more sober, orthodox approach that focused on the original teachings of the Prophet.

The Sanussiya doctrine was particularly well received by the illiterate Bedouin of Cyrenaica, who were described by one observer as 'an undemonstrative people'; it was difficult to imagine them 'piercing their cheeks with skewers, eating glass or swaying into convulsions'.[13] Yet their receptiveness was driven not so much by an attraction to the theological arguments of the order, as by its simple message, which sought to strip Islam back to basics, and by the charisma of its pious leader, who claimed descent from the Prophet Mohamed. Aside from the educated elite who actually lived in the lodges, most Bedouin who followed the Sanussiya had only the slightest knowledge of the brotherhood's religious teachings. Its simple adherents rarely knew any of the special prayers or litanies – their use of such things was restricted to having a scribe write the words on paper, to be sewn up in leather and tied to their bodies for protection.[14]

The success of the Sanussi order in Cyrenaica was also down to the fact that the region had a strong tribal system. The order was able to capitalize on this great social organizer, coordinating its lodges with existing tribal structures and creating alliances with tribal leaders.[15] This also enabled the order to benefit from the fact that there was close interrelation between tribal power and control of the trade routes across the Sahara from Central Africa to the Cyrenaican coast and Egypt.[16] In this way, the Sanussiya came to control much of the trade in the area and beyond, enabling the order to spread far and wide. By the late 1880s, it had extended not only throughout Cyrenaica (excluding the urban areas) and into the deserts of western Egypt, but also down into Chad, Niger, Nigeria and Sudan. Interestingly, the order failed to really take hold in the more cosmopolitan Tripolitania, especially near the coast, where it had to compete with other urban-based religious orders.

Thus the Sanussiya became not only the dominant religious force, but also the most important political force in Cyrenaica. The order acted as a kind of independent state, which at the peak of its power provided security, education and justice to the entire region. As a result, the east evolved into a kind of self-contained unit, where tribalism and Islam – both still defining features of the region today – were preserved.

Given the order's immense power, the Ottomans ultimately concluded that the best approach was to work with the Sanussiya, rather than against it. They therefore allowed the order in the hinterland to operate more or less independently, agreeing to award it suzerainty status within the empire – something that gave it tax-exempt status. Meanwhile, they focused their efforts on securing Tripolitania and the Fezzan, bringing some newfound order and security to the western and southern regions. This new sense of order had a major impact: trade began to flourish, settlements began to be established in rural areas, and there was greater urbanization in the northern regions. From the mid- to late nineteenth century, these areas were sufficiently secure for the Ottomans to begin instituting some of the administrative reforms they were introducing to other parts of their empire. By the early 1880s, the Ottomans had introduced a relatively comprehensive administration in Tripoli, and education and commerce were beginning to blossom. These changes created a new urban elite, many of whom joined the Ottoman administration.

Tripoli changed even more dramatically with the emergence of the Young Turks movement in the Ottoman Empire in the early twentieth century. This modernist and progressive movement opposed the sultan's regime and demanded more extensive reforms. There were plenty of these Young Turks in Tripoli. The city had become something of a centre of Turkish dissidence, after Constantinople had taken to banishing troublesome officials there as a kind of hardship post, hoping it might knock some of the rebellious spirit out of them. A number of local young, upwardly mobile men began to imitate these young Turkish rebels and, despite the traditionally conservative nature of society, began to drink alcohol and to talk politics. Newspapers also appeared at this time, as did new courts and proper postal services. The changes were so great that one European visitor to Tripolitania in 1907 remarked: 'during the last twenty years the capital of Tripolitania had been enriched by a whole series of institutions concerning justice, finances, commerce, public education, and even hygiene and public assistance: One thinks oneself at first glance in an important European centre.'[17]

However, beyond these urban developments, during all their centuries of rule the Ottomans were never able to unify the three distinct provinces of Tripolitania, Cyrenaica and Fezzan, and never succeeded in creating a common identity among the people they governed. Moreover, just as these urban developments were advancing, Libya was to experience its next colonial invasion: the arrival of the Italians in 1911 was to change the course of Libya's history in the most dramatic of fashions.

The Italians

Italy's bid to conquer Libya was a reflection of its own changing circumstances. Following Italian unification in 1861, Rome sought to emulate its European counterparts, who were deep in the throes of imperial expansion, by acquiring some colonial possessions of its own. Given that Tripolitania, Cyrenaica and the Fezzan were the only provinces in North Africa to have escaped European colonial advances at this time, they were the obvious targets for Rome's new colonial ambitions. Italy began by establishing an economic presence in Tripolitania and Cyrenaica, opening branches of the Banco di Roma in Tripoli, Benghazi and other key cities, and investing in local agriculture, light industry, mineral prospecting and shipping.[18]

In 1911, however, the Italians embarked upon a full-scale military invasion. They were able to occupy the coastal cities of Tripoli, Benghazi, Derna, Homs and Tobruq easily enough. But, like so many before them, the Italians found themselves unable to expand beyond the coast. The somewhat 'green' Italian forces were shocked to find themselves up against fierce resistance from a number of

Ottoman garrisons, which were supported by local volunteers who may not have had any particular love for the Turks, but who preferred to support a fellow Muslim power against an invading Christian force. However, the Ottomans were not what they used to be. With their empire weakening, they concluded that their best bet would be to sign a secret treaty with the Italians. This accord, signed in October 1912, gave Rome nominal control of Tripolitania and Cyrenaica, while the Ottomans retained residual rights, including the supervision of religious affairs.

The fact that these two colonizing forces had cut such a deal was stupefying to the locals, who, when they discovered what had happened, felt utterly abandoned by the Turks. Determined not to give any more ground to these foreign invaders, the local inhabitants fought back. This was particularly the case in Cyrenaica, where the Sanussi Order, now led by Ahmed Al-Sharif Al-Sanussi, the grandson of the order's founder, led the resistance. Groups of hardy tribal fighters holed themselves up in the eastern mountains and waged a guerrilla campaign against the Italian forces. They were not unsuccessful. Although the Italians pushed hard into Cyrenaica in 1913, and took a number of coastal towns, like so many of their predecessors they were unable to penetrate into the deserts below.[19] Indeed, despite their ambitions, the Italians were essentially left with just the coastal strip to call their own.

Yet it was not only the locals' determination to defend their land that prevented the Italians from expanding their presence beyond these coastal areas. In May 1915, Italy entered the First World War, and this forced the country to redirect its military energies elsewhere. Rome was also experiencing growing economic and political challenges at home, which meant that it simply did not have the resources to pursue its colonial ambitions in North Africa. As a result, less than a decade after it had embarked upon its colonial adventure, Italy was forced to scale down its presence in Libya. In

1919 it issued the Legge Fondamentale – laws under which Tripolitania and Cyrenaica were granted their own parliaments and governing councils. The following year it awarded Idris Al-Sanussi, head of the Sanussi Order since 1916, the position of Emir of Cyrenaica, enabling him to administer a number of oases autonomously. This appointment was to have important implications for the future of Cyrenaica, essentially legitimizing the Emirate of Cyrenaica as a virtually autonomous region led by the Sanussiya.[20]

Italy's granting of autonomy to the east was not lost on the Tripolitanians, who wanted to secure a similar deal for themselves. In 1922, they made a formal request that Idris Al-Sanussi extend his emirship into the western region. However, by then it was too late. Rome had appointed a new governor in Tripolitania, the hardnosed Giuseppe Volpi. Volpi introduced martial law, annulled the Legge Fondamentale, and set about reconquering the province for the glory of Italy. His efforts were to be given a major boost in October 1922, when a Fascist government came to power in Rome. Fascist leader Benito Mussolini, who was determined to turn his back on the woolly policies of Italy's previous liberal governments, sought to amplify Italy's role as an imperial power. He therefore reinvigorated Italy's assault on Libya and made it clear that this time around there would be no half-hearted attempt at subjugation.

Yet for all their zeal, it still took the Fascists nine years to bring the whole of the territory under their control. Once again, the east proved the hardest challenge. With the support of the local population, the tribal fighters continued the resistance from their hideouts in the rugged Jebel Akhdar (Green Mountains) of Cyrenaica. They were led by Omar Al-Mukhtar, a Sanussi sheikh and Qu'ranic teacher, who hailed from Janzour near Tobruq on the eastern coast, and who was a master of guerrilla tactics. It was Al-Mukhtar's skill and steadfastness which meant that the guerrilla fighters, who were greatly outnumbered by the Fascist forces, were able to stave off Italian domination for almost a decade.

The Italians responded to such determined resistance with a ruthlessness and brutality that was shocking even by the standards of the time. They engaged in savage campaigns of repression, killing fighters (as well as suspected rebels and civilians) with what can only be described as detached abandon. According to certain reports, some 12,000 Cyrenaicans were executed during 1930 alone, and a similar number the following year.[21] Indeed, the gallows were a regular feature of life during the nine-year struggle. Such was the ideological vigour behind the campaign that the Fascists went so far as to make postcards depicting Libyans being hanged; they would exchange these 'keepsakes' on special occasions. There were horror stories, too, of rebels being dropped from aeroplanes.

The Italians knew that the key to defeating the stubborn east was to isolate the fighters from their supply lines and from the local population that was giving them support. They therefore built a 300km fence along the Egyptian border to cut off supplies, sealed wells and confiscated herds. They also rounded up two-thirds of the civilian population of eastern Libya and deported them to concentration camps, thus depriving the resistance of its social base.[22] Thousands of men, women and children were forced to walk hundreds of kilometres to these camps in the harsh winter of 1929, many of them dropping dead from illness or exhaustion along the way.

Such tactics eventually proved too much for even the most resilient of guerrilla fighters. In September 1931, Omar Al-Mukhtar was finally ambushed, put on trial and publicly hanged in the Suluq concentration camp. The seventy-year-old Al-Mukhtar's last words were the Qu'ranic phrase often used at time of death: 'To God we belong and to Him we shall return.'

After Al-Mukhtar's death, Rome officially proclaimed the pacification of Libya and set about trying to turn the North African territory into an extension of Italy. In the spirit of Fascist civilization building, the Italians established large-scale agricultural and land-reclamation projects. Italian settler families were shipped en masse to Libya, where they were given small farms to work under special subsidized schemes. In 1938 alone, some 20,000 Italians, mostly peasants, were settled on specially prepared farms in Tripolitania and Cyrenaica.[23] A further 12,000 followed the next year. The Italians also hired Libyan labour to work on these schemes. Italy went about building infrastructure, too. As one British observer wrote in 1942, 'The building, town-planning and sanitary activities of the Italians have been remarkable.'[24] The whitewashed, tree-lined, arcaded boulevards in the centre of Tripoli are testimony to these acts of Fascist town planning.

With Libya now considered Italy's fourth shore, the native inhabitants found themselves completely pushed aside, as the colonizers enjoyed the pleasures they had created out of this Mediterranean heap of sand. Indeed, the Fascists rejected Rome's earlier policy of collaborating with local elites, regarding the locals as little more than a pool of manpower that could be used to build what was officially declared in 1939 to be the nineteenth region of Italy. They permitted Libyans to be educated to elementary level only, and much of this education entailed 'civilizing' the 'savages' by teaching them Italian values. However, Mussolini did make some concessions to popular sentiment. In a deeply misplaced bid to counter the growing feelings of anti-Italianism, at a special ceremony in Tripoli in 1937, Il Provolone (the nickname for Mussolini, who, it was deemed, resembled the round Italian cheese of the same name) declared himself to be 'The Protector of Islam'. At this event, the Fascist leader was presented with the 'Sword of Islam' (which, according to accounts of the time, had been manufactured in Tuscany and engraved by Libyan Jewish goldsmiths!). One historian wrote in 1941: 'Having purchased "The Sword of Islam" as near to home as Florence ... the Duce presented it to himself with grotesque solemnity.'[25]

Libyans thus became like shadows in their own land. The famed British adventurist Freya Stark captures some of this feeling as she recounts her experiences in Benghazi under Italian rule:

> Something was missing and I noticed that it was the raucous Arab voice of the Levant. The crowds moved in a silence that sounded European to anyone familiar with the East ... I began to feel a quagmire beneath this gay little town, a deadening substratum of fear. 'There must be Arabs somewhere,' I thought and spent what remained of the daylight trying to find them; and did eventually, in a little ghetto of squalid streets far back from the sea. A throttled horror made me wish never to visit Benghazi again.[26]

It is hardly surprising, therefore, that this brutal period in Libya's history is still deeply ingrained in the Libyan psyche. Tales of resistance by locals against Italian forces continue to be common currency in what is essentially an oral culture. The strength of such sentiment should not be underestimated. The father of Ali Attia Mohamed Bujafool Zwai, a young Libyan from Benghazi who joined the jihad against US and British forces in Iraq in 2006, recounted how his son had been brought up on his grandmother's stories of resistance to the Italians. The young man's grandmother had repeatedly stressed that, while some members of the family's tribe had been killed in the struggle against the Italian colonizers, his father's particular branch had not produced any 'martyr' of its own. Desperate to redeem his family's honour, the young man determined to martyr himself in Iraq.

Given the depth of feeling about this era, it is not surprising that Omar Al-Mukhtar is still held up as the country's greatest national icon, especially in the east. For many Libyans, the resistance leader symbolizes honour, strength and pride. Such is his aura that Qaddafi, who was himself brought up on stories of bravery against the Italian occupiers, regularly used Al-Mukhtar's image to try to bolster his own popular legitimacy. Who could forget the images of the Libyan leader arriving on his first ever visit to Italy in 2009, decked out in full military regalia, with a picture of Omar Al-Mukhtar in the hands of Italian captors pinned provocatively to his chest? The image of Al-Mukhtar was just as iconic during the 2011 revolution, during which Libyan youths referred to themselves as the 'grandsons of Al-Mukhtar'. And Libya's new leaders have been no less keen to claim the desert hero as their own. The new governing body, the National Transitional Council (NTC), included a page specially dedicated to Al-Mukhtar on its website. Thus, while Libya's history has been a tale of domination by a range of colonial forces, each of which has imposed its own particular catalogue of horrors, it is the Italian period that left the deepest scar.

Heading towards independence

For all that Libyans yearned to be free of Italy's colonial yoke, it took another world war to liberate them from their imperial masters. Indeed Libya's journey to independence was shaped more by international than by internal forces, and the local people were little more than bystanders in the deliberations over their fate.

Fascist Italy joined the Second World War on the side of Nazi Germany; the decision turned out to be a mistake. Following the Allied powers' victory over Germany and Italy at the famous battle of Al-Alamein in Egypt in 1942, it was all over for the Axis powers in North Africa. The Italians were forced to retreat, at last freeing Libya's three provinces from the clutches of its uncompromising colonial master. By the end of 1942, all the Italians in Cyrenaica had been evacuated, and some of the thousands of destitute Libyans who had been forced into exile were able to return.[27] Not that there was much to come back to. While Tripolitania had largely escaped the fighting between the Allied and the Axis powers, Cyrenaica was badly damaged. Benghazi alone was subjected to more than a thousand air raids, which all but destroyed the infrastructure that the Italians had built. Even the farms that the Italians had abandoned were in a pitiful state, with farm buildings so devastated that some Libyan families who returned lived outside in tents while their herds took over the farmhouses.[28]

While Libyans were jubilant at the departure of the Italians, the exit of their imperial overlord did not mean that they could now become masters of their own destiny. The three provinces fell straight into the hands of the victorious Allied powers; Britain set up military administrations in Cyrenaica and Tripolitania in 1942 and 1943 respectively, while the French, who had pushed up into the Fezzan, established their own administration in the south. The arrival of these new European powers did not prevent the local population from making a push for independence. The Sanussi order, in particular, saw the new British administration in Cyrenaica as an opportunity to try to wring some concessions for themselves. Sayyid Idris Al-Sanussi, who had shrewdly built up good relations with the British during his post-1922 exile in Egypt, from where he had offered them military support against the Axis powers, declared a Sanussi Emirate over Cyrenaica.

However, the British were in no mood to offer any such concession on a formal basis. This was hardly surprising: by this point Libya's fate had been catapulted fully into the international arena. When the Second World War ended in 1945, the four Big Powers that had emerged victorious – Britain, France, the US and the USSR – were faced with the issue of what to do with their enemies' former territories. Although Libya's three impoverished regions were of little economic worth, they were of key strategic value to all four countries, particularly at this time of profound international upheaval. After reverses in Egypt and Palestine, Britain was keener than ever to keep a base in the Mediterranean that could also serve as a location for staging posts on its air routes to East Africa, the Indian Ocean and the Far East. With nationalist movements gaining in strength in its colonial territories, France wanted to maintain the Fezzan as a buffer zone to protect its highly prized possession of Algeria. Although the Americans were not actually on the ground in Libya, they were not without strategic interests there either. In 1943, the US Air Force had taken over the Mellaha air base, east of Tripoli, which they renamed Wheelus. The USSR meanwhile, concerned about being sidelined, also wanted its share of the pie.

Given that the four powers had such divergent interests, they struggled to come to any mutually acceptable arrangement over what to do with this 'gigantic dust bowl of sand'.[29] Despite the various proposals that were thrown up, deadlock prevailed.

Unable to come to any workable agreement, the big players sent a Four Power Commission to the three provinces to elicit local views. Although still extremely limited, the Italian departure had opened up space for some indigenous political activism. Much of this activism was influenced by the return of exiles from Egypt, bursting with the new ideas of nationalism and Arabism that they had encountered there. Unsurprisingly, it was the more cosmopolitan city folk of Tripoli who proved the most open to these ideas, and by 1947 there were half a dozen political parties operating in the city. These parties were small and confined to the urban elite. Some comprised only a handful of members who could be seen almost daily, 'sitting round a single table at a "Corso" café'.[30] However, these parties were broadly united in their belief that the three regions should be brought together as a single independent country. In Cyrenaica the political activity that had emerged largely reflected the tight tribal structures and the domination of the Sanussi elite. The main political actor, dominating the scene, was the National

Congress – a political party that was established in 1946 by Idris Al-Sanussi and that included most of Cyrenaica's tribal elders and a number of traditional urban leaders. The Congress boldly told the Four Party Commission that it wanted nothing short of independence under Sanussi rule. In the Fezzan, meanwhile, there was also a relatively strong pro-nationalist current.

In the summer of 1948, the Commission reported back to the Four Power Conference that there was an overwhelming desire among locals for full independence. However, it also concluded that the country was politically, economically and socially unprepared for such a step. This left the Big Powers stumped; in the absence of any other solution, they threw the problem at the United Nations, hoping that this body could succeed where they had failed.

However, patience with the United Nations soon wore thin. The Cold War was hotting up and preventing the Soviets from gaining a foothold in the Mediterranean became the overriding priority for Britain, France and the US in their deliberations over the future of this impoverished land. Unable to wait any longer, the British decided in 1949 to take unilateral action: they released plans for Cyrenaican self-government under the rule of Idris Al-Sanussi. While Britain announced that its actions would in no way prejudice the eventual future of Libya, the move cemented the dominance both of Idris and of the east.

This was a ground-breaking moment for Cyrenaica. Although the British plans did not equate to full independence (Britain was to retain control of foreign affairs, defence and military bases), they at least gave Cyrenaicans power over their internal affairs. A jubilant Idris proclaimed the birth of the Sanussi Emirate from his Al-Manar Palace in Benghazi on 1 June 1949. The following year, in the Fezzan, France followed Britain's lead and handed over responsibility for internal affairs to a local government headed by Ahmed Bey Saif Al-Nassir. However, the Big Powers soon realized that they needed to go further; it dawned on them that, if the three regions entered some form of trusteeship under UN auspices, then the future of the military bases they had there would be brought into question. Under the UN trusteeship system, the administering power was not permitted to establish bases on the land it was administering; it was only as an independent country that Libya could freely enter into treaties and agreements governing such bases. The Western powers determined, therefore, that the best way of maintaining their all-important bases, and of keeping the Soviets fully out of the picture, was to grant Libya independence under a compliant pro-Western leadership. Only this approach could be sure to bind Libya firmly to the Western camp. Therefore, on 21 November 1949, the United Nations General Assembly adopted a resolution stipulating that Libya should become independent as soon as possible, and no later than 1 January 1952.

Libya was to be free at last. Yet for all the happiness this news engendered, it was tainted slightly by the fact that independence was a direct result of manoeuvrings on the part of the Big Powers, rather than of a hard-earned liberation struggle. Indeed, the Libyans had been relegated to the very lowest rung of the decision-making ladder – as with so much in their historical experience, independence was something that happened to them and in spite of them.

However, the Libyans did at least have a say in what kind of governing system this newly independent country should have. Under the auspices of the United Nations, the three provinces formed a National Assembly, which, at its first meeting on 2 December 1950, agreed that Libya was to become a federal state under a constitutional monarch, with Idris Al-Sanussi as head of state of a United Kingdom of Libya. That it was to be a federal system was hardly unexpected, given the enormous differences between the three regions. The fact that Idris was to be the country's monarch was hardly more surprising: the Sanussi leader had emerged as the only figure of any real political significance and already had

Cyrenaica in his hands. Moreover, the British – and the Western powers more widely – wanted someone in the post whose allegiance they could be certain of.

In 1951, the National Assembly drew up Libya's first constitution. This was no easy matter. Given the divergent interests of the different regions, and particularly those of Cyrenaica and Tripolitania, what emerged was a complex and cumbersome political system, comprising a parliament, a federal government and powerful provincial councils, whose heads were appointed by the king. Indeed, such was the desire for local autonomy that the provincial governors and councils became powerful bodies in their own right.

Perhaps most indicative of the competing claims of the two main regions, however, was the squabbling over where Libya's capital should be located. Unable to settle on one location, it was eventually decided that the capital would alternate every two years between Tripoli and Benghazi. This rather ludicrous solution meant that every couple of years the entire government and diplomatic corps had to pack up and make the arduous journey across thousands of kilometres of desert. To make matters worse, in a bid to avoid the punishing heat of the summer, government offices were later constructed in the Green Mountains at Baida, as a summer seat.[31] The moves between these administrative capitals were complicated by the fact that the diplomats needed to have their passports checked in order to move from one province to another, and differing customs tariffs meant that duties were imposed on goods moving between the regions.

Yet, for all its weaknesses, this system was a valiant attempt to forge a single nation from something that had essentially been operating as three different countries. It was certainly deemed sufficient by the Western powers: on 24 December 1951, the United Kingdom of Libya was born. The new country could finally start to put its colonial past behind it, and to look forward to a new era of independence, full of hope and promise.

CHAPTER 2

Ripe for Revolution

On 24 December 1951, the newly installed King Idris Al-Sanussi, accompanied by the country's first prime minister, Mahmoud Muntasir, proudly proclaimed Libya's independence from the balcony of the Al-Manara Palace in Benghazi. Draped over the balcony was the country's new flag, its colours and symbols representing the coming together of the three regions as a single unit for the first time.[1] It was a moving experience for the crowds who thronged below and who lined the rooftops of the buildings opposite, straining to catch a glimpse of their new monarch. One attendee at the palace celebrations recounted: 'As the tears fell from my eyes I felt that the Libyan people had got their spirit back and that they had returned to history.'[2] For a country so long ravaged by the interests of outside powers that had spared little thought for its indigenous inhabitants, this was a time of hope and of new beginnings.

However, this new start was not to prove the great awakening that many had hoped for. The challenges at independence were immense. The Italians had left the country with a population that was, for the most part, uneducated. Illiteracy rates stood at a shocking 90 per cent or more, and the country could boast only some sixteen graduates.[3]

There were almost no Libyan doctors, teachers or other technically trained people, and no real professional class. Local inhabitants were sorely lacking in administrative know-how, as not only were there no indigenous institutions, but Libyans had been excluded from Italian colonial administrative and bureaucratic offices. The kingdom had to build itself from scratch.

The country was also utterly impoverished. At the time of independence, Libya was ranked the poorest nation in the world. Things were so bad that a former prime minister, Abdelhamid Bakkoush, recalled how the arrival of an Egyptian ship bringing a gift of rice prompted Tripoli's inhabitants to come out into the streets in celebration.[4] Such dire financial conditions meant that, until the discovery of significant reserves of oil in 1959, the new kingdom had to rely almost exclusively on foreign aid for its survival, much of it from Britain and the US. For all its newfound freedom, Libya was still bound to the whims and wishes of the Big Powers.

To make matters worse, though the country was officially united, the differences between the three regions could not be surmounted overnight. Although there was a broad consensus about being a single nation, suspicions and rivalry persisted, as each province sought to serve and secure its own interests in the new power structures that had been drawn up under UN supervision. The long years of physical separation, differing colonial experiences and diverse cultural traditions could not simply be whitewashed over by a new name and a new constitutional system. As a former British ambassador to Libya, Alec Kirkbride, observed in 1957, the use of the word 'United' in the country's official name was an expression of hope rather than a statement of fact.[5]

Yet perhaps most important of all, the newly created Libya was hampered by the fact that it had not really achieved its own independence. There had been no struggle for independence, or movement that could claim to have won a hard-fought battle for freedom. This meant that independence came as something of a shock. Libyans seemed to have emerged into independence in a sort of 'incredulous daze' and still felt there must be a catch somewhere.[6]

More importantly, unlike in neighbouring Algeria or Tunisia, where nationalist liberation movements were to bring a unity of purpose and an almost undisputed degree of legitimacy to the post-independence regimes, Libya's new leaders had no such clout. Although the new king had a natural authority and religious legitimacy on account of his leadership of the Sanussi order and his claim of descent from the Prophet, Idris was in his post largely by virtue of his alliance with the British. Moreover, the Sanussiya leader had always been something of a compromise figure. While he was much loved in his native east, the Tripolitanians gave him their support largely in the interests of securing independence as quickly as possible, rather than out of any strong sense of loyalty. Those in the Fezzan, meanwhile, supported him partly to ensure that they were not dominated by Tripolitania. Thus Idris became king more by default than by virtue of his personal leadership qualities.

The sixty-one-year-old was not exactly what one would look for in a king. The frail Idris, who suffered from repeated bouts of illness, was known primarily for being a deeply religious man. Born in 1890 in the Sanussi oasis of Jaghboub, in the eastern desert, Idris had grown up in an atmosphere of piety and learning. He was accustomed to a sedentary life and had never been considered a man of action or a man of a 'hardy constitution'.[7] However, he was deemed a man of piety and high moral standing, who had readily adopted the Sanussiya traditions of asceticism and austerity. Although Egyptian King Faruq once called him 'an ignorant dervish',[8] Idris, with his trademark round spectacles, also had a reputation as something of a scholar. It is hardly surprising, therefore, that he struggled to make the leap from being the head of a religious order to being the monarch of a nation. As one British official posted in

Libya at the time recalled, Idris was 'more of a mistake than a modern day ruler'.[9]

Idris's inability to step up to the mark was partly related to the fact that the role of monarch was not one the new king had ever craved. While happy to take on the Emirship of Cyrenaica, the Sanussiya leader seems to have accepted the throne more out of a sense of duty than from any serious desire to rule over the new-born nation. He thus remained firmly a man of Cyrenaica, and proved unable really to go beyond the local. As Henry Villard, the first US ambassador to Libya, commented, the unfailing subject of interest to him was the past, present and future of Cyrenaica, and he gave the impression that he would be content to reign over that territory alone.[10]

With such an attitude, Idris soon gained a reputation for being a reluctant king who 'found the exercise of power rather tiresome'.[11] In stark contrast to Qaddafi, whose images were emblazoned across the country, Idris refused to have his face printed on the currency or to have any landmark (other than Tripoli's civilian airport) named after him. The infirm monarch also shied away from the day-to-day running of the country, relying heavily on his closest advisors to manage affairs on his behalf. He hated detail and complicated arrangements, was acutely indecisive, and had 'an aversion to direct-ness in either thought or action'.[12] He was so retiring that whenever things got too much, he threatened to abdicate. Following the assas-sination in 1954 of his trusted advisor, Ibrahim Al-Shelhi, who was killed by a rival faction in the Sanussi family, Idris shut himself away in a simple apartment on the top floor of a local government building in Tobruq, like a recluse. It was only the pleading of then Prime Minister Mustafa Ben Halim that convinced him not to relinquish the throne and to stay on in office.

Yet it would be wrong to equate the king's character and apparent lack of political acumen with weakness. Despite his frail and disinterested air, Idris created a highly paternalistic ruling system, in which all power was focused in the palace. Idris surrounded himself with strongmen from loyal tribes in Cyrenaica, such as the Bara'asa, the Al-Obeidat and the Al-Awaqir, placing them in the all-powerful *Diwan* (royal office) that became the key focus of authority throughout his rule. Although he was careful to include a number of important commercial figures from Tripolitania among this royal entourage, it was, for the most part, dominated by those eastern tribes that had traditional links to the Sanussiya.

Idris also ensured that the new government structures were dominated by close allies. He retained the right to appoint ministers to the key portfolios of defence, interior, finance and petroleum affairs, and the new king gave these posts to faithful tribal notables or to prominent Tripolitanian families whose loyalty could be assured. He also appointed the local *walis* (the heads of the powerful local provincial councils), who, during the first decade of independence, came to act more like heads of independent states. Thus politics under Idris became the assertion of family, factional, tribal and parochial interests.[13]

Indeed, anyone hoping for a robust parliament and a healthy political life was to be sorely disappointed. Idris also dismantled all semblance of an effective opposition. He had already banned the troublesome Omar Al-Mukhtar Society in 1951, after the members of this militant group (which had been set up in 1942) staged a demonstration against a government hospital in Benghazi that had failed to bury a dead man within twenty-four hours, as dictated by Muslim tradition. The protest soon turned against the government and the British, giving Idris the excuse he needed to rid himself of this irritant. In 1952 the new king went further. He outlawed the National Congress, the most important political party in Tripolitania, after it had staged a demonstration to protest against the results of the country's first ever parliamentary elections in 1952, which it had expected to win.[14] The demonstration turned violent, and clashes with police resulted in a number of deaths. This was the perfect excuse for Idris to rid himself of the country's most potent opposition party. In fact, much like Qaddafi after him, the king had a longstanding suspicion of political parties per se, fearing that such new-fangled modernist inventions could be used as Trojan horses by foreign powers.

Thus the king created a kind of court government, made up of loyal tribal notables reliant on patronage. This bypassed the official structures of the state that had been so arduously thrashed out in the constitution. Indeed, despite the façade of government, power lay with what was essentially a benign oligarchy, centred around existing power patterns in Cyrenaica. Yet perhaps one should not be surprised by this. Idris was not a modern man, and he ruled in the only way he knew: more like a localized tribal and religious leader than a state builder. He regarded the country's new political structures as secondary to his own understanding of government, which was based upon Sharia (Islamic law).[15] In line with Islamic tradition, Idris seems to have believed that ruling should be a *shura* (consultation) process, in which he listened to the views of others and then made his own decisions in accordance with his personal moral and religious principles. For Idris, the realities of modern-day ruling were always going to remain elusive.

However, one reality that Idris could not ignore was the discovery of large reserves of oil in 1959 – something that was to have perhaps the most profound impact on the newly independent Libya. Foreign energy companies, many of them American, rushed into the country in search of the 'black gold', and Libya, which had relied almost exclusively on foreign aid, began to see new possibilities for itself. Yet in order to realize its potential, the country had to get its act together fast. Not only did it need to create a climate that was conducive to foreign investment, but it also needed to overcome its regional differences, so as to develop and manage a national oil industry. The need for income clearly outweighed political considerations, and in

1963, just two years after the first shipment of oil left Libya's shores, Idris issued a royal decree abolishing the federal system; the United Kingdom of Libya became simply the Kingdom of Libya.

The new status meant that the powerful provincial councils and their judicial systems were abolished, and the national government was given authority for the first time over economic development, transportation, finance and taxation. Despite the fact that there was strong resistance to these changes at the provincial level, where local loyalties still pulled the heart strings hardest, the king proved wise enough to realize that, in order to become an oil exporter, Libya needed to at least act like a unified nation. The decision certainly paid off. The Libyan economy boomed almost overnight. Per capita annual income (which at independence had stood at $25–35) had rocketed to $2,000 by 1969.[16]

But the good-news story was not all roses. Libya's new role as an oil exporter brought problems as well as benefits, not least of which was corruption. While patronage had always been the king's chosen method of ensuring compliance, the opportunities for making a fast buck increased with the new income flows. Taking up a post in a state institution became a byword for lining one's own pocket. This was especially true of ministerial posts, where serious money could be made. Close links also developed between the foreign oil companies and the Palace, with ministers often acting as go-betweens. Thus the key beneficiaries of this new oil wealth were predominantly the old tribal elite that had been at the helm since independence. As one commentator observed, 'the king's entourage included too many individuals for whom personal self-enrichment had become an all-consuming passion'.[17]

This oil wealth also created a new class of rich that cut across tribal links and that began to change the social fabric of Libyan society. An emerging class of bureaucrats and technocrats, who had benefited from the new education programmes that had accompanied independence, formed the beginnings of a local bourgeoisie. They started moving into government positions and into the new institutions created around the energy sector, enabling them to move up the social ladder. The expanding oil sector was accompanied, too, by a boom in service trades and industries. There were suddenly jobs to be had in the construction and hotel trades, among others. The lack of skilled workers in the country meant that truck drivers or stenographers who knew English could command almost any wage they demanded.[18] The upshot of these changes was that a small number of individuals became very rich very quickly.

At the same time, Libyans from the arid and desolate rural areas began to pour into the cities in search of work. Between 1954 and 1964, the population of Tripoli mushroomed from 130,000 to 213,000, while Benghazi's doubled from 70,000 to 137,000.[19] Predictably enough, there were nowhere near enough jobs to go round, and many of these new arrivals found themselves struggling to survive in the fetid shanty towns that fast grew up around Tripoli and other key urban centres. One Benghazi shanty town named Sabri, which housed around a quarter of the city's inhabitants, yielded

> ... a clear picture of a primitive and miserable society living on the lowest margins of human subsistence. In winter, the people suffer from dirt, mud and rain. Summer conditions are better than those of winter, but millions of flies live on the dirt and sewage found all over the place ... Neither modern dwellings nor medical services, sanitation, hygiene, piped water or electricity are yet known, despite the fact that the eastern part of the area lies along the main northern entrance to the city.[20]

This migration – and the misery that awaited those who had uprooted themselves to go in search of their fortune – prompted an extreme dislocation and a disruption of traditional and social links.

This only served to accentuate feelings of marginalization. It is hardly surprising, then, that as these individuals saw the old and new elites (as well as foreign oil companies) benefiting from the oil boom and getting richer and richer, resentments began to build.

The power of ideology

While Idris struggled with being a modern statesman, his greatest challenge turned out to be dealing with the tide of Arab nationalism that gripped the Arab world during the 1950s and 1960s. The nationalist creed preached that the Arabs could regain their former glory if they united as a single nation. Young Libyans proved no less immune to the pull of this ideology than their contemporaries across the region. Such progressive and self-affirming concepts were appealing, especially in a country that had been in the pockets of Western powers for so long. Next to Libya's traditionalist monarchy, the new Arab nationalist regimes of President Nasser of Egypt and Abdul Karim Kassem of Iraq seemed like a welcome breath of fresh air.

These new ideas spread easily enough in Libya through the media – and in particular through the Voice of the Arabs radio station that was broadcast from Cairo and that pumped out relentless nationalist propaganda. Thanks to the availability of cheap transistor radios, many young Libyans tuned into the crackly airwaves, this being their only access to the outside world. Nationalist ideas were also disseminated via the hundreds of Egyptian, Palestinian and Sudanese teachers who had been brought in to staff Libya's schools and universities on account of the dearth of qualified locals. Arab nationalist ideas were also circulated by Libyans who had studied at Egyptian universities, as well as by Libyan military officers who had graduated from the Military Academy in Baghdad.[21] Thus there was a small but emerging class of educated and salaried middle classes in Libya who looked to Arab nationalism to save them from the political and economic marginalization they experienced at the hands of the outmoded monarchical system.

These young nationalists not only objected to what they viewed as the backwardness of their own monarchy, but also took umbrage at its continued dependence on foreign powers. This dependence was not insignificant. Given its sorry financial state at independence, in 1953 Libya had signed a twenty-year friendship treaty with Britain. Under this agreement, the British were granted the military facilities and overflying rights they so craved, in return for £1 million a year in economic development aid and £2.75 million a year in budgetary aid for the years 1953–58. The following year Libya signed a similar treaty with the US, promising it the use of the Wheelus airbase in return for generous financial support. These income flows were critical for the country's survival and development. Yet they provoked serious resentment among the nationalists, who viewed them as an extension of colonial domination.

The foreign military bases provoked particular anger. This was a time when a common Arab consciousness was developing, and the nationalist creed preached that all Arabs were members of a single Arab nation. Libyan nationalists, therefore, feared that these bases might be used against a fellow Arab state. Their anxieties were not unfounded: when President Nasser nationalized the Suez Canal in 1956, Britain seriously considered using its Libyan bases to launch attacks against Egypt. When news of Britain's intentions leaked out, anti-British demonstrations erupted, and some of them turned violent. There was rioting in Benghazi, and dock workers went on strike, refusing to unload British military cargo. As one British Foreign Office official trenchantly observed at the time, 'Arab blood is thicker than foreign subsidies.'[22]

Idris was shaken by these displays of popular anger and by the growing tide of nationalist sentiment. The king knew he could not ignore the growing resentment on Libya's streets that was threatening to provoke serious instability. However, he was in a difficult position. He still needed ongoing financial support from the British, to whom he felt a deep sense of personal loyalty that arose from their longstanding commitment to him. Idris also wanted continued British protection, not only from the Libyan nationalists, but also from Egypt. The frail king was deeply mistrustful of President Nasser and his brand of modernist nationalism, which threatened the traditional way of life that Idris loved so much. He repeatedly voiced the view that Egypt was bent on sowing dissent in other countries, and when asked for his opinion on the Suez Crisis, the king confided to one British official in 1957: 'Speaking secretly ... I consider that Britain should have waited until the Jews had smashed Egypt.'[23] So paranoid was Idris about Egypt that he was convinced it was conniving with Algeria to divide Libya up, before moving on to take Morocco and Sudan.[24]

In the face of these conflicting interests, the king tried to strike a balance. His government asked the British to insert a clause into the 1953 treaty promising not to use their Libyan bases for an attack on any Arab state. It also requested that British troops be withdrawn from the big towns, and that those soldiers who went into a town did so only in civilian clothes. The British responded with a partial troop withdrawal, leaving sufficient numbers in place to be able to protect the king. They also established a military academy in Benghazi in 1957 to train up Libyan troops so that the country could defend itself. This was to prove pivotal: it was at this very military academy that the young Qaddafi was trained.

Despite these moves, the young ideologues took to the streets of Benghazi again in January 1964. What had fired them up this time was the king's decision not to attend a meeting of Arab states in Cairo, at which Arab heads of state were to discuss what action to take against Israel's proposal to divert waters from the River Jordan. The monarch chose to send the unpopular crown prince instead, a move that was taken by the nationalists as an indication of his lack of commitment to the Arab cause. The authorities dealt harshly with these protests, wading in and killing and injuring a number of students. If this heavy-handed response was meant to cow the nationalists into submission, it had the opposite effect: it provoked further demonstrations against the monarchy and the foreign bases, including in Tripoli, where protesters marched on the office of Prime Minister Muhi-Al-Din Al-Fikini, forcing him to resign.

Given the obvious upsurge in popular feeling, parliament felt it had no choice but to step in and exert some authority with the Palace. In March 1964, the new prime minister, Mahmoud Al-Muntasir, acting on parliament's orders, told Britain and the US that the government would not renew or extend the base agreements. Such audacity on the part of the official institutions of state shook the king to his core. Despite his threat to abdicate over the affair, parliament pressed ahead, and by August 1966 Britain had evacuated its Libyan bases, although small British garrisons remained at a number of locations in Cyrenaica. Wheelus continued to operate, although withdrawal discussions were being held with the Americans.

Yet even this was not enough to pacify the nationalists. By this point there was little the government or the king could do to calm the growing nationalist tide. The Six Day War with Israel in 1967 prompted another explosion of nationalist frenzy on Libya's streets. On 5 June, mobs, incited by Egyptian broadcasts, rampaged through the streets of Tripoli, killing terrified local Jews and attacking their property. Angry protesters also attacked British and American property in Tripoli and Benghazi, in the belief that both countries had participated in the war on Israel's side.[25] Protesters, demanding the evacuation of Wheelus, also sacked the US information office in Benghazi. The US was so alarmed by the trouble that it evacuated 6,300 American citizens from the country. Oil production was also halted as oil workers joined the Arab embargo.

The popular anger was fuelled as much by frustration at Libya's failure to help its Arab brothers as it was by hatred of the imperialist powers. All the Libyan government had done was to issue a statement stressing Libya's pride in and support for the Arab nation and its determination to fight for the liberation of Palestine. As far as the nationalists were concerned, such limited action was utterly humiliating. By the time a Libyan battalion was actually given permission to go and join the Arab forces that were fighting Israel, it was too late: before the battalion could even reach its destination, the Egyptian army had been routed and the struggle was over. Among those who had joined this battalion was one young Muammar Qaddafi, who later claimed that he had returned to Libya from the escapade determined to mount an attack on the bases of those countries that had helped the enemy.[26]

By this point it was becoming increasingly apparent that the king was no match for the power of the Arab nationalist ideology, and that he could not contain the growing nationalist fervour. It is true that any Western-backed monarch would have struggled to survive in the face of such potent ideology. Yet Idris's inability to break free from the parochial nature of his own rule made his position all the worse. So did the fact that, as the king got older and frailer, power was increasingly being transferred into the hands of the Al-Shelhi family – the family that had spawned Idris's closest advisors. As Idris had been unable to produce an heir, the nationalist camp feared that the Al-Shelhis were closing in and were trying to ensure the continuation of their privileged position. To many Libyans, the whole system was looking utterly rotten, from the inside out.

That is not to say that Idris's rule was entirely without its achievements. Libya's first and only king oversaw a difficult transition that turned a shattered land of three disparate parts into a functioning unified state that boasted a thriving energy industry. He also invested the country with some sense of national identity, albeit a limited one.

It is perhaps for these reasons that some Libyans look upon this short-lived period with a certain fondness. Not that they want a return to the monarchical system. But for all its failings, the monarchy is generally viewed as having been a fairly benign institution. While repression, censorship and corruption did exist under the king, they never reached anything like the astronomical levels they attained under the Qaddafi regime. It is partly for these reasons that the protesters who took to the streets of Benghazi in February 2011 were proud to adopt the Libyan flag of the post-independence era, and why it became one of the enduring symbols of the revolution.

Yet nostalgia aside, Idris's failure to build a modern state, to distribute wealth and power in an equitable fashion, and, most importantly, to understand the demands of a newly empowered generation that wanted to be the master of its own destiny helped to sow the conditions that made revolution all but inevitable. Things were so bad that the country seemed almost to be waiting for someone to take over. Even the king had given up, telling one of his former prime ministers, Mustafa Ben Halim: 'What is important to me is my relation to Allah. My relation to others is not important . . . I want to leave. I am incapable.'[27] By 1969 Libya was well and truly ripe for change.

Towards a new dawn

Such change was only going to come through the army. While nationalist feeling was strong, it hardly constituted an organized force that could mount a full-scale popular revolution. Moreover, this was the time of the military putsch; the nationalist regimes that had overthrown Western-backed monarchies in the region had, for the most part, come to power via military coups, this being the quickest route to power. As Qaddafi himself was later to recall, 'The army was the only thing capable of imposing the People's will by force.'[28]

This reality was not lost on some of Libya's foreign backers. As early as 1967, the Americans were expressing their concerns about possible internal subversion, and specifically urged the Libyans to improve their local security agencies so that they would be able to deal with such an eventuality.[29] By the summer of 1969, when the king, accompanied by his wife, Queen Fatima, decided to take a prolonged respite – first in Greece and then in Turkey, ostensibly for health reasons – the air in Tripoli and Benghazi was thick with murmurings of plots and coups.

Such rumours were not unfounded: there were several groups plotting in the wings at the time. Among them was a group of young officers, led by one Muammar Qaddafi. Its plot had been a long time in the making. It had all started a decade earlier, while Qaddafi and his fellow revolutionaries were at secondary school in Sebha in the Fezzan. Intoxicated with nationalist fervour, these schoolboys considered the Libyan monarchy to be the epitome of weakness and reaction and the antithesis of the modern Arab state that they aspired to. In the words of Qaddafi:

Our souls were in revolt against the backwardness enveloping our country and its land, whose best gifts and riches were being lost through plunder, and against the isolation imposed on our people in a vain attempt to hold it back from the path of the Arab people and from its greatest cause.[30]

It was during this time that Qaddafi determined to launch a revolution of his own – a revolution that his idol, President Nasser, could be proud of. He began to organize this little band of students into something akin to an underground revolutionary movement, dividing them up into cells that Qaddafi himself described as the beginnings of 'planning and preparation for the revolution'.[31] There were no strict recruitment criteria. Rather, Qaddafi sounded out those he thought were Nasser's men, who sympathized with nationalist ideas. However, there were some conditions: the recruits should not drink alcohol and should not 'run after women'.[32]

It seems that many of these young men were so taken with the nationalist creed and so keen for action that they were waiting for someone like Qaddafi to come along. Mohamed Belqassim Zwai, who was at a nearby secondary school in Sebha and who stuck by the Leader until the bitter end in 2011, described how, after meeting and speaking to the young Qaddafi, he felt as if he had been born anew and that he had found the right path at last.

The group took to holding secret meetings; as Qaddafi recounted: 'We used to meet under a palm tree near the Sebha Fortress using a light we had made by our hands. Under this light, I used to give my lessons in secret revolutionary organizations.'[33] Right from the start, Qaddafi imposed strict discipline on these recruits, forbidding them all pleasurable distractions, including nightclubs, gambling and other vices. He also demanded total obedience and utmost secrecy. Indeed, this was a serious business. As Qaddafi recalled: 'We met as a group of friends to plan a long hard path for ourselves. It would, however, lead to a goal we had promised ourselves to achieve.'[34]

However, their plans were cut short in 1961 when Qaddafi landed himself in hot water after getting involved in a demonstration in the town centre of Sebha against Syria's decision to secede from the United Arab Republic, which it had established with Egypt in 1958. The little band of protesters carried pictures of President Nasser and collected money to send a telegram of support to the Egyptian leader. Qaddafi went further and gave a rousing speech condemning the presence of British and American military bases in Libya. While this speech was to make him a legend in Sebha, it not only got him expelled from school, but also banned from studying in the province.

Undeterred, Qaddafi packed up his belongings and, after an emotional farewell to his family, travelled the many kilometres to the unfamiliar town of Misarata on the coast. After a struggle over his papers, he managed to enrol himself in a secondary school in the town. As in Sebha, he set about recruiting for the cause among his fellow students, not only in Misarata but in other nearby towns and cities. It was not long before he sparked the nationalist spirit in the local youth and established cells in Tripoli, Janzour, Zliten and Homs, as well as in Misarata itself.

In 1963, as the students came of age, Qaddafi determined that the best course of action for him and his fellow revolutionaries would be to enrol in the army. This way they could begin to lay the ground-work for their military coup. The following year, Qaddafi enrolled at the military academy in Benghazi and urged his colleagues to do the same. Some were less than enthusiastic about signing up to a life in barracks. Abdelsalam Jalloud, who went on to be Qaddafi's right-hand man, was not keen; neither was Omar Al-Meheishi, who also went on to become one of Qaddafi's inner circle. But both men felt they had little choice after Qaddafi insisted and ordered them to present themselves at the military academy with their documents immediately.[35]

As they became military men, the group reorganized itself. In a direct imitation of Nasser's Egyptian revolution, it renamed itself the Free Unionist Officers Movement and set up a Central Committee (later renamed the Revolutionary Command Council) that held its first meeting on the rugged beach at Tolmetha in Cyrenaica in 1964. It was not easy getting these young cadets, who were posted at various camps around the country, together for meetings. In order to avoid suspicion, the band of revolutionaries used to meet on public holidays and in remote locations, where they 'slept in the open, met under trees or behind rocks or in Bedouin shacks'.[36] Romantic it may have been, but the commitment was not easy, especially given that most of the recruits came from the lower classes: buying a car – something they were all charged with doing, in order to allow them to move around – was a challenge in itself.

The group's members spent the next few years recruiting as far and wide as they could, but mainly within the armed forces, which they believed were their 'gateway to the revolution'.[37] They tried unsuccessfully to pull in some higher-ranking army officers, but focused most of their efforts on the military cadets, who would then graduate to become low-ranking military officers. These officers were organized into sub-committees and were tasked with recruiting their own cells and preparing for the revolution. They also set about amassing live ammunition, stealing it from official sources and hiding it among rocks and trees. It was a risky business. In 1967, the aunt of Abu Bakr Younis Jaber, one of the core group of revolutionaries who went on to be Qaddafi's chief of defence staff, had to fling a stash of ammunition that her nephew had hidden in her house into the sewers to avoid detection when the police came looking for her son.[38]

By 1969, having recruited enough members, the revolutionaries felt sufficiently prepared to seize the moment. Although there is no way of knowing the exact size of the movement at this time, Qaddafi claimed that it comprised hundreds of officers. This is likely to be something of an exaggeration; but with cells posted at the various military camps across the country, the movement's leaders concluded that they were in a position to be able to control the whole of the army. It was time to set a date.

The day of the coup was fixed for 12 March 1969. But nervous anticipation soon turned to disappointment, when the revolutionaries discovered that the date clashed with a concert due to be given by famed Egyptian singer Oum Kalthoum. Not only were a number of key royal and military figures going to attend the performance, but it was also a benefit concert for the Palestinians.[39] Interrupting a concert by the Arab world's most revered singer would certainly have been in bad taste and would have done little to endear the young revolutionaries to the people. Moreover, arresting key figures from the regime amidst a crowd of thousands would not have been easy; so 'for ethical and human reasons, it was decided they would be spared apprehension during the performance night'[40] and the plans were shelved.

A new date was set for 24 March. Once again fate intervened: having got wind that something untoward was up, the military authorities spirited King Idris away to Tobruq so that he could be under the protection of the British forces stationed there. They also stepped up security measures in the key centres. Given that the revolutionaries' plan had been drawn up on the assumption that both the king and the crown prince would be in Tripoli, the coup was scuppered. Qaddafi abandoned the plot and ordered the movement to go underground.

The young revolutionaries were shaken by the realization that the establishment had got wind of the plot, and they feared they had an informer in their ranks. This may well have been the case, as the military authorities were never very far behind them. Qaddafi, who was under special monitoring, was repeatedly hauled in for questioning by his superiors, and fear of discovery was always close at hand. Qaddafi recalled one such grilling in 1969:

> At such disturbing moments I used to think not of tomorrow, or paradise, or the people. I thought of what I had in my pockets such as papers or leaflets, names, notes I might have written. My fingers moved unconsciously to my pockets.[41]

Yet time and again, Qaddafi and his fellow Free Unionist Officers escaped detection, sometimes only by a hair's breadth. Indeed, the path to revolution was so full of mishaps and accidents that the whole saga unfolds almost like a farce. There was the time in early 1969, for example, when Qaddafi was driving back to Benghazi in a Volkswagen, after a secret meeting with some of his comrades. They had waited until late at night to travel, in order to avoid detection. However, after losing their way among the sand dunes in the dark, they suffered a puncture, which caused the car to suddenly career out of control and crash. As some locals approached to give them a hand, all that Qaddafi could think about was the handwritten secret leaflet that was in his possession. With beating hearts, the panicked revolutionaries managed to disguise the incriminating leaflet; they wrapped it in cloth and used it as a stopper for an old alcohol bottle that they had filled with distilled water for the car battery. When the rescuers discovered the bottle, the teetotal recruits were more than happy to go along with the assumption that they had been drinking and were little more than young men out for a good time. Though the men were taken to a military camp at Ajdabia for questioning, the authorities failed to get to the bottom of what they had really been doing so late at night. A few months later the revolutionaries feared detection again when they had another car crash. This time Qaddafi was returning to Benghazi with Mustafa Kharroubi, another figure who went on to become part of Qaddafi's inner circle. Kharroubi, who was driving, was so busy reciting verses from the Qu'ran that he failed to notice a large cow that had wandered onto the road near Al-Marj. The vehicle crashed into the beast; though it escaped unscathed, the car was badly damaged.[42]

It was perhaps this air of complete amateurism that enabled the seemingly shambolic group to escape arrest throughout the long years of preparation. According to Colonel Aziz Shenib, the third in command of the Libyan army at the time, he and other senior officers did not take Qaddafi and his men seriously: 'We always thought it was rubbish, that Qaddafi and his group would never be able to do anything.'[43] However, Qaddafi and his band were to prove them wrong.

After yet another false start, when the coup had to be postponed again because some of the units had not received instructions in time, a new date was finally set. This new date was 1 September 1969 – and this time there was to be no going back. This was partly because the plotters were aware that the authorities were edging ever closer to discovering them, and partly because, after so many failed attempts, some of the young recruits were getting disillusioned and were having second thoughts. Most importantly, however, the date was fixed because a number of the Free Unionist Officers were due to be posted to Britain for a training stint at the beginning of September. The announcement that these officers were about to be sent abroad sparked panic among the revolutionaries. Qaddafi knew that if he did not act, he risked losing his dream forever.

In a mad rush, he and the Revolutionary Command Council set about preparing themselves. Operational plans were drawn up, put in envelopes that were then sealed with red wax, and distributed among cell leaders. Qaddafi and his cohorts spent a frantic couple of days at the very end of August travelling around the country, informing their fellow revolutionaries that the time had finally come. It was a jittery time all round, and fear that their plans would be leaked at the last moment was on everyone's mind.

To make matters worse, some of the Free Unionist Officers had got so accustomed to the coup being postponed that they simply did not believe it when it actually went ahead. This included Omar Al-Meheishi, who refused to believe it when he was told on 31 August that he needed to get back to his unit in Tarhouna (western Libya), to carry out his part in the plot. As Qaddafi recalled:

> I asked Kharroubi to go to Al-Meheishi in Al-Barka [Cyrenaica] and he met him. He found that he had no intention of joining his unit in Tarhouna. So Kharroubi gave him 30 dinars to encourage him to travel on the aeroplane. Al-Meheishi took the 30 dinars but decided not to travel and said 'I want to meet Muammar.' When it came to my knowledge that that was what he wanted I asked him

to come to the Gar Younis camp. He came and I confirmed that we had decided that the revolution would be on that night and that he had to join his battalion in Tarhouna ... he was so happy when I personally confirmed to him that the revolution was that night and he congratulated me.[44]

Finally convinced that the plot was going ahead, Al-Meheishi rushed to the airport in order to get to Tripoli; but to his dismay, when he got there he found that there were no seats left on the plane. He only managed to get onto the flight by pulling strings with an employee he knew in the airline. After arriving at Tripoli airport at 9.30 p.m., with just hours to spare before the coup, he eventually found someone to take him to Tarhouna; but in his rush to get to his base, he left his revolver and ammunition in the car.

On the eve of the coup, Qaddafi insisted that the revolutionaries carry out their usual duties until noon – the end of the working day – and try to act as normal as possible. He recalled: 'I didn't allow enthusiasm or fear to show.'[45] However, some of his fellow revolutionaries were less able to contain their emotions. As Qaddafi described it:

[Emhamed] Magrayef[46] seemed worried and from time to time he moved to try to get my attention but I deliberately ignored him. As for Abdelfatah [Younis Al-Obeidi],[47] his enthusiasm was such that he looked drunk to the point of being paralysed. As for Kharroubi, the signs of faith appeared upon him and he looked like a believer who was approaching martyrdom.[48]

Qaddafi was later to attribute some of his calmness to his belief that the divine was on his side. On the night of 31 August, after all the preparations were in place, he and Mustafa Kharroubi lay on the same bed in his room and listened to the Voice of the Arabs radio from Cairo as they awaited the 'zero hour' of 2.30 a.m. The station broadcast some Qu'ranic verses that included the line: 'Allah will not deny the faithful their reward.'[49] Taking this as a sign, Qaddafi explained: 'These verses made us secure and calm. We started repeating the last part of them over and over to ourselves, "Allah's help is all-sufficient for us. He is the best protector" and we were assured of success.'[50]

Needless to say, the actual operation was as peppered with mishaps as the years of preparation had been. Khweildi Al-Humaidi, another loyalist who was to remain at the very core of Qaddafi's regime, could not find the Tripoli radio station that the movement was supposed to occupy. When some other revolutionaries drove him there, a group of soldiers opened fire on them, believing that they were Israeli invaders who were trying to 're-enact their raid on Beirut'![51] Meanwhile, the tank commanded by Abu Bakr Younis [Jaber], which was packed full of explosives and ammunition, burst into flames because of a short circuit. As the flames licked the side of the tank, Younis only just managed to disconnect the wire in the tank in time, preventing the whole lot from exploding.

Even Qaddafi was caught up in a misadventure of his own. As the soon-to-be leader was driving his jeep at the head of a convoy on its way to take over the radio station in Benghazi, he came to a fork in the road. Qaddafi took the left turn, as planned, expecting the train of vehicles to follow him. However, in the excitement of the moment, the other drivers went hurtling off down the right fork. He later recounted:

I had stopped my jeep to await the rest of the column when I suddenly saw all the other vehicles tearing like demons towards the main road. It then dawned on me that the entire Gar Younis Barracks were streaming along in the one direction and that the drivers in their enthusiasm were following one another without worrying much about where they were supposed to be going.[52]

Indeed, despite the meticulous planning, some of the revolutionaries displayed a kind of recklessness. Yet for all the sense of farce, one should not underestimate the bravery of these young men, who were ready to risk their lives to bring about change. Nor should one underestimate their determination. Few would have believed that this group, which started out as little more than an idealistic gaggle of schoolboys, would ever actually achieve its dream.

As it turned out, the revolutionaries met with little real resistance; most of the regime simply melted away. The Cyrenaican Defence Force, an elite force built up by King Idris to protect the monarchy, fell with remarkable ease after its commander, Brigadier Sanussi Fezzani, was arrested at home in bed. Even the head of the Libyan army, Colonel Abdul Aziz Al-Shelhi, put up no resistance. When Al-Meheishi and Abu Bakr Younis went to his house to arrest him, the military chief dived into his swimming pool in his pyjamas, flummoxing his captors, who were unable to discover his hiding place until the next morning. The king, meanwhile, was still away on his summer break, while the crown prince simply turned all the lights in his palace out and hid on his own in the dark, causing the rebels to believe that he had deserted the building. It took two different sets of rebels to actually discover and arrest him.

Upon hearing of the coup, Idris is alleged to have dismissed it as a 'trifling affair' and vowed to return to take over again. The king was clearly banking on getting help from the British; he sent a special emissary to London the day after the coup to request assistance. However, he had not understood that times had changed. As one of his former prime ministers aptly noted, his greatest mistake was to believe that history moved extremely slowly.[53] By this point Britain was fully engaged in the policy of Harold Wilson's government of 'progressive withdrawal' from its former colonies. As early as 1961, Britain had concluded that 'it would be most impolitic for us to use British troops for the purpose of maintaining a particular Libyan regime in power, which would entail interfering in Libyan politics and possibly killing Libyans.'[54]

With no foreign power to defend it, the whole country fell quickly and with minimal bloodshed. Even Cyrenaica, the home of the monarchy and all that it stood for, put up almost no fight at all. Yet this reflected the fact that, by 1969, the regime had become so inert that there was a gaping political vacuum that was waiting to be filled. Moreover, although the success of the coup was largely due to the incompetence of the old regime, Qaddafi and his Free Unionist Officers had tapped into the mood of the time, as reflected by the popular demonstrations that were to erupt on the streets as news of the demise of the old regime spread. Although they were still largely unknown, these young revolutionaries, with their nationalist ideals, appeared to be the very embodiment and articulation of the desire for change that was felt by so many Libyans at this time.

Thus it was that, at 6.30 a.m. on 1 September 1969, Libyans awoke to the unfamiliar voice of Qaddafi breaking onto the airwaves. In a rousing proclamation, which he claimed to have jotted down at the very last moment, the young Qaddafi, who had first dreamed of this moment a decade earlier, proudly declared:

People of Libya! In response to your own free will, fulfilling your most heartfelt wishes, answering your incessant demands for change and regeneration and your longing to strive towards these ends; listening to your incitement to rebel, your armed forces have undertaken the overthrow of the reactionary and corrupt regime, the stench of which has sickened and horrified us all ... From this day forward Libya is a free, self-governing republic ... She will advance on the road to freedom, the path of unity and social justice, guaranteeing equality to all her citizens and throwing wide in front of them the gates of honest employment where injustice and exploitation will be banished, where no one will count himself master or servant, and where he will be free, brothers within a society in which, with God's help, prosperity and equality will be seen to rule us all.[55]

Libya had finally embarked upon a new dawn.

CHAPTER 3

The Rise of the Jamahiriyah

As dawn broke on the morning of 1 September, Libyans had no idea who had toppled their king, yet alone what they stood for. However, as the identities of the twelve-strong Revolutionary Command Council (RCC)[1] emerged four months after the coup, it became clear that the country's new leaders were of a very different breed from the established political elite. In stark contrast to those who had prospered under the king, most of the RCC, as well as the wider circle of Free Unionist Officers, came from minor tribes and were either from lower middle-class stock or from poor families. The majority were the children of nomads or lowly cultivators; most were part of the upwardly mobile generation who had benefited from the nascent education policies established by the monarchy and who sought a better lot in life than their parents.

Qaddafi was no exception. Born into a Bedouin family in a small desert village in Qasr Bu Hadi, south of the coastal town of Sirte, the future leader had a tough beginning. Although undeniably beautiful, the Libyan deserts are harsh, with freezing winters and relentlessly hot summers. They are also subject to the *Ghibli* – the hot, dry, dust-bearing desert wind that has a dramatic effect on the landscape, moving vast quantities of sand and making life even more difficult for the desert dwellers. Little grows on the surface of the golden sand where 'the blue dome of the sky seems to seal off the entire landscape in an absolute silence'.[2] It was into these harsh and silent surroundings that Muammar Abu Miniar Al-Qaddafi was born. It is not clear in exactly which year he made his entrance to the world; he maintained that it was in 1941, although others have suggested it may have been later, possibly in 1943.

Muammar was the only son of goat herder Abu Miniar and his wife Aisha Ben Niran, both poor, illiterate tent-dwellers. Qaddafi was the youngest child and had three older sisters. The family was part of the Qaddadfa, an Arabized Berber tribe comprising several sub-clans that are spread across the country. The tribe, whose name means 'to throw', traces its roots back to a well-known *wali* (saint), Sidi Qaddaf Al-Dam, who is buried in Gharyan, south of Tripoli.[3] It is no coincidence that Gharyan proved loyal to Qaddafi during the last days of his regime.

The Qaddadfa moved away from Gharyan over two centuries ago. Some parts of the tribe settled in the lush pastures of the Cyrenaican plateau, but were subsequently driven out to the barren deserts around Sirte by an alliance of eastern tribes led by the Bara'asa and the Magharba.[4] Although originally a small tribe by Libyan standards, following the move out of Cyrenaica the Qaddadfa became one of the largest and most dominant in the Sirte region. However, it was still essentially semi-nomadic and impoverished. Qaddafi himself describes how the inhabitants of the little hamlet of tents he grew up in used to go out looking for scrap metal, empty ammunition casings and other remnants of World War II that could be used as improvised household articles.[5] Things were so difficult that Qaddafi's father was forced to migrate with his herd to the south in the winter in order to survive.

We do not know very much about Qaddafi's early life. However, from the snippets available, the young Bedouin comes across as a serious boy, who was on a higher plane than those around him. He is also portrayed as a figure for whom leadership was somehow preordained. As his father described him: 'He was so different from the others! ... Of course he planted and sowed like the rest of us; he looked after the goats and the camels. But he was so serious, so quiet; not sulky, no, on the contrary he was always smiling. Yet he didn't much enjoy playing; aloof from his cousins, he seemed always to be musing.'[6] Similarly, his old history teacher at secondary school, Shalan Abdelkhaliq, recalled: 'Always Muammar was seen during the break standing alone in the courtyard of the school as if he was an individual island.'[7]

One should, of course, be careful about taking such descriptions too literally. Qaddafi's childhood and early years were carefully reconstructed after the revolution to create an image that befitted his position as leader. The Colonel's early experiences became an integral part of the narrative of the revolution; so much so that scenes from his youth were immortalized in garish colours on enormous billboards that were erected in public spaces across the country. Thus it is sometimes difficult to distinguish truth from fiction.

However, it is clear that, as the only son, Qaddafi held a special place in his parents' hearts, and his father was keen for the little Muammar to get an education. There was no school in the oasis where the family lived, but his father arranged for the local roving *faqi* (religious teacher), to come and teach his son the basics. It was at the hands of this *faqi* that Qaddafi learned some Qu'ranic verses by heart.[8]

Qaddafi seems to have had an appetite for learning; in 1954 he persuaded his father to allow him to attend primary school in Sirte. The family's knowledge of educational matters was such that, when the eager, curly-haired boy turned up to begin his studies, he was disappointed to discover that it was already exam time and almost the end of the school year. However, he returned a few months later and was enrolled in the second year on account of his knowledge of the Qu'ran. It was a tough existence for a small boy. As his father recounted, 'I had no money to pay for lodgings! He slept in the mosque, where else?'[9] Qaddafi went back to his family home every weekend, walking the 30km or so each way. He also returned to the family every harvest time, interrupting his studies to help out at home.

Qaddafi was marked out immediately as different from his peers. Not only was he older than the other pupils in his class, but he was of Bedouin stock. This brought no end of abuse. His cousin, Muftah Ali Subaya Qaddafi relates: 'There were three or four of us Bedouin at the school, and we were held in utter contempt. We were so poor that we often had nothing to eat at break. What an atmosphere for children!'[10] Yet in a sign of his resolve, such taunting seems to have spurred the future leader to work even harder. As Qaddafi commented, 'My motivation to learn was huge, especially when the pupils confronted me with their comments deriding this desert dweller.'[11]

After a couple of years at school in Sirte, Qaddafi's family moved to Sebha, in the south of Libya, which his father described as a place that 'seemed forgotten in a sea of sand'.[12] Qaddafi enrolled at the local secondary school, and it was here that the young pupil began to develop a political awareness. Like many young men of his day, Qaddafi's imagination was fired by the nationalist revolution in Egypt, and he loved to listen to the Voice of the Arabs radio station. Qaddafi became so captivated by President Nasser that he began memorizing the Egyptian leader's speeches and reciting them in front of his classmates.

Despite his youth, Qaddafi was clearly already a charismatic figure; his fellow pupils took to carrying around a small stool for him that he would stand on in order to deliver his speeches. He also began organizing little demonstrations against the colonialist powers; he led his fellow pupils in a general strike every 2 December to protest against the 1917 Balfour Declaration, the British statement supporting the establishment of a home for the Jews in Palestine. The young Qaddafi also convened regular protests outside the French consulate in Sebha, where, from his stool, he would deliver speeches about the injustices the French were committing in Algeria and elsewhere.

But it was not just the imperial powers that Qaddafi protested against: he also railed against Libya's ruling elite. Inflamed with his newfound political consciousness, he led a little band of schoolboys as they smashed the windows of a Sebha hotel because it served alcohol – something they considered symptomatic of the morally lax, westernized and un-Islamic behaviour of the ruling class.[13] Ironically, such actions were more in line with the Islamist groups that at the time were challenging the Nasser regime in Egypt than they were with the ideology of the nationalists, who tended to have a more liberal outlook. Yet they reflected Qaddafi's puritanical streak, something that was part and parcel of his Bedouinism.

After being expelled from school in Sebha for his outspoken attacks against the British and American bases, Qaddafi continued to make an impression at his new school in Misarata. The leader was becoming increasingly hardened in his hatred of the weak monarchy and the imperialist powers behind it, and he was not afraid to let it show. One target for his invective was the English school inspector, Mr Johnson, whom Qaddafi dismissed as 'no more than an agent of imperialism'.[14] On one occasion, Qaddafi refused to stand up when Mr Johnson entered the room and, in a provocative gesture, waved a key chain bearing an image of President Nasser at the haughty inspector. Upon being ordered to leave the room, Qaddafi coldly told the inspector, 'You are the one who should leave for good, not this room but the whole country.'[15]

The future leader's entry to military college in Benghazi failed to tame his rebellious streak: if anything, it seemed to spur it on. The new cadet refused to learn English – the language of the occupier – and went out of his way to be rude to his superiors.[16] A visit in 1966 to Britain, where he was sent for signals training at Beaconsfield, only served to increase his hostility towards the 'imperial power'. The proud young nationalist, who was remembered for his aloofness and general disdain for British society, seems to have revelled in the challenge of being in the land of the colonizer. He later remarked: 'I put on my *Al-Jird* [Arab robes] and went to Piccadilly ... I was prompted by a feeling of challenge and a desire to assert myself.'[17]

It was at the Benghazi military academy that Qaddafi's more sinister side came to the fore. A British officer at the academy, Colonel Ted Lough, described the young revolutionary as 'inherently cruel'.[18] By Lough's account, Qaddafi was responsible for the murder of a young cadet at the Benghazi military academy who was accused of committing a sexual offence, possibly involving homosexuality.[19] The terrified cadet, his hands and feet bound, was dragged to a firing point, where Qaddafi and a group of other cadets began shooting at him, before a Libyan officer finished him off with a *coup de grâce* while the others laughed.

However, Qaddafi also experienced his share of punishment at the academy. He was regularly penalized for insolence, and on one occasion was forced to crawl on his hands and knees across gravel, a rucksack filled with sand on his back and the harsh sun beating down. Such humiliations can only have strengthened the young revolutionary's determination to unseat the system and its colonial backers.

Indeed, reconstructions of his past aside, Qaddafi was clearly a man of charisma who, from a young age, marked himself out as someone who was going to follow his own destiny. He was always a larger-than-life figure; so much so that the history of modern Libya reads like a biography of his ambition and the lengths he was willing to go to fulfil it.

Qaddafi to the fore

If Qaddafi was no ordinary man, the events of 1 September 1969 were no ordinary coup d'état. This was to be more than a simple military putsch: it was to be a full-scale revolution that would not only replace Libya's corrupt and complacent elite, but would also transform the country's entire way of being. It was a revolution that was to eat into every part of life, and that would shake the country to its core.

There was never any question of who would lead this transformation. The whole revolution had been Qaddafi's brainchild right from the start, and it was always going to be his project. This Bedouin from the desert was determined to mould the backwards, reactionary kingdom into his own vision of what a progressive and modern Arab state should be. Not that this vision was conceptualized into any real plan as yet; that was to come later. However, at the outset there was no doubt that the enigmatic Qaddafi would lead the way and that his fellow revolutionaries were more than happy to follow. As one of his former comrades, Mohamed Belqassim Zwai remarked, 'everything from start to finish always revolved around Gadafi'.[20]

How Qaddafi was going to persuade the rest of the population to follow his lead was another matter. It is true that, in the first days after the revolution, the country's new leaders were greeted by throngs of enthusiastic supporters. It is also true that the humble origins of most of the young revolutionaries in the RCC separated them in the minds of Libyans from the privileged and corrupt elite that was associated with the monarchy. This gave the RCC a special legitimacy that Qaddafi was keen to play up right from the start, telling the French newspaper, *Le Figaro* on 30 September 1969:

The officers have the conscience to recognise the people's claims better than others. This depends on our origin which is character-ised by humbleness. We are not rich people; the parents of the majority of us are living in huts. My parents are still living in a tent near Sirte. The interests we represent are genuinely those of the Libyan people.[21]

Yet, for all their claims to represent the people, these new revolu-tionaries were still an unknown quantity. They had not been born out of a popular liberation movement, and to most Libyans they had literally come from nowhere. Moreover, they could not escape the fact that they were essentially a group of naïve young men with no political or worldly experience. All were in their late twenties or early thirties, and none had progressed education-wise beyond secondary school and the first years of military training. Aside from Qaddafi, most had a strong suspicion of intellectuals, considering their humble origins enough of a qualification to rule. They took up the reins of power with little more than a zealous belief in Arab nationalism and anti-imperialism.

Aware of their lack of experience, the young revolutionaries looked immediately to Egypt. A surprised President Nasser immedi-ately dispatched his trusted advisor, Mohamed Heikal, to Benghazi to ascertain the lie of the land. Heikal was stunned at what he encountered, reporting back that Libya's new leaders were 'shock-ingly innocent' and 'scandalously pure'.[22] He was also surprised when, in all simplicity, Qaddafi told him: 'We have carried out this revolution. Now it is for Nasser to tell us what to do.'[23] Nasser was to be no less shocked by Qaddafi's naivety when he met him in person. The Egyptian President recounted one occasion when the young leader was served a shrimp during dinner: a horrified Qaddafi asked: 'What are these? ... Locusts? Do you eat locusts in Egypt?' Nasser patiently explained that they were shrimps and a kind of fish, but Qaddafi flatly refused to eat them, allegedly declaring that they had not been slaughtered in a *halal* (Islamically permitted) fashion.[24]

Aware of the need to take this nascent nationalist republic under its wing, Egypt sent a contingent of its security forces to help guard against any kind of counter-coup, as well as a special advisor, Fathi Al-Deeb, to guide Libya's new leaders. Al-Deeb was no less astonished at the inexperience of the young revolutionaries, but set to work trying to steer them in the right direction. The main focus was on turning what was essentially a military coup into a full-scale revolution. Abdelsalam Jalloud later reflected that many of the policies adopted by the RCC in the early years were designed to achieve precisely this.[25]

One of the first tasks in this respect was to rid the country of the vestiges of the former regime. The revolutionaries set about weeding out those who were loyal to the former king, who was still abroad and who was tried and sentenced to death *in absentia*. Members of the royal family, politicians and prominent officials were arrested, as were hundreds of senior army and police officers.[26] Many suffered the humiliation of being subjected to televised trials, although – belying the brutality that came to characterize the Libyan regime in later years – the sentences were generally light, and there was little sign of retribution.

The RCC also worked to break the power of the country's traditional tribal leaders who had worked as a prop for the monarchy, moving against a number of tribal chiefs, especially in Cyrenaica and Fezzan. They also redrew administrative borders so that they no longer followed tribal boundaries, and local governors and mayors, whose positions were linked directly to their tribal standing, were dismissed and replaced by a younger modernizing class with more humble backgrounds. At the same time, the RCC did its best to break what was left of Sanussiya influence over the eastern parts of the country: in November 1970, for example, they closed the Sanussi

Islamic University at Al-Baida. They also bolstered the army, and Qaddafi was persuaded by the Egyptians to enlist some personal bodyguards.

Getting rid of the past was one thing, but the revolutionaries also had to build a present. They knew that one of their first tasks in this respect was to establish some sort of ruling body that would go beyond the RCC. Their plan had always been to hand power back to civilian rule; this had been agreed upon at a meeting in March 1969, when the revolutionaries decided that they would declare a civilian government within a month of taking over.[27] It was with this in mind that, one week after the coup, the revolutionaries set up a government. They brought in new faces from outside the RCC, five of them civilians and two from the military – both of them officers who held higher rank than they did themselves. They also appointed a civilian as prime minister – Mahmoud Suleiman Al-Maghrebi, a Palestinian with strong left-wing tendencies.

While the plan may have been to hand power over to this civilian-dominated government, Qaddafi had other ideas. It was no coincidence that, at the same time as the cabinet was formed, he promoted himself to the rank of colonel and made himself commander of the armed forces. He also insisted that all cabinet decisions had to be approved by the RCC, meaning that the military body continued to be the main focus of power.[28] Indeed, it became increasingly apparent to Qaddafi's fellow revolutionaries that this man from the desert had no real intention of handing power over to anyone, let alone a civilian government. His stance frustrated those in the new government; so much so that the two military officers in it – Colonels Adam Hawaz and Musa Ahmed – tried (and failed) to stage a coup in December 1969. Qaddafi's refusal to go with the original plan also angered some within the RCC, especially Mohamed Najm, who was perhaps the strongest advocate of democracy among the group. Yet at this stage, the other revolutionaries were still so dazzled by Qaddafi that they largely went along with whatever the Colonel decided.

Moreover, the revolutionaries were consumed with putting their nationalist agenda into practice. They embarked upon a series of populist gestures, first closing down the hated foreign military bases and expelling the colonizing forces: the last British troops left Tobruq in March 1970, and the Americans evacuated the Wheelus base a few months later. The revolutionaries also expelled what was left of Libya's Jewish community, as well as the last of the Italian settlers, appropriating their land and assets in the name of anti-imperialism – an act that prompted a triumphant Qaddafi to declare: 'the feeling of holy revenge runs today in our veins'.[29] Libya could no longer be accused of being subservient to the imperial powers. The revolutionaries also applied their nationalist ideas to the economy, undertaking a number of measures to 'purify' the country of foreign influence. More than half the capital of foreign banks operating in the country was seized and oil distribution networks were nationalized. Although some of these measures may have appeared harsh, such moves went down well with the population, who welcomed them as an assertion of national pride and independence after the ineffectual, soggy days of the monarchy.

In line with Qaddafi's purist Bedouin principles, the RCC also moved to invest some religious authority in itself. Given Qaddafi's devout religious beliefs, Islam was always going to be a core part of the revolutionary discourse. The RCC clamped down on pleasures associated with 'Western vices', closing down casinos and nightclubs and banning alcohol. In 1972, the payment of *zakat* (compulsory charitable donation) became a formal legal obligation, and shortly afterwards sharia law and sharia courts were integrated into what had been a largely secular legal system. The following year, Qaddafi established the Islamic Call Society – a missionary body that served as a mass propaganda machine that was pumped full of oil money to promote Islam and Libya internationally. He also restored the Islamic calendar and insisted that both Christian and Islamic dates be used on all official documents. This return to Islamic values was reassuring to a population that was still largely illiterate and that was struggling to come to terms with the modernization that had accompanied not only the colonial experience, but also the oil boom.

Less reassuring may have been the new regime's efforts to ensure that there could be no challenge to the revolutionary state. In the interests of conformity, all political activity outside the official framework of the state was banned – something that culminated in the controversial Law No. 71 of 1972, which made engaging in party politics a crime punishable by death, and which remained in place until the fall of the regime. Unofficial trades unions were also barred, and the new unions that were established all came under the supervision of the Ministry of Labour. The press was also emasculated, with ten newspapers having their licences suspended, and even the main state newspaper *Al-Thawra* (*The Revolution*) periodically being stopped from going to press when its content did not meet with the approval of the new leadership. Indeed it was clear from very early on that there was only going to be one way of doing things.

However, it would be wrong to think that these moves were part of any coordinated or coherent plan. Beyond the populist gestures, little thought had been given to how actually to manage the day-to-day affairs of what was a relatively new state that was still finding its feet after independence. Having got rid of the most competent officials after taking power, Libya's inexperienced new leaders were essentially grappling in the dark; they talked for hours, but could agree on nothing. So nothing got done and the country slipped into a kind of chaotic stasis: the economy ground to a halt, unemployment began to rise and planned projects failed to get off the ground. Libyans, who had hoped for so much from this group of young soldiers, began to have their doubts.

It was in this tense and shambolic atmosphere that Qaddafi began to differentiate himself from those around him. He took to behaving as though he was far above the rest of the RCC, and began venting his frustration at the way things were going on around him. The camaraderie of the pre-coup days dissolved, as the new leader turned on his fellow revolutionaries, blaming them for the chaos and openly insulting them; he regularly admonished them in public, telling them in the most disparaging of terms that they 'didn't understand anything' and that they were not up to the job. Within a few weeks of the coup, he also began undermining them in front of their staff, cancelling decisions they had made and accusing them of incompetence.

This did not go down well with his fellow revolutionaries, who were hurt and troubled by this sudden change of behaviour. Despite their loyalty to him, they became increasingly irritated, too, as Qaddafi took to lording it over them. He began convening meetings and then making them wait for hours before he deigned to turn up (or sometimes did not turn up at all). These meetings were often held at 2 a.m., a time that suited his unorthodox hours, but that left others struggling to keep awake. The new leader also expected the rest of the RCC to adopt his rather austere lifestyle. So 'pure' was Qaddafi that he refused to stump up the cash for two RCC members, Khweildi Al-Humaidi and Abdelmonem Al-Houni, who travelled to Cairo in 1970 for medical treatment. The indignant revolutionaries were forced to go cap in hand to the Libyan embassy in Cairo to borrow money from the officials there.[30] The RCC members were so fed up that they regularly complained to Al-Deeb that their leader, who refused to have his own chauffeur, was a miser.

RCC members became increasingly frustrated, too, that Qaddafi took to behaving like a spoiled and sulky child when he did not get his own way: he stopped talking to his colleagues for two or three days at a time if they upset him, and regularly stormed off and sat at home, threatening to resign unless he got his own way. Sometimes his outbursts were over the most trivial of matters. On one occasion, Qaddafi insisted that all RCC members should wear military uniforms and carry pistols at all times. Abdelmonem Al-Houni objected to this decision and turned up to the next meeting wearing civilian clothes.[31] This prompted a furious Colonel to disappear into the deserts of Sirte in a huff for an entire week. On another occasion when things were not going his way, Qaddafi announced dramatically that he had decided to leave Libya to go to fight alongside the Palestinians in Jordan. Needless to say, this turned out to be another empty threat, aimed at getting his own way.

While such outbursts were difficult enough for Qaddafi's fellow RCC members, what really upset them was that he took to taking unilateral policy decisions. Showing scant regard for their views, he forged ahead as he saw fit. In May 1970, for example, he took a group of soldiers and closed down two casinos that were still in operation, arresting and imprisoning the foreign artistes and customers he found there. When the RCC complained that such a heavy-handed approach would misrepresent the revolution abroad, Qaddafi retorted by telling them that they didn't understand a thing.[32]

Sometimes the other RCC members only learned what the Colonel was up to by tuning into the radio. This was the case in 1970, when he paid a visit to Algeria. There he struck a number of agreements with Algerian President Houari Boumedienne to work towards unifying the two countries. This move shocked some of the RCC members, who were suspicious of Algeria's real intentions. Indeed, while the RCC was largely supportive of Arab unity, some members were concerned at the speed with which the young Qaddafi was recklessly trying to forge ahead with it. Abdelsalam Jalloud in particular believed the Colonel's rush to try to forge unions with other Arab states to be ill-advised.

Yet Qaddafi was a man with a vision. Indeed, it was clear very early on that there was only going to be space for one man and that no one was going to hold him back. As he declared while holding his gun aloft during a speech in Misarata in 1971, 'We will achieve unity even if it is only me who does so, even by the force of this gun.'[33] All this was becoming too much for some of his fellow revolutionaries. On another occasion, after Qaddafi had made a fiery public speech in which he attacked the rest of the RCC for not being sufficiently keen on Arab unity, Omar Al-Meheishi exploded in his face and pointed a machine gun at him.[34] According to Al-Houni, Qaddafi, who was himself armed with a pistol, was only saved when Al-Houni and Jalloud pounced on the furious Al-Meheishi and wrestled the gun away from him.

Qaddafi's behaviour pushed some RCC members over the edge: Mukhtar Abdullah Qarawi was so fed up with the insults that he resigned in 1972, followed by Mohamed Najm the following year. One group of RCC members went further. In 1975 Omar Al-Meheishi (who, thanks to his intellect and more middle-class origins, could have been a powerful figure in his own right) tried to stage a coup against the Colonel with two other members, Bashir Hawadi and Ali Awad Hamza. The plot was uncovered, and the men were forced to flee, along with Abdelmonem Al-Houni, who was also accused of involvement.

Yet such extreme episodes were rare within the RCC. For all that they may have been infuriated by Qaddafi's behaviour, the rest of his fellow revolutionaries remained loyal, many of them until the very end. Mustafa Kharroubi, Khweildi Al-Humaidi and Abu Bakr Younis Jaber, for example, stayed with their leader even when it became apparent to all that his days were numbered. Their unswerving loyalty may have been because, deep in their hearts, they knew that it was Qaddafi who had made them: the Colonel had picked them out when they were simple schoolboys from lowly tribes and had lifted them out of their surroundings. Indeed, without him they were nothing. As Al-Houni was later to reflect, the RCC members were essentially 'mundane' and their mental capacity was far below the historic task they had been given.[35] Even Qaddafi himself callously described them as 'lackeys'.[36] As such, those from the RCC who remained loyal were little more than a bunch of followers who were in no position to challenge the unstoppable force that was Qaddafi.

In any case, almost from the beginning, the wily Colonel had begun to sideline the RCC by bringing in and relying on others whose loyalty and obedience he could be assured of. These included groups of Free Unionist Officers who had not previously been part of the inner circle. They also included members of Qaddafi's own family and tribe. Al-Deeb reported back to Cairo in the early 1970s how Qaddafi's relatives, especially Hassan Ishkal and Khalifa Hannesh, were playing a major role, and how this was upsetting some RCC members. Yet Qaddafi had understood early on exactly what he needed to do in order to build his dream.

However, consolidating his power structures was not enough to turn the coup into a revolution. Despite the Colonel's best efforts to rally the masses with his populist rhetoric, the Libyan people were still not seriously behind (or even engaged with) the revolution, particularly on the ideological level. This came as a bitter disappointment to the young Qaddafi, who was becoming increasingly frustrated that the Libyan people were failing to live up to his lofty ideals. The youth were not enlisting in the army as they had been instructed to do; agricultural and resettlement schemes had been set up, but Libyans were refusing to work in remote parts of the country; and university 'perverts' were engaged in subversive activity.[37] The Colonel was clearly running ahead of his population, failing to appreciate that, while most Libyans were happy that the old regime had been toppled, they were not ready to make a complete break with the past and to accept his new-fangled ideas.

An increasingly sulky Qaddafi did not hesitate to take his frustrations out on the populace, admonishing it for its poor performance. In a speech in October 1971 in the coastal town of Sabratha, he complained:

We have ascertained that even under the revolutionary regime nobody is doing anything except for the sake of remuneration, and that nothing is performed, no mission accomplished, save in exchange for some reward … There will have to be a real change of heart among the Libyans: the revolution of 1 September was only a beginning.[38]

Qaddafi became so disenchanted with his revolutionary experience that it became increasingly common for him to withdraw to his family home in Sirte or to his beloved desert for long stints of contemplation. In a particularly serious episode in 1972, after yet another quarrel with the RCC, Qaddafi announced his resignation and stormed off to Egypt with his family in tow, telling President Sadat, 'I came to reside here as a normal citizen.'[39] Despite this assertion, the Libyan leader spent his time in Egypt giving lectures, touring factories, and meeting intellectuals. After fifteen days, the impetuous Qaddafi returned to Libya where, at an RCC meeting, his fellow revolutionaries, who were confused by events, informed him that they accepted his resignation. Qaddafi retorted: 'Unfortunately you were not elected so I cannot give you my resignation. You are imposing yourself on the people by the force of a Kalashnikov.'[40] When some RCC members reminded Qaddafi that he had not been elected either, he responded: 'I have popular support and I will give my resignation directly to the people.'[41]

It was therefore agreed that Qaddafi would put his resignation to the masses at a specially convened meeting at Zawara, to the west of Tripoli, to mark the anniversary of the birthday of the

Prophet on 16 April 1973. However, when the time came, the RCC was in for a shock.

The beginnings of 'Qaddafism'

From a stage erected in the centre of this unprepossessing coastal town, Qaddafi made a speech that was to change the course of Libyan history. After dramatically declaring that the revolution was in mortal danger, and after attacking the Libyan people for their laziness and lack of revolutionary zeal, he announced not his resignation, but the launch of a cultural or 'Popular Revolution'. The audience was stunned. So too was the RCC, which clearly had no idea that its leader was about to spring this on it; Jalloud was flabbergasted.[42]

But Qaddafi's fellow revolutionaries, who had had the carpet pulled from under their feet, could do little about the situation. As a group, they were not strong or united enough to do anything to stop Qaddafi. More importantly, for all their exasperation, most still had an overriding sense of loyalty to their leader, even though this was the clearest sign yet that he was leaving them far behind. Indeed, this speech – which was to serve as a blueprint for the rest of his four decades in power – represented the real beginnings of the intense personalization of politics that was to characterize Libya under the endlessly eccentric Qaddafi. Such was the force of the Leader's personality that those around him had no choice but to follow.

Sweeping away the existing political structures, the Colonel declared a new five-point programme that would mobilize Libya's citizens and save his cherished revolution. This programme advocated: a) the repeal of all existing laws and their replacement by revolutionary enactments; b) the weeding out of all anti-revolutionary elements by taking appropriate measures against 'perverts and deviators'; c) the staging of an administrative revolution to destroy all forms of bourgeoisie and bureaucracy; d) the arming of the people to create a people's militia that could protect the revolution; and e) the staging of a cultural revolution to get rid of all imported poisonous ideas that are contrary to the Qu'ran.

The plan was to be enacted through popular committees that were to be formed by 'every village, town, college, factory and school'. The members of these committees were to be elected directly by the people and were to run everything from schools to companies to government offices. This was essentially an attack on the administration and was meant to weed out the last vestiges of the old bureaucracy, including local mayors and managers, university administrators and members of local municipal councils, who were all forced out of their posts. It was to be a complete purge of anyone deemed to be 'obstructing the path to revolutionary progress'. As Qaddafi told students at Benghazi University, 'Trample under your feet any bourgeois bureaucrat who closes the doors of government offices in your face ... Tear up all the imported books which do not express Arabism, Islam, socialism and progress. Burn and destroy all curricula that do not express the truth.'[43]

By August 1973, there were over 2,000 such committees in operation. Some of the more zealous among them took their work seriously: acting on their recommendations, the police arrested between three and four hundred regime opponents, including communists, Ba'athists, members of the Muslim Brotherhood and Hizb ut-Tahrir (Islamic Liberation Party).[44] However, predictably enough, others used their new positions to settle old scores and pursue their own interests. Moreover, the impractical nature of this system and the inexperience of those elected to the committees soon showed, resulting in further bureaucratic chaos – yet another feature of Qaddafi's revolution that was to endure. By mid-1973, the country's bureaucratic structures had nearly doubled in size and had become both a means for social advancement and, importantly, a mechanism for the new regime to control activity at every level of society.[45]

Meanwhile the regime began recruiting for a people's militia that would augment the army. This militia – which was open to both men and women – managed to enlist some 40,000 recruits during its first year.[46] Its members received training, uniforms and weapons, but no pay, and their function was mainly to guard buildings and to man checkpoints and border points. However, they could be mobilized at a time of crisis. More importantly, the militarization of society in this way served to create a loyal force that could serve as a counterbalance to the armed forces, if need be.

The five-point plan clearly marked an extension of some of the concepts of 'people power' that had already characterized the rhetoric of the first years after the coup. However, it was also a reflection of Qaddafi's realization that, if the masses were not going to come on board, he would have to impose his revolution by force. As he asserted, he was ready to 'take people to paradise in chains'.[47]

So it was that, from this point forward, the Libyan revolution came to be equated with what can only be described as 'Qaddafism'. Indeed, the popular or cultural revolution was based on Qaddafi's unique and personal vision that he had been developing during his periods of quiet contemplation in the desert. This vision was the Third Universal Theory, which came to serve as the ideological underpinning of his revolutionary state. He first announced this theory in May 1973, a month after his Zawara speech, at an international conference for Arab and European youth. With a characteristic lack of modesty, Qaddafi told his audience that his new theory would be based upon 'universal truth' and that it would 'serve all humanity'.

The theory was essentially a new 'middle way' to replace both communism and capitalism. The Colonel shunned both systems, arguing that capitalism had transformed society into a circus that had handed over the reins to the individual without any restraints, while 'godless' communism had turned humans into sheep because of its claim to solve economic problems by the total abolition of private property.[48] His theory was an alternative for the Third World and would enable the weak to fight back against the strong. It was also a reflection of Qaddafi's belief that the answers to society's problems lay in Islam. As he explained in his speech to the youth forum, 'The Third Theory or ideology ... is an ideology which calls for mankind to return to the Kingdom of God ... When we speak about the Third Universal Theory we stress that it is not made by man nor is it a philosophy, but it is based on truth ... truth is firm and unchangeable.'[49]

Yet for all the heady talk of new concepts and universal truths, the essence of the theory appears to have been socialism with an Islamic flavour. Qaddafi believed that socialism was inherent in Islam, that both abhorred exploitation of the weak by the strong, and that both had a respect for justice. As he declared, 'Islam provides for the realisation of justice and equity; it does not allow any rich person to use his wealth as a tool of oppression nor to exploit people ... Islam stands against poverty, and firmly stands by the side of the working classes.'[50]

For Qaddafi this was a theory that could resist the imperialism of the two dominating political-ideological systems, and that could ensure the protection of individuals in societies in the developing world. Yet while this theory may have been clear to Qaddafi, it is doubtful whether the masses – whose lives it sought to transform – were able to fully grasp its meaning. Even the educated found the theory utterly confusing; one Libyan studying in the UK at the time recalled: 'We didn't understand a word of it.'[51] Mansour Kikhia, Qaddafi's foreign minister between 1972 and 1973, who was abducted on a visit to Cairo in 1993, recalled:

Whenever new intellectuals arrived Qadhafi would tell me to invite them to visit him. Then as we talked he would take notes. He would ask them how to remedy this or that problem. The trouble for him was that he couldn't digest their ideas. He didn't have a basic scientific approach. When he himself offered an opinion, he came out with immature and confused analyses, such as were later to form the basis of his Third Universal Theory.[52]

Moreover, there was nothing particularly new in the theory. The erudite Mohamed Heikal commented: 'As one who has lived through the experience of Nasser's revolution I am still puzzled by the Third Theory. It reminds me of something Nasser once said to his companions: "Don't invent electricity; somebody had done that already ... Our task is to learn to use it, not to re-invent it." '[53] Bona Malwal, the Sudanese minister for information and culture, visited Libya in 1974. During his stay, the Libyan leader spent two days trying to convince him to apply the theory to Sudan, but Malwal concluded, 'I didn't find an original idea in it.'[54] Rather it was a mish-mash of confused ideas and concepts, wrapped up in a fervent anti-imperialism and a simplistic belief that Islam and social justice could make the Arabs great again.

Yet the importance of the Third Universal Theory was that it was something that could lift Qaddafi and his revolution above and beyond the local. Qaddafi always believed he was a thinker of world-class calibre, and for him this theory was proof of that – so much so that he embarked upon a mass publicity campaign aimed at spreading his ideas on an international scale. He invited Muslims and thinkers from around the world to conferences in Libya, where he and his RCC members would expound on his theory and on his revolution.[55] He also took his ideas on touring roadshows. In Cairo, in the summer of 1973, he enraged Egyptian intellectuals and President Sadat by calling on them to carry out their own cultural revolution, and condemning them for the fact that they permitted bars, nightclubs, alcohol and gambling: 'How can a drunk make progress in society?

How can a drunk battle in Sinai against the enemy?'[56] It also emerged in 1974 that the very day after Qaddafi had offered to allocate $3 billion over five years to raise production levels in Egyptian factories, Jalloud had demanded that, for such funds to be agreed, Egypt must commit itself to the Third Universal Theory and the popular revolution.[57]

In his bid to publicize his new ideology, Qaddafi made some very curious alliances. One of the strangest was his dalliance with a hippy group called the Children of God (COG). The Children of God were led by an American preacher, Moses David, who, according to his daughter, had started to receive 'special revelations' about Qaddafi in 1971. Moses David seems to have come to the conclusion that Qaddafi was someone special, who 'may either be the Antichrist himself, or … is preparing the way for the Antichrist. But it is God-ordained, and it's obvious God has predicted it.'[58] The group decided that it should assist Qaddafi in whatever way was necessary, and in his writings Moses David heaped praise upon the Colonel, his Third Universal Theory and his 'Godly Socialism'.

Qaddafi's links to this group certainly came as a surprise to members of the RCC. Al-Meheishi recalled how, during the opening in March 1972 of the Tripoli International Fair, he noticed the presence of 'girls wearing gypsy clothes with unkempt hair' who were carrying leaflets and musical instruments.[59] When Al-Meheishi asked who the girls were, he was told they were 'the girls of Allah'. Some of these women approached him while he was visiting the stall of the USA and told him they were friends of Qaddafi. According to Al-Meheishi, 'they started singing a song in which the word Qaddafi was repeated so many times'.

When Al-Meheishi questioned the Leader about the wisdom of befriending such a group, Qaddafi's motives were abundantly clear. He replied: 'they promote my name in Europe through their songs'.[60] It took until 1975 and a month-long stay in Tripoli for Moses David to cotton onto the fact that Qaddafi was only interested in the group for what it could do to promote his revolution. His daughter recounts:

> Dad spent about a month in Libya, but things weren't going the way he thought they would. He had taken with him a troupe of girls and started an FF [flirty fishing] ministry[61] among some military leaders and Qadahfi's personal staff. But Qadahfi was not interested in prostitution – the Koran forbids it – even though his officers were. Rather, the Libyan wanted only to make use of the ten thousand COG disciples who were distributing literature around the world ... But Moses David was not interested – he was in over his head, and he knew it. He realized that Qadahfi could crush him like a bug if he wished.[62]

Yet it was not just cult groups like the Children of God who heralded Qaddafi and his new revolutionary spirit. The young leader also found popularity among other parts of the developing world. He visited Pakistan for the 1974 Islamic summit and was reportedly received like a hero. Yet all this international notoriety was clearly going to his head. According to Al-Meheishi,

> After Qaddafi's return from Lahore, I noted that he wasn't the man I knew. He started saying repeatedly that he was no longer the chairman of the Revolutionary Council but that he was the leader of the world, especially the Islamic world. He started rejecting the idea that he was the head of Libya only ... After that he stopped receiving ambassadors and stopped receiving heads of state in the airport.[63]

It was not long after his return from Pakistan that he was to immortalize his thinking in his most famous work, the *Green Book*.

The *Green Book* and the Jamahiriyah

The *Green Book*, the first part of which was published in 1975, was Qaddafi's attempt to bring his revolutionary thoughts into a single written treatise. Divided into three parts – the first dealing with politics, the second with economics and the third with social issues – it is a kind of handbook for society that lays out Qaddafi's utopian, but hopelessly simplistic, vision of the ideal form of governance. The basic thrust of the text is that, in order for true democracy to flourish, state institutions should be abolished and society should take charge of its own problems and rule itself in a 'stateless society'.

Given the enormity of the subject matter, one might expect the *Green Book* to be a hefty tome, requiring hours of study. Yet it is not a big book. In fact, it is remarkably slim. As Italian journalist Oriana Fallaci once rather condescendingly told Qaddafi during an interview, 'Oh yes I have read it! It doesn't take very long. A quarter of an hour, tops. It's so tiny. My powder compact is bigger than your little green book.'[64] Qaddafi appears not to have taken offence at Fallaci's comment, replying: 'You sound like Sadat. He says it sits on the palm of your hand.'[65] Even one of the Libyan regime's most fervent ideologues, Rajoub Bu Dabbous, once described it as 'A summary of a book that hasn't been written yet.'[66]

What the *Green Book* lacks in size it does not make up for in coherence. It is not an easy read: it is repetitive and packed with heavily laboured examples that do little to clarify the ideas (or rather the germs of ideas) that they are supposed to illustrate. Certain passages are baffling or just downright bizarre, such as that included in the part of the book about 'sport, horsemanship and shows', in which Qaddafi declares:

Sport is like praying, eating, and the feeling of warmth and coolness. It is stupid for crowds to enter a restaurant just to look at a person or a group of persons eating; it is stupid for people to let a person or a group of persons get warmed or enjoy ventilation on their behalf. It is equally illogical for the society to allow an individual or a team to monopolize sports while the people as a whole pay the costs of such a monopoly for the benefit of one person or a team.[67]

The first, and arguably most important, part of the *Green Book*, entitled 'The Solution of the Problem of Democracy', is hardly more sophisticated in its intellectual approach. It is based primarily around the notion that parliaments and political parties are obstacles to true democracy because, by their very nature, they involve the surrendering of individual sovereignty to whoever is elected. All forms of representation are rejected; parliaments are dismissed as 'a misrepresentation of the people' and political parties are 'the modern dictatorial instrument of governing'.[68] Qaddafi declares, too, that the parliamentary system cannot be called true democracy, because a political party may win an election with 51 per cent of the vote, leaving the other 49 per cent of voters ruled by a party they do not support. This, for him, is the antithesis of what it means to be democratic.

Having dismissed such political systems, Qaddafi goes on to lay out his solution for rule by the people, namely 'direct democracy'. Building on the ideas in his Zawara speech, Qaddafi asserts that the only way to achieve true democracy is through the establishment of a system of people's congresses and people's committees – something he describes as 'the final fruit of the people's struggle for democracy'.[69] This is a mind-bogglingly complex system; crudely described, at the bottom of the hierarchy are the 'basic people's congresses', in which every citizen is supposed to participate. These congresses are tasked with debating and voting on policies of national and local interest, after which their decisions are fed up to a General People's

Congress (a kind of parliament), which in turn passes decisions on to a General People's Committee (a kind of cabinet) for implementation. Under this system, in theory at least, every citizen participates in the process of governing, and the general will of the masses is eventually implemented.

The second part of the *Green Book*, entitled 'The Solution of the Economic Problem', adopts an equally egalitarian approach. Qaddafi argues that in his stateless society all citizens should be allowed to share and profit equally from the country's wealth. He rejects the idea that people should be 'wage workers', as this only leaves them open to exploitation and means that they are not consuming any of the production they have generated. The book states: 'Wage-workers are a type of slave, however improved their wages may be.'[70] Qaddafi puts this exploitation and the development of the world's unjust economic systems down to the fact that society has strayed from the natural order of things. Indeed he writes as if there is an innate natural law that is inherently just and that has been corrupted by wages, class and ownership.

In order to return to this 'natural order', wages should be abolished and people should be freed by becoming 'partners in production', taking control of economic enterprises themselves. In this way everyone is able to profit equally. As Qaddafi asserts, 'For man to be happy, he must be free, and to be free, man must possess his own needs.' He thus argues that everyone should take an equal share of whatever they produce, and that this share should be commensurate with their needs.

Under this system, the *Green Book* declares, individuals should not possess economic assets that could be used to exploit others. The renting out of houses, for example, is forbidden: 'No one has the right to build a house, additional to his own and that of his heirs, for the purpose of renting it, because the house represents another person's need, and building it for the purpose of rent is an attempt to have control over the need of that man and thus "in need freedom is latent".[71] Similarly it forbids the employment of domestic servants or the hiring of taxis, because these non-productive activities also amount to exploitation.

The third and final part of the *Green Book*, entitled the 'Social Basis of the Third Universal Theory', is a curious mix of eclectic subjects covering sport, music, women and slavery that provides an insight into Qaddafi's conception of the world. Demonstrating that, for all his aspirations to progressiveness, the young leader still clung tightly to traditional values, the *Green Book* insists that the family is the most important unit in society. It states that if an individual is separated from his family he 'has no value or social life' and 'To the individual man the family is of more importance than the state. Mankind acknowledges the individual man and the individual man acknowledges the family which is his cradle, his origin and his social "umbrella".' Qaddafi takes this idea further by explaining that a tribe is a large family, and that the nation is 'a tribe which has grown through procreation'.

Qaddafi's thoughts on women are rather less traditional: 'woman and man are equal as human beings. Discrimination between man and woman is a flagrant act of oppression without any justification.' However, alongside these more progressive statements about equality are more reactionary proclamations about woman's role in society. He asserts, for example: 'According to a gynaecologist, woman menstruates or suffers feebleness every month, while man, being a male, does not ... When a woman does not menstruate she is pregnant. If she is pregnant she becomes, due to pregnancy feeble for about a year.' He goes on: 'Afterwards woman breast-feeds the baby she bore ... Breast-feeding means that a woman is so inseparable from her baby that her activity is seriously reduced. She becomes directly responsible for another person whom she helps to carry out his biological functions, without which it would die.' From this

Qaddafi concludes: 'All these innate characteristics form differences because of which man and woman cannot be equal.'

Such obvious contradictions highlight the fact that the *Green Book* is in essence a naïve and idealistic expression of youthful revolutionary fervour. It was written by a man whose view of the world was uncomplicated by any real experience or knowledge of it, and who, for all his pretensions to internationalism, struggled on the intellectual level at least to move beyond the local. If anything, it is a reflection of his Bedouin roots. For all he thought of himself as progressive, Qaddafi always clung closely to his Bedouin heritage – something that, for him, as for many Arabs, represented purity and honour, and a life free from the materialist trappings of the modern westernized world. The strength of Qaddafi's attachment to this somewhat romanticized image of the Bedouin is nowhere more evident than in one of his own short stories, where he warns:

> Flee, flee the city and get away from the smoke … Flee from the lethargy and waste, the poison and boredom and yawning. Flee from the nightmare city … Leave the worm-like existence behind … Depart the city and flee to the village, where you will see the moon for the first time in your lives … Leave the cemetery neighbourhoods for God's wide and wondrous land … In the countryside, look up and see the divine lanterns suspended in the dome of the sky, and not the ceiling of a filthy tomb in the city.[72]

He goes on:

> In complete happiness, go to the village and the countryside, where physical labour has meaning, necessity, usefulness, and is a pleasure besides. There, life is social, and human; families and tribes are close. There is stability and belief. Everyone loves one

another, and everyone lives on his own farm, or has livestock, or works in the village's service sector. Deviation is unacceptable, because the people in the village know one another, unlike those in the city ... The conscience is healthy.[73]

In fact, Qaddafi sought to play up his Bedouin heritage throughout his rule, milking it for all it was worth; Bedouin life became totally idealized in the regime's discourse. So much so that state television regularly carried what felt like endless footage of Bedouin women in tents grinding what appeared to be wheat, accompanied by men singing traditional Bedouin songs. The Leader always made a point, too, of hosting meetings in his Bedouin tent, sometimes making foreign dignitaries travel all the way to Sirte, and controversially erecting massive tents whenever he travelled; when Qaddafi arrived, it was as though the circus had come to town![74] So great was Qaddafi's bid to push his Bedouin heritage that it became a stick for his detractors to beat him with: a favourite complaint among the urbane mercantile Tripolitanians was that they were ruled by a handful of 'ignorant and backward' Bedouin from the desert.

Yet for all that it may have been unsophisticated, Qaddafi believed that his book contained the ultimate answer to all society's ills. As with his Third Universal Theory, he was in no doubt that the *Green Book* would change the world; it was the book to end all books and to render every other political system utterly invalid. Following the publication of the first chapter, Qaddafi announced: 'With the establishment of this unique democratic experiment, all political theories in the world have collapsed.' In a speech to the final session of the General People's Congress on 18 January 1976, he proclaimed: 'I am not exaggerating if I say that all philosophy books that have tried to come up with a view on how to solve the problem of democracy before the dawn of 1976 are all now in the rubbish bin.'[75] In interviews with the international media, Qaddafi even went so far as to declare that the *Green Book* was the new gospel – the gospel of the modern age and the masses.[76]

It was this 'new gospel' and the ill-conceived political system contained in it that was to be Libya's fate for the following three decades and more. Things would never be the same again; Libya had well and truly moved into 'the dawn of the era of the masses' and, as far as Qaddafi was concerned, there was no going back.

CHAPTER 4

Jamahiriyah in Practice:
A Revolutionary Decade

Having presented his new gospel to the world, the Colonel was ready to put his ideas into practice. On 2 March 1977, in the town of Sebha, where he had staged his first rebellions against the king, Libya's young leader announced the 'Declaration of the Establishment of the Authority of the People'. This announcement marked the birth of the Jamahiriyah, or 'State of the Masses', and formalized the cumbersome political system that Qaddafi had laid out in the first part of his *Green Book*. This was to be 'people power' in action: every Libyan was to participate in governing through the jumble of people's congresses and committees that made up this 'stateless society'. It was time for the masses to rule themselves.

To reflect this historic transformation, the country's name was changed to the decidedly un-catchy 'Socialist People's Libyan Arab Jamahiriyah', and a few months later the flag was changed to what must be the blandest national emblem in history – an expanse of plain, unadorned green. As befitted this momentous occasion, Cuban revolutionary Fidel Castro was invited to be present at the announcement of the declaration, as a special guest of honour. Qaddafi brimmed with pride as the famed Cuban leader addressed the

General People's Congress in Sebha, full of praise for the Libyan revolution. Celebrations in Tripoli, meanwhile, reached a crescendo: crowds filled the streets, chanting their support for the birth of the first ever Jamahiriyah, as military aircraft flew overhead in tight-knit formations and the ships in the port blew their sirens. Direct democracy Qaddafi-style was up and running.

Yet, for all that the declaration was billed as the handing over of power to the people, it was clear who was going to steer the ship. Qaddafi appointed himself head of the Secretariat of the 970-member General People's Congress, a body that was to implement the will of the people, as expressed in the 'basic people's congresses'.[1] From now on, 'Qaddafism' was to seep into every part of life, and everything familiar was to be swept away, as the new leader endeavoured to turn his utopian vision into a reality.

The Colonel may have believed that this Jamahiriyah was the answer to all humanity's problems, but most Libyans remained less than convinced by the 'new dawn'. The masses were, for the most part, utterly bewildered by the changes that were suddenly being foisted upon them in the name of the people's authority. Most were not the slightest bit interested in grand notions of 'people power' and, to the Colonel's frustration, there was a widespread popular indifference to his 'people's democracy'. Attendance at the basic people's congresses that were planted in every locality was pitiful: in Tripoli and Gharyan, for example, more than half the members were routinely absent from meetings; and in some areas of Misarata absenteeism reached 90 per cent.[2]

Moreover, those who did bother to turn up to the congresses often had no idea what they were supposed to be discussing there. To Qaddafi's displeasure, those who attended often continued to pursue local or regional interests, and had little appetite for his new-fangled political innovations. The congresses were also proving administratively inept; they were often led by careless or absent officials and, even at this early stage, corruption was eating its way through the new revolutionary bodies.[3] The purity that the Bedouin from the desert had dreamt of was already being soiled.

To make matters worse, in some quarters popular indifference was hardening into outright resistance. If Qaddafi had hoped that the country's universities would serve as intellectual powerhouses for his new revolutionary theories, he was to be sorely mistaken. Students had begun showing their displeasure at the new regime even before the announcement of the Declaration of the Establishment of the Authority of the People. As early as January 1976, young students began staging demonstrations, demanding freedom of expression and objecting to the authorities' insistence on imposing their own student union leaders. They demanded, too, that the regime amend its newly introduced policy of compulsory conscription, mainly because the timing of what was being proposed interfered with their studies. Such demands were hardly extreme; they were relatively mild in comparison with the kind of student activities taking place in neighbouring countries, where Islamist and militant leftish elements were battling it out on university campuses.

However, Qaddafi's was an ideology of absolutes, and conformity was the name of the game. The Colonel moved quickly to nip the protests in the bud. Following a major demonstration on 7 April 1976 on the campuses of both Tripoli and Benghazi universities, the regime sent in its forces, arresting and detaining hundreds of unsuspecting students. Given that the 1969 coup had been a largely bloodless affair, this sudden heavy-handed approach came as a shock.

Things took an even more sinister turn the following year, when, just a month after the Declaration of the Establishment of the Authority of the People, a number of students who had been involved in the protests were publicly hanged on the campus of Tripoli's Al-Fateh University. Their fellow students were forced to watch the grisly proceedings that were also broadcast repeatedly on state television. On the same day, four Libyans and one Egyptian were hanged in Benghazi's main square after having been convicted of acting for Egyptian intelligence. It was also at this time that twenty-two army officers were executed in their military units for their involvement in Al-Meheishi's 1975 coup attempt. From then on, 7 April was reserved as a special date for public executions.

This baptism of blood was a stark warning: the People's Authority was not going to tolerate dissent. Libyans were learning fast that this uncompromising 'prophet of the desert' was not going to allow anything to stand in the way of his vision. As he once declared, 'It [the revolution] is a moving train. Whoever stands in its way will be crushed.'[4] If the Libyans were not willing to come along with him on his revolutionary journey, then he would have to drag them along by force.

Yet Qaddafi knew that force alone would not be enough to quell the popular apathy or the outright resistance to his vision. He also knew that, if he let the revolution rest on its laurels, dissent would worm its way even further into his perfect vision. He feared, too, that his Jamahiriyah would be swallowed up by the state, that his immaculate conception would be sullied by the day-to-day business of running the country.

His answer was to instigate a revolution within the revolution, to create a separate revolutionary authority that could serve as a monitor and guide for the formal political structures that made up the Jamahiriyah. Such an authority could act as a kind of whipping force to keep the country in a state of perpetual revolution and to bend it utterly to his will. On the anniversary of the revolution, at the 1 September celebrations of 1978, the Colonel announced that, henceforth 'revolutionary authority' was to be separated from the 'people's authority'. The following March, he and his fellow former RCC members resigned from the Secretariat of the General People's Congress, leaving it to deal with the everyday business of running the country, while they devoted themselves to the higher cause of furthering the revolution.

Although he still retained the role of commander of the armed forces, from now on Qaddafi was to have no formal position in the state. Instead he insisted on being referred to as 'Leader of the Revolution', or, more often, 'Brother Leader'. Not having an official role in this way appealed to Qaddafi's sense of himself as an intellectual and thinker, busy with the supreme mission of advancing the revolution and way above the mundane role of head of state. As he declared before he resigned from the General People's Congress, 'I will return to my natural place, which is the revolution, not the authority.'[5] Qaddafi clearly saw himself as a Che Guevara figure, a true revolutionary in its most romantic sense, restlessly pushing the country forwards, ceaselessly moulding it to his revolutionary vision.

Of course, it would be wrong to think that Qaddafi was no longer involved in the affairs of the state. Despite all his protestations, Brother Leader was still in complete control: from foreign policy to the budget to deciding who held what position in the General People's Congress, Qaddafi and his coterie of revolutionaries (who were increasingly coming to include members of his own family and tribe) continued to take all the key decisions.[6] Indeed, the creation of this revolutionary authority meant that, from now on, real power was to lie in the informal structures that were centred even more firmly around Qaddafi and his entourage. Within a year of the establishment of his Jamahiriyah, Qaddafi had effectively rendered its formal political institutions impotent, turning them into little more than a façade. Now, unfettered by the constraints of the cumbersome political system he had created, Qaddafi became a behind-the-scenes grand chess master, cannily moving the pieces around his board.

Having created this revolutionary authority, Qaddafi now needed some sort of revolutionary body to people it, in order to mobilize the masses and connect him to the base. Unlike his fellow leaders in the region, Qaddafi had no official political party to back him or to provide any real sense of cohesion or nationhood. He therefore wanted to create a truly populist force that would enable him to rally the masses in support of his vision. He also wanted a force that would be capable of monitoring and controlling the structures that made up the people's authority, and that could bulldoze anything that stood in the revolution's way.

It was to this end that Qaddafi created the 'Revolutionary Committees Movement'. This paramilitary body was to become one of the most feared institutions of Qaddafi's long rule. Although the movement was formally established in 1979, revolutionary cells were operating as early as 1976. They were established first on university campuses and were primarily an instrument of repression.[7] Groups of students, imbued with ardent revolutionary fervour, were brought together in these committees and charged with rooting out and liquidating dissenting students and members of staff. In November 1977, the official media began broadcasting news of the formation of revolutionary committees in different cities across the country, mainly to give the impression that these bodies had sprung up naturally from the midst of the masses.

Almost a year later, Qaddafi outlined the duties that the new revolutionary committees were to be tasked with. Unnervingly, the Colonel declared:

> The mission of the revolutionary committees is to be everywhere, secret or public ... to carry out the duty of urging the masses to revolt in order to seize power and to destroy any organization that stands in the way, including political parties [and] reactionary conventional tools of government such as tribes, families, sects and classes.[8]

In other words, they were to act like an enormous, omnipresent enforcer, overturning anything that stood in the way of Qaddafi's supreme mission. They soon established their *mathabas* (meeting places) in every town. These highly distinctive (and exceptionally ugly) constructions, supposed to replicate Bedouin tents, sprang up across the land, planting a sense of foreboding in every local community.

The members of the new revolutionary committees were mostly young men from lowly backgrounds who had benefited from the early education policies of the new regime. They were part of the new generation, eager to seize the opportunity to better themselves and to be part of the new Libya. Not only did membership provide access to jobs and privileges, but, more importantly, it offered power and prestige. Qaddafi imbued the committees with near immortal status: just as he compared the *Green Book* to the new gospel, he referred to the revolutionary committees as 'the prophets of the age of the masses'.

These prophets moved quickly to assert their revolutionary authority: the young revolutionaries also marched on all the formal mechanisms of the Jamahiriyah, penetrating the hierarchy of people's congresses and committees from the very top to the bottom. From 1979, for example, they were put in charge of coordinating elections to the basic people's congresses and they could veto candidates they did not approve of. In January 1980, their superiority over these institutions of people's authority was confirmed. The Secretary General of the General People's Congress, Abdel Ati Al-Obeidi, announced: '[A]ll People's Congresses, no matter what their level, as well as the Secretariat of the General People's Congress are under the permanent control of the revolution and the revolutionary committees.'[9]

In this way, the revolutionary committees came to be the highest authority in the land. Yet, demonstrating his political acumen, Qaddafi was careful to tie these revolutionaries very tightly to his own mast. He created an executive body for the movement – the Revolutionary Committees Liaison Office – and filled it with members of his family and his branch of the Qaddadfa tribe. These included key figures, such as his cousins Ahmed Ibrahim, Omar Ishkal and Abdullah Othman, who continued to play a major role in the country's political life throughout the following decades.[10] This all-powerful office was headed by one of Qaddafi's relatives and most loyal supporters, Mohamed Majdhoub, who held the post until his death in 2007. In this way, loyalty at the top of the movement was more or less guaranteed. At the same time, Qaddafi took steps to ensure that the base could not become a force in its own right. He shrewdly prevented revolutionary committee groups from contacting each other without going through the Liaison Office. Indeed, there was no structural horizontal relationship between the various revolutionary elements.

Yet the power of the revolutionary committees was not limited to the formal institutions of the Jamahiriyah. As Qaddafi had asserted, these fearsome revolutionaries were to be everywhere; they were to be part of what the Colonel dubbed the *Zahf Al-Akhdar* ('Green March') that would take his revolution to every part of Libya. No institution was to be left untouched, as the revolutionary committees infiltrated universities, professional organizations and even the security apparatus. Revolutionary committee units were set up inside the army, where they enforced petty regulations, such as banning officers from carrying weapons in a personal capacity or prohibiting them from entering barracks after working hours.[11] They also infiltrated the police, where they worked to combat speculation and corruption.

The revolutionary committees also moved in on the economy. In a bid to impose Qaddafi's mantra of creating partners not wage workers, in January 1980 groups of young men, bursting with revolutionary fervour, descended upon factories and companies across the land. These ideologues pushed the workers in these places to kick out the owners and managers and to form people's committees that would run the concerns themselves. This was a disastrous policy: the people's committees were completely inexperienced in running businesses, so that the factories and companies quickly fell into decline. Yet for Qaddafi, ideas were more important than state-building.

To spread these ideas, the revolutionary committees also took over the media, turning everything to the service of 'the people'. They established the *Zahf Al-Akhdar* and *Al-Jamahiriyah* newspapers and took over all broadcasting facilities. These outlets regurgitated endless regime propaganda, and the tone was uncompromisingly militant. However, reflecting his personal paranoia, Qaddafi became anxious that some elements in these media outlets might become personalities in their own right. Indeed, there was to be space for one personality only in the Jamahiriyah. When a presenter started to become too well known, the Leader ordered 'the people' to take over. The Libyan broadcasting house was suddenly inundated with ordinary Libyans, queuing up to have a turn at reading the news in what were live broadcasts – something that prompted no small degree of amusement among Libyans at large.[12] In a similar vein, Qaddafi insisted that officials be referred to by their position, rather than by their name, and that footballers only be known by the numbers on their shirts.

The impact of this media and cultural takeover served to isolate the Libyans from pretty much everything aside from Qaddafi's revolutionary ideas. In an era that pre-dated satellite dishes, Libyans were left largely cut off from the world. Foreign media and publications were banned, and state television, which in the 1980s broadcast for just six hours a day, pumped out little more than the Leader's speeches and conferences on the *Green Book*. One Libyan woman recalled: 'We had no idea what was happening in the world. Everything was propaganda, everything revolutionary.'[13]

This censorship was the start of the overwhelming and suffocating isolation that came to characterize Libya and the bizarre world that

Qaddafi created in it. Indeed, the surreal was never far away; on one occasion, for hours on end state television broadcast a photograph of a pair of military boots with the words 'From a viewer to the broadcasting house' underneath them.[14] Even after state television started having to compete with foreign satellite channels, such as Al-Jazeera, in the late 1990s, the broadcasting got little better. In 2006 Libyans were treated to hours of footage of a seemingly endless dirt road in sub-Saharan Africa, shot from the window of a moving vehicle, because this was the road that Qaddafi was travelling along during one of his many visits to that part of Africa!

As well as revolutionizing the state, the revolutionary committees were given a far more sinister remit. In February 1980, they were tasked with liquidating the opponents of the revolution. To help them complete this gruesome mission, the regime established a new system of 'revolutionary courts', in which the revolutionaries were given free rein to try 'reactionary' and 'deviant' elements. These courts, which were staffed by revolutionary committee members, acted completely outside the country's justice system and, unsurprisingly, committed gross abuses of power; mass trials became commonplace, as did retrials of political prisoners who had been arrested after the cultural revolution of 1973. Many of these prisoners had their sentences increased to life imprisonment; many others who went through these kangaroo courts found themselves sentenced to death.

The revolutionary committees took to the task of rooting out deviant elements with great gusto. This is hardly surprising: each year, every member was charged with uncovering and taking to the revolutionary court five elements who were hindering the revolution. Fear began to fill the air and seep through doorways, as scruffily dressed young men, rigid like their ideology and filled with self-righteous certainty, began arresting and carting off anyone they suspected of anti-revolutionary behaviour. One Libyan university professor recalled: 'People were afraid of expressing their views and thoughts because they were afraid of being accused of treason and treachery.'[15] This fostered a climate of crushing fear and intimidation that was not to be broken until the uprisings of 2011.

In such an environment, violence was never far off. Aggressive interrogations by revolutionary committee members were regularly broadcast on state television, with the victims frequently showing signs of torture. The shocking scenes, aimed at instilling fear, remained imprinted on the minds of the masses. One Libyan recalled:

> The first person to be interrogated on television was Omar Shalouf. I still remember his face very well. He was wearing a white shirt that had blood spots on it and we could see signs of torture on his face ... These kinds of interrogations came on every day after the news bulletin and the broadcaster would announce, 'and now we will see the confessions of the stray dogs'.[16]

In one interrogation of Sheikh Al-Bishti, the imam of Tripoli who had dared to question Qaddafi's views on Islam, the terrified preacher had his beard set alight.

These court interrogations and confessions were sometimes carried out as major public events. In 1984, crowds of unsuspecting Libyans, including schoolchildren, were brought to a sports stadium in Benghazi. It soon became clear what kind of spectacle they had been called to witness. A young man, Sadiq Hamed Shwehdi, sat cross-legged on the ground, utterly alone in the middle of the large pitch, his hands tied behind his back.[17] At one end of the pitch, seated at a table draped with crudely painted banners sporting revolutionary slogans, were three hardnosed revolutionary committee members. Shwehdi, his face contorted with fear, was certain of his fate. There was only one sentence for 'dissent': execution. Even so, the young victim was forced to confess his 'crimes' into a microphone, as Houda Ben Amar (who went on to become one of the most powerful women in Qaddafi's inner circle) whipped the crowd up into a frenzy, until it was baying for his blood.

Shwehdi's execution, like so many others that darkened the public squares and stadiums at this time, was broadcast on state television. These public executions seemed to engender a grisly sense of triumphalism among the revolutionary elements, who almost revelled in the violence. Television footage from the era (April 1984) shows one female revolutionary committee member kicking the corpse of a young man who had been hanged; in the same footage, another member sits on the corpse of a victim, repeatedly hitting him in the face.[18] In a similar vein, following a failed attack on Qaddafi's Bab Al-Aziziya compound in Tripoli in 1984 by members of the opposition group, the National Front for the Salvation of Libya (NFSL), revolutionary committee members were shown chanting over the dead bodies of those who had been killed in the attack. As a warning to others, the corpses were left for days until they rotted.

Qaddafi could clearly be certain of his loyal creation. Yet this was not enough for the Colonel; his was a mission of global proportions and he wanted his new revolutionary forces to make their presence felt abroad. In 1982, he established the International Mathaba to Resist Imperialism, Racism and Reactionary Forces, with the aim of mobilizing the masses the world over. It was headed by the charismatic and much-feared Musa Kusa, who answered directly to Qaddafi (and who went on to become the highest-level defector from the regime in the 2011 uprising). However, this new international revolutionary force was not only a way of spreading the revolution; it was also a means of dealing with those Libyans abroad who were increasingly coming to express their opposition to the Qaddafi regime. Teams of rough and ready revolutionaries moved in and took over the Libyan embassies (now named 'people's bureaus') around the world and began rooting out the 'stray dogs' who were engaged in anti-regime activities. Eliminating the opposition was far more important to Qaddafi than the niceties of foreign diplomacy.

This extreme approach was a reflection of Qaddafi's increasing paranoia about the opposition outside the country. It is true that opposition elements abroad were creating their own organizations and trying to counter the revolutionary propaganda with propaganda of their own. However, these fragmented groups hardly amounted to a serious challenge, and were more of an irritant than anything else. Yet the Leader could not tolerate such open displays of hostility. Former Austrian Chancellor Bruno Kreisky once described the opposition abroad as Qaddafi's 'weakest spot', recalling: 'I have talked to him about it and cannot get a real answer. He is paranoid about this opposition, he cannot think about it logically.'[19] The extent of the paranoia is evident in some of the exploits the Colonel engaged in to try to hamper his opponents. In March 1984, an Algerian working for the Libyan regime hijacked a French plane that was on its way from Frankfurt to Paris and tried to redirect it to Tripoli, because Qaddafi believed it had Libyan opposition elements on board.[20] In a more sinister incident, on 16 March 1984 a Libyan plane raided a Sudanese radio station, killing five people – all because Qaddafi believed that members of the opposition group, the NFSL, were broadcasting from the building.[21]

The Libyan opposition abroad were terrified. They had good reason to be. On 11 April 1980, Mohamed Ramadan, a Libyan journalist with the BBC's Arabic Service, who had been publishing open letters to Qaddafi in the Arabic media, was shot at point-blank range in the courtyard of the Regent's Park mosque after Friday prayers. The Libyan authorities refused to accept his body back for burial. Ramadan's death was not a one-off: the same month Libyan lawyer Mahmoud Abu Nafa was shot dead in the offices of a legal firm in Ennismore Gardens in London, a street that at the time also housed the education offices of the Libyan People's Bureau. What followed was a spate of bloody murders. In May 1980, a wealthy Libyan timber merchant was murdered in his hotel bed in Rome. The following month Izzadine Al-Hodeiri, a Libyan living in Bolzano in northern Italy, was shot dead in the railway station in Milan. At the same time, a naturalized Italian of Libyan birth, Salem Fezzani, was shot at in the Rome restaurant he owned. The attacker told the police: 'I was sent by the people to kill him. He is a traitor and an enemy of the people.'[22]

One of these bids to silence the opposition landed Libya in very hot water. In 1984, a young British policewoman, Yvonne Fletcher, was shot dead as she policed a demonstration of Libyan dissidents outside the People's Bureau in St James's Square in London. The shots, which came from inside the building, were clearly meant for the protesters, but they hit Fletcher instead, prompting the British to break off diplomatic relations with Libya.

The Yvonne Fletcher killing, as well as the other assassinations, demonstrated Qaddafi's complete lack of understanding of the wider world. The Colonel clearly believed that there was nothing wrong with killing those who stood in the way of his revolution – even if that meant doing so in the streets of foreign capitals. The regime revealed its naivety in comments made by Musa Kusa to *The Times* on 11 June 1980: 'We killed two in London and there were another two to be killed ... I approve of this.'[23] Similarly, the British ambassador to Libya at the time recounted how the Libyan reaction to the condemnation by European ambassadors in Tripoli of the killings was incredulity. He was asked by one Libyan official 'What do you care if these are not your citizens?'[24] Indeed, for Qaddafi, this most Machiavellian of leaders, the ends always justified the means, and nothing was going to stand in the way of his revolution. As he once commented, 'Some people will die and people will forget about them but the result will be that right will triumph, good will triumph, progress will triumph.'[25]

Turning lives upside down

Qaddafi not only turned Libya's political world upside down, but he also unleashed a whirlwind of revolutionary economic policies that were to jolt the country to its core. In his efforts to create a socialist-inspired economy, he set the revolutionary committees to work, charging them with putting the second part of his *Green Book* into practice. These changes affected more than just large companies and economic concerns: the long arms of the revolution reached deep into the pockets of almost every Libyan, often to devastating effect. The people did not know what had hit them, as Qaddafi put his scorched-earth economic policies into effect. In 1977, for example, the government confiscated all land and only allowed individuals to lease back enough to satisfy their own subsistence needs. This measure, which was meant to prevent anyone from making a profit out of farming and which was accompanied by the destruction of all land tenure records, shattered age-old ways of life. The following year, all properties and real estate were confiscated by the state, after which no one was permitted to own more than one dwelling or to rent property.

Even more intrusively, in March 1980, when the regime decided to devalue the Libyan dinar, it called on all Libyans to come forward and declare their assets. People were instructed to exchange any old dinars they had for the new notes at government banks. The policy created untold chaos and panic, as the regime only gave its citizens one week in which to exchange their money. What was worse was that it also limited the amount that could be exchanged to 1,000 dinars; any deposit in excess of that sum was frozen. For a cash-based society, in which people hoarded their savings under the bed, this was devastating. Fearful of losing their hard-earned cash, Libyans rushed to the *souqs* (markets) and bought up as much gold as they could lay their hands on.

It was becoming clear that the reality of this 'classless society' was that the state moved in to take control of everything. From 1979, private traders and small merchants were squeezed out through a series of measures culminating in Law No. 4 of 1984, which abolished all private commerce and trade.[26] An entire merchant class found itself disenfranchised almost overnight, as the state took over all import and export distribution networks and became solely responsible for the sale of goods. State supermarkets were set up across the country, and Libyans were given ration books entitling them to buy certain goods from these outlets every month. However, the goods on offer were not up to much, and with all the country's imports controlled by just ten state import agencies, which purchased everything from oil technology to basic foodstuffs, supplies were limited.

These state supermarkets were grim places, in which the people of this oil-rich country suddenly found themselves scrabbling for sub-standard goods in the most humiliating fashion. One Libyan woman paints a very depressing picture of this time:

Despite the fact that the goods were bad, we saw people pushing each other out of the way to get hold of them, as there was nowhere else to buy the things they needed, like clothes and furniture. People stood in arbitrary queues in front of these markets, especially during Eid. We would see closed bags that contained some clothes which were unsuitable both in size and quality being thrown at them. Some people who had a bit of money were forced to travel to Turkey and Syria to buy goods that weren't available in Libya. Children at that time didn't even know bananas or apples because the state markets only distributed necessary goods such as sugar and flour.[27]

Consumer shortages became commonplace at this time. Qaddafi glibly told the *New York Times* in 1986: 'Sometimes we make items disappear to force people to work harder and produce them.'[28] But the real reason behind the shortages had less to do with a policy of deliberate deprivation and more to do with bureaucratic inefficiency and corruption: these public markets were sometimes burned down by those running them, in a bid to cover their tracks after they had looted the goods inside for sale on the black market.[29] Such incidents left the local population temporarily bereft of even these paltry second-rate supplies.

Private professional activities were also prohibited. As part of Qaddafi's grand egalitarian vision, doctors and lawyers were prevented from practising privately and were forced to work for the state. With private activity banned, everyone turned to the public sector to provide them with a living. Secure in its oil revenues, the regime was happy to keep on expanding the state, finding it a useful way of buying acquiescence. The ordinary budget, which covered salaries and wages, increased from 583 million Libyan dinars (LYD) in 1977, to LYD 950 million in 1980 and to LYD 1.52 billion in 1983.

Most Libyans opted for office jobs in this mushrooming state sector. But because the majority were not properly qualified, foreign nationals still had to be brought in to fill managerial and professional positions. Foreign labour was also imported for the manual jobs that Libyans did not want to soil their hands with. Indeed, the state became like an enormous paper towel, absorbing all and sundry, regardless of their expertise. The growth of the public sector also bore no relation to actual need. Workers got paid for simply turning up, and several people were employed to do the same job. This was a feature that was to endure up until the 2011 revolution; changing just a small amount of foreign currency into Libyan dinars was a laborious process that could take several people, all fully engaged in discussion about the task in hand, well over half an hour!

However, having a job in the state sector did not mean that Libyans' needs were satisfied. It is true that the regime had set up an admirable and comprehensive welfare system. One of the plus sides of Qaddafi's socialist-style vision was that everyone was provided with a place to live, access to education and healthcare, and even their own car – all at the state's expense. This was significant progress from the poverty-stricken days of the monarchy. Yet people were still struggling. State salaries were generally low and were always paid late.[30] To make matters worse, the regime introduced Law No. 15 of 1981, which froze all public sector wages. With inflation running at around 20 per cent throughout the decade, making ends meet was becoming increasingly hard. Many professionals, including those of senior level, were forced to double up as taxi drivers in the evenings – something that was common right up until the fall of the regime. Others engaged in black-market activities – something in which almost every Libyan family found itself inadvertently involved, just in order to survive.[31] Incredibly, this freeze on public sector pay remained in place until the late 2000s.

The result of all these economic directives was chaos. This was hardly surprising: Qaddafi's was an economy driven by ideology rather than by sound economic planning. Indeed, the regime ended up investing in all sorts of ludicrous and costly schemes in order to turn the Colonel's dreams into reality. In the bid to achieve self-sufficiency, for example, the state invested in a number of large-scale agricultural projects that made bad financial sense. These included a project to irrigate several thousand acres of soil at Kufra using advanced technology, with the aim of producing wheat. Although grain was produced at the project, just the transport costs of getting a tonne of the grain to the coastal areas were some 10–20 times higher than contemporary world prices for a tonne of wheat.[32] Agricultural production dropped during the 1980s as a result of the regime's encouragement of mechanization, which led to over-irrigation and which lowered water tables in a country thirsting for water.[33] For Qaddafi, such trivialities were unimportant; this was mere detail when set beside the greater effort of establishing his revolutionary ideals. As far as he was concerned, his grand vision would be enough to carry the country forwards.

Qaddafi was equally reckless when it came to military spending. The Leader wanted a military arsenal that was worthy of his Jamahiriyah, and buying weapons became a kind of personal obsession that started early on. Omar Al-Meheishi, who once referred to Qaddafi as a 'dangerous psychopath', recounts how, in 1973, Abdelsalam Jalloud had come to him one day with a terrified expression on his face.[34] The reason for Jalloud's alarm was that Qaddafi had just written to the Kremlin asking for 6,000 tanks, 1,000 warplanes and 200 naval ships. Despite his best efforts, Jalloud was unable to convince the Colonel to reduce these ridiculously huge requests. Things got worse: from the late 1970s, Qaddafi embarked upon a period of unrestrained military spending, buying up military kit as if it were going out of fashion. Defence spending soared from $709 million in 1982, to $1,149 million in 1984.[35] Many of these purchases were from the Soviet Union, and in 1979 there were some two thousand Russian military advisors in Libya.[36]

All this buying meant that the Libyan army was unable to absorb all the weapons being thrown at it. In 1979, there were only 150 competent pilots for over 160 operational warplanes, when the norm was at least two pilots per aircraft.[37] Such was the mismatch that Libya was forced to bring in foreigners from a host of countries – including Pakistan, Cuba and the Czech Republic – to man and maintain its newly acquired military equipment. Yet, as was so often the case with the Colonel, image was more important than substance. It was all about projecting the greatness of his Jamahiriyah to the rest of the world. So much so that Qaddafi even sought to acquire a nuclear weapon – something that would put his Jamahiriyah on a par with the big nations of the world. To this end, Libya made official approaches to China, France and India; all of them were politely turned down.

Never one to think small, Qaddafi also set about militarizing the whole of Libyan society, in a quest to turn the Libyan people into soldiers for his ideas. Although a number of Arab dictators employed military-style discipline in support of their regimes, Qaddafi took things to a whole new level. In the early 1980s, he began militarizing the country's schools: school uniforms were replaced by military uniforms, and military science became a compulsory subject. Pupils were suddenly at the mercy of military officers, who took over from school heads and teachers, and these new 'teacher officers' dished out military punishments at whim. These chastisements included leaving disobedient students out in the scorching sun for long periods. Pupils were likewise forced to go on military marches and parades, displaying their loyalty to the new Jamahiriyah.[38]

These grand schemes were all bankrolled by the country's vast oil reserves. Indeed, it was thanks to the abundance of energy supplies that Qaddafi was able to use the country as a grand laboratory, frittering away cash as each hare-brained experiment took his fancy. Compared to his fellow Arab leaders, Qaddafi had it easy. Libya's small population and enormous wealth made it possible for him to enforce conformity and to stamp his personality on the country to an extreme degree.

Yet even energy economies need careful planning, as well as regulation. This fact appears to have eluded the young revolutionary, who was too caught up in himself to worry about such trivialities. With his constant spending, Qaddafi seemed to pay no heed to the fact that global oil prices fluctuate.[39] Due to the world decline in oil prices in the early 1980s, Libyan oil revenues plummeted from US$24 billion in 1980 to less than US$14 billion in 1981.[40] Yet Qaddafi was a man who lived in the present, and he certainly was not going to let a simple drop in income stop him from realizing his Jamahiriyah.

That is not to say that there was no economic planning at all: the regime came up with a series of five-year economic plans, laying out a blueprint for the economy. However, the planning that did go on was hampered by the sheer lack of experience of those in charge. It was also hindered by administrative chaos, made worse by Qaddafi's habit of suddenly issuing grand pronouncements about what shape the economy should take. This left his inexperienced officials scratching their heads as they tried to fathom out how to implement the unrealistic ideas. As if that were not enough to contend with, the Colonel kept changing his mind about how many secretariats (ministries) there should be in the General People's Committee (cabinet) and what their responsibilities should be. While the energy sector was generally left alone – since it needed to function in order for the regime to survive – other portfolios, including those related to the economy, were renamed, merged or dismantled every couple of years.[41]

Coming up with any kind of stabilized economic policy in such an environment was clearly impossible. No one knew who was responsible for what, and the secretariats were too busy trying to deal with their own structural changes to be able to issue or implement policies with any coherence. Things were so bad that these secretariats were unable to collect even the most basic of economic data that could provide them with the economic indicators necessary for making policy. Data about inflation levels, internal and external trade figures, types of consumption and income levels just were not available.[42] Moreover, without any clear direction from the top, regulation was almost non-existent. It was not that the regime did not try to regulate the economy; rather, the situation was so chaotic that everyone began issuing monitoring decisions, many of them completely contradictory, meaning that actual regulation got lost. Libya became what one analyst has aptly coined a 'centrally unplanned economy'.[43]

Yet this lack of planning and regulation had its advantages: it enabled Qaddafi to distribute largesse and to buy people off whenever he saw fit. The regime soon got into the habit of dishing out special perks and benefits to those whose allegiance it wanted to secure. The revolutionary committees, for instance, were given their own farms in the countryside, where members would go at the weekends to relax amidst the fruit trees and date palms; the security services were provided with top-of-the-range cars, which they sold on for a tidy profit. In this way, Qaddafi was able to build a faithful 'army' of ideologues, ready to do whatever it took for his Jamahiriyah. Yet perhaps the greatest irony in all this is that, by the mid-1980s, the new revolutionary regime, which had taken power promising to strip away the 'backward' practices of the past, had come to operate in a fashion not entirely dissimilar to the way the monarchy had worked. Here was Qaddafi and his coterie of close advisors bypassing the official institutions of the state and relying on patronage to buy loyalty. Had Libyans not seen this somewhere before?

What was different, however, was that the end result of the adoption of these extreme revolutionary economic policies was that every family became reliant on the state for almost every aspect of life. In this 'stateless society', the state had become everything. This in turn meant that, whatever Qaddafi's dreams of making Libya completely self-sufficient, it became ever more dependent on its energy sector. Indeed, Libya became a distributive state par excellence. While all this may have had short-term political advantages – ensuring that every family had a stake in the future of the revolution – its longer-term consequences were to prove disastrous for Qaddafi in the coming decades.

Qaddafi as messiah

Not only did the revolution seep into every pore of Libya's political and economic life, but it also took a grip on the most sacred of areas – the country's religious life. It is no surprise that Islam was to be at the very core of Qaddafi's revolution: the deeply pious Bedouin was profoundly committed to his faith and saw Islam as an essential component of his idealized Jamahiriyah. It was also integral to his mission to cleanse Libyan society of the corrupt moral practices of the 'aristocratic Sanussi' of the past. Therefore, while for the other Arab nationalist leaders of the day, Islam was predominantly a legitimizing force, for Qaddafi it was so much more.

In fact, Qaddafi saw himself as a religious leader, as much as he considered himself a political thinker. As early as 1971, he shocked the *ulema* (religious scholars) by leading prayers for the holy celebration of Eid Al-Fitr in Tripoli's large Moulay Mohamed Mosque. This was highly unusual practice for a political and military leader, yet alone for someone so young, who should have known his place in matters of the faith. Yet Qaddafi's precociousness was driven by his unswerving belief that he had the divine on his side. This lowly desert dweller, who spent a lifetime comparing himself (albeit indirectly) to the Prophet, believed himself to be a kind of modern-day messiah, emerging from the vast empty sands with a new truth.

This new messiah certainly had an unorthodox take on Islam. Stunning the entire Islamic world with his boldness, the eccentric colonel took on some of the more heterodox ideas that were doing the rounds in Arab intellectual circles at the time. In doing so, he was to set himself at odds with the entire tradition of Sunni Islam. Most fundamental was Qaddafi's assertion that the Qu'ran, as the revealed word of God, was the one and only basis of true Islam. As far as he was concerned, the second source of authority in Sunni Islam, the Sunnah (the acts and the sayings of the Prophet, as told by his companions), was not essential to the faith. Qaddafi viewed the Sunnah as human rather than divine, while for him only the Qu'ran represented the pure foundation of Islam. He also argued that Sharia (Islamic law) was a normative set of laws that had been made by humans.[44] Such assertions were hugely controversial. To almost deny the Sunnah as the second source of authority of Sunni Islam was deeply offensive and sacrilegious to many Muslims. It is difficult to express just how shocking this denial was to Sunni Muslims at the time (and indeed today). Yet for Qaddafi it was part of stripping Islam back to its basics, instilling it with a Bedouin simplicity that was pure and untainted by humanity.

Qaddafi set out his highly provocative ideas to a stunned audience at a speech to mark the anniversary of the birth of the Prophet in the pink-domed Moulay Mohamed mosque on 19 February 1978. As well as insisting on the Qu'ran's being the only true basis of the faith, the Leader went so far as to almost accuse Muslims of polytheism and of idolizing the Prophet rather than God, declaring: 'If I say Mohamed, you all jump to say "Peace be upon him", but if I say Allah, you say nothing. This is a kind of paganism ... This means we are more frightened of the Prophet than Allah and the Prophet is closer to us than Allah.'[45] These were scandalous words for the leader of a Muslim country. Yet Qaddafi pressed on, seemingly taking pleasure in the challenge. Indeed, the Colonel loved to swim against the tide, to be the lone voice, struggling to be understood. He also revelled in the role of teacher and wise man, believing it was his mission to uncover the truth for the rest of the world.

Five months later he presented the same electrifying ideas to an international audience, at a stormy meeting of Arab religious scholars, who spent several hours trying to force him back into the ways of orthodoxy.[46] But Qaddafi was not to be persuaded. Nor was he to be dissuaded from his heterodox views by the unforgiving condemnation of religious groups and individuals, who were horrified at his reductionist ideas. What Qaddafi, with all his Bedouin simplicity, saw as extreme purity, others saw as little more than heresy. The militant group Hizb ut-Tahrir, which had a small presence in Libya in the 1970s, was so outraged that it accused him of being *kafir* (heathen) and an enemy of Islam.[47] Yet it was not just extremist groups that condemned Qaddafi in this way; by the early 1980s a series of fatwas had been issued against him, including one from the highly influential Council of Senior Ulema in Saudi Arabia, which proclaimed him a heathen.

This was a devastating indictment and a label that Qaddafi was never to overcome. However, the ever proud 'visionary' remained undeterred. Refusing to bow down to conformity, he continued to mould Islam to suit his revolution, in moves that verged on the narcissistic. In 1979, for example, casting centuries of tradition aside, the Brother Leader declared that the Muslim calendar would no longer be dated from the time of the Prophet's migration from Mecca to Medina; instead it was to begin ten years later, from the time of Mohamed's death – an event he deemed to be far more important in the Prophet's life. Not only was this shocking to most Muslims, but its practical application left the country reeling.

To say that Libya's traditional religious establishment was deeply uncomfortable with the Leader's unorthodox views is an understatement. They were horrified. They were particularly unnerved, too, by his assertion, aimed directly at undermining them, that man could have a direct relationship with God. As he once reflected, 'People are the masters on earth. They decide what they wish. Allah is in heaven. There is no intermediary between us and Allah.'[48] With this reasoning, Qaddafi was not only extending the egalitarian spirit of his revolution to the realm of Islam; he was driving a stake right into the heart of the religious establishment, emasculating it at a single blow.

Some members of this religious establishment dared to challenge Qaddafi – and they often came to an unsavoury end. In 1978, after the revolutionary committees had been charged with purifying certain mosques and putting an end to the activities of certain preachers, the ninety-year-old Sheikh Tahir Al-Zawi, Mufti of Libya, who had resigned in protest at Qaddafi's unorthodox ideas, was placed under house arrest. Two years later, the popular imam of Tripoli, Sheikh Mohamed Abdelsalam Al-Bishti, who had articulated his disapproval of Qaddafi's denial of the Sunnah, was to meet a worse fate. On 21 November 1980, a group of revolutionary committee members burst into the Al-Qassar mosque in Tripoli and dragged the imam away. Soon afterwards a petrified Al-Bishti was shown on television publicly confessing that he had been part of an armed group that had been receiving money from Saudi Arabia to spread the Saudis' rigid Wahabist interpretation of Islam.[49] Al-Bishti was never to be seen again. Although the exact circumstances of the imam's death are not clear, Qaddafi's son, Saif Al-Islam, asserted in 2008 that Al-Bishti had been killed at the hands of security men in one of Libya's forests.[50] Mosques, meanwhile, were closed down. This included the tiny mosque of Sidi Hammouda, which was symbolically blown up to make way for the enlargement of Tripoli's main square – renamed Green Square – a space that, when it was not being used for large celebrations, was to become a giant car park.

The mindless destruction of this little mosque represented the extreme iconoclasm and violence that characterized this first, blood-stained revolutionary decade. For all his lofty ideals, Qaddafi had essentially created an authoritarian state of extreme proportions, in which the cult of personality knew no bounds. Libyans came to understand that once again they were to be merely spectators in their own history, as the country was violently transformed into the outward expression of all that was in Qaddafi's head. As all the foundations of what constituted a normal state were stripped away, the country was plunged into an all-encompassing idiosyncrasy that was to last until the regime's dying days. It was also what made Libya so ill-equipped to deal with its own transformation to the post-Qaddafi era in 2011.

CHAPTER 5

Foreign Adventurism

Libya was always going to be too small for Qaddafi; he believed himself a revolutionary of international proportions, and Qaddafism was not about to be confined to the domestic sphere. With a self-belief that knew no bounds, the prophet of the desert immediately set about projecting his revolution beyond Libya's borders. The world became the Colonel's oyster, as he employed the immense oil wealth at his disposal in the quest to put himself and his revolution on the map.

While some of this foreign adventurism was about seeking domestic legitimacy – winning over the masses with bold and rabble-rousing anti-imperialist exploits – it was also about creating a foreign policy that befitted a leader of world-class calibre. It was about establishing, too, a distinctive foreign policy, free of interference from other quarters; Qaddafi was not content to simply slot himself into one of the two Cold War camps, choosing instead to forge his own path and to take up the mantle of leader of the weak against the strong.

That is not to say that there was any clear strategy about his litany of foreign exploits. The intense personalization of the foreign policy process in Libya meant that, while grounded in a set of ideological principles – Arab nationalism, Islam and anti-imperialism – Qaddafi's foreign policy was as arbitrary, contradictory and whimsical as the man himself. It also meant that ambition took over all sense of reason, as the Colonel crashed through successive foreign policy adventures, wreaking havoc and destruction wherever he went. So much so that Qaddafi's foreign policy reads rather like a catalogue of calamities, for which Libyans were to pay a heavy price.

The first arena in which Qaddafi sought to project himself was the Arab world. Arab nationalism had always been at the core of Qaddafi's revolutionary discourse, and it was his first and enduring passion. It was also the ticket upon which he had come to power and was a sure way of bolstering his popular legitimacy. It was only natural, therefore, that he should turn first to the Arab world, where he dreamed of uniting Arab peoples into a single Arab nation that would regain the glories of the past.

Unfortunately for the Colonel, his fellow Arab leaders were not so enthusiastic. They were wary of this rough and ready revolutionary who had emerged from Libya's deserts, big on dreams but short on experience. While they may have appreciated his sincerity (and his ready supply of petro-dollars), the seasoned rulers of the Middle East were not about to be swept up by the ideas of the zealous young upstart. They were certainly not over-impressed when, less than a year after the coup, Qaddafi and his foreign minister, Saleh Busair, embarked on a tour of the Middle East, touting a military plan to bring Arab forces together to annihilate Israel. To the Colonel's crushing disappointment, the simplistic plan, which smacked of the inexperience of those who had drafted it, met with derision and even resentment from states, such as Syria and Jordan, which understood what it meant to be at war with Israel. The plan met with equally short shrift in Egypt, where they were told that they may have understood revolutions but they did not understand military plans.[1]

The leaders of the Arab world were even more shocked in June 1970, when they gathered in Tripoli for a celebration to mark the evacuation of the Wheelus airbase. Reflecting the fact that Qaddafi was always a populist before he was a statesman, the Colonel got so carried away during his speech that he began threatening his guests. He warned that if the meeting failed to achieve unity, he would tell the Arab masses what their leaders were really like, so that they could launch revolutions against them. Qaddafi's inopportune comments prompted a severe reprimand from his hero, the Egyptian president. Nasser was so furious that he brought his fist down hard on the table and warned the young upstart that if he did not shut up, he, Nasser, would tell the Libyan people just how disrespectful their new leader was.

Nasser's admonishment did not deter the eager revolutionary; quite the opposite. With his desert upbringing and limited experience of the world, Qaddafi seemed to have a completely unreal sense of his own limitations. It seemed perfectly obvious to him that, following Nasser's death in 1970, it would be he who would inherit the role of leader of the Arab nationalist struggle. Hardly had the dust settled than the young revolutionary muscled in on the act: at the Egyptian leader's funeral, Qaddafi surprised his fellow mourners by joining President Numairi of Sudan and Palestinian leader, Yassir Arafat, in receiving the official condolences of the attending delegations.[2] Despite his youth and the fact that he had seized power seemingly overnight in a backward state of just a few million people, Qaddafi clearly believed himself to be the next 'Father of the Arabs'.

More than that, the Colonel also believed he could go beyond Nasser. Imbued with his own sense of greatness, this 'visionary' genuinely thought he could do what no other Arab leader had done before him: bring the Arab world, with all its complexities and divisions, together under his leadership. As he exclaimed in 1971,

I envisage that this small people will play the role that Prussia played in the unification of Germany, and that the Libyan people will play this role in the unification of the Arab nation. I also feel that this small people and this small republic will play the role that Piedmont played in the unification of Italy.[3]

The preposterousness of these comments demonstrates the extent to which the raw revolutionary had failed to comprehend the world around him. While his fellow Arab leaders may have lauded the concept of pan-Arabism, using it as a useful rallying cry to bolster their popular standing, they were in no mood to actually unite their political systems. With all his naivety, Qaddafi had failed to discern that it was solidarity, rather than union, that his fellow Arab leaders sought. The Colonel had also failed to understand that, by the time he came to power, the heyday of Arab nationalism was already over. Following the Arabs' shattering defeat at the hands of Israel in 1967, the nationalist project fell into decline, and by the early 1970s the new ideas in the region were being forged around Islamist rather than nationalist agendas. The Colonel had missed the boat. This was not lost on some young Libyans. One Islamist-leaning student told the Colonel after one of his speeches to the medical college in Benghazi in May 1972: 'Brother Muammar, there is no call for nationalism in the Qu'ran. The Qu'ran didn't say, "oh Arabs", not even once and the mention of the Ummah [nation] in the Qu'ran is the Islamic one.' A shocked Qaddafi did not take kindly to the challenge; he shouted at the student: 'No, no, you are sick! I blame this college … you are sick and you have to be treated … and we must put you in a clinic … You are not suitable to be a doctor. You have to leave and go and read the Qu'ran.' The young student was arrested, and two days later appeared on television meekly repenting.

Qaddafi's car-crash insistence on swimming against the tide soon began to irritate those around him, who were sometimes forced to engage in rapid damage-limitation exercises, mopping up the mess he had left in his wake. One could never afford to rest on one's laurels when Qaddafi was around. In 1972, while speaking at a popular rally in Tunis, the Libyan leader surprised his hosts by suddenly calling for union between the two countries. The panicked Tunisian president, Habib Bourguiba, who was at home listening to a live broadcast of the speech, was forced to hurry to the rally to put the impudent newcomer in his place. The veteran Bourguiba, a heavyweight by any standards, took the microphone and, in a withering putdown, declared that the Arabs had never been united, that Qaddafi's ideas about Arab unity were misplaced, and that Libya itself was fragmented and backward.[4] Although Bourguiba flirted briefly with the idea of union with Libya in 1974, the Tunisian president ultimately rejected the notion of harnessing Tunisia to Qaddafi's experimental state.

This was no isolated case. Time and again, the Colonel's attempts to link Libya with other Arab nations, including Syria and Egypt, proved an unmitigated disaster. Yet Qaddafi was not content to accept the realities of the world around him. If others were not going to come round to his way of thinking, he was going to force change in whatever way he could – even if that meant doing so in an underhand manner. In 1976, he was accused of being behind an assassination attempt on Tunisian Prime Minister Hadi Nouira; four years later, he was accused of training a group of Tunisian rebels, who launched an attack on the mining town of Gafsa in the south of Tunisia, near the Libyan border.[5] After France and the US rushed in to provide Tunis with additional military assistance, Libya permitted angry mobs to attack and burn the French embassy in Tripoli and the consulate in Benghazi. This was looking seriously like the politics of revenge.

Similarly, after taking a personal dislike to the Moroccan king on account of his 'royal behaviour' at the Rabat Arab Summit in

December 1969, Qaddafi voiced his support for an attempted coup by senior Moroccan army officers in July 1971, announcing on state radio that Libyan troops were ready to fly to Morocco to fight on the side of the people.

The story in Egypt was no different. When things were not going his way, Qaddafi took to trying to foment subversion and unrest among the tribes of Egypt's western deserts. He had never got on with President Nasser's successor, Anwar Sadat, believing the new Egyptian leader to be unqualified to lead Egypt, let alone the Arabs. The Colonel also disapproved of Sadat's more pro-Western orientation. For his part, Sadat, who once dismissed Qaddafi as 'a boy', was deeply suspicious of the new regime's massive build-up of arms. Tensions reached such a point that, in July 1977, the two countries embarked on a four-day war, after the Egyptians launched ground and air raids across the border. Who would have thought that, less than a decade after the revolution, Libya would have locked horns with the state that had been its guiding light in the run-up to the coup and after it?

Demonstrating just how much Qaddafi had already alienated others in the region, Sudan and Saudi Arabia rushed to Egypt's defence. Both states were keen to quell this new and decidedly disconcerting Libyan adventurism. Sudan, in particular, wanted to put a stop to Qaddafi, whom it accused of having trained up rebel mercenaries to launch a bloody coup against the regime in Khartoum in July 1976.

Their efforts to subdue the young revolutionary were short-lived, and the experience did not give the Colonel pause for thought: in his desire for perpetual revolution, there was to be no space for reflection. The only way was forward, and he took to backing and bankrolling whichever movement or faction he believed would further his revolutionary objectives at any given time. Sometimes these objectives appeared utterly contradictory. Flying directly in the face of his cherished Arab nationalism, for example, he supported the Iranians in their long war against Ba'athist Iraq in the 1980s. Given that Saddam Hussein was one of the foremost Arab nationalist leaders in the region, one might have expected Libya to take the side of the Iraqi president against the non-Arab enemy. Yet for Qaddafi, the Iranian revolution's anti-Westernism and its Islamic credentials made Tehran a more worthy recipient of support than Arab Baghdad. Qaddafi also had a soft spot for the Iranian revolution of 1979, which he had supported at the time, viewing it as the first real expression of popular revolt against the West.

Yet there was another reason why Qaddafi favoured Persian Iran over Arab Iraq: he could not abide Saddam Hussein, whom he regarded as little more than a thug. His dislike for the Iraqi leader began even before the famed Ba'athist became president. In the mid-1970s, when Saddam was still deputy president, Qaddafi had gone to Baghdad to try to convince the then Iraqi president, Ahmed Hassan Bakr, to get rid of Saddam.[6] When it came to choosing sides in the Iran–Iraq war, therefore, a combination of personal considerations and blatant opportunism overrode Qaddafi's ideological concerns. These personal considerations also drove him to support the Iraqi Kurds in their struggle against the Ba'athist regime in Baghdad, making him the first (and only) Arab leader ever to champion the Kurdish cause. Although the Colonel came up with a fitting Arab nationalist pretext for supporting the Kurds – claiming that he wanted to prevent them from falling into Zionist hands[7] – the real reason was to agitate against Saddam Hussein. Backing the Kurds also played into Qaddafi's quest to be the leader of revolutionary causes, and suited his penchant for supporting the oppressed against the oppressor. Arab nationalism could play second fiddle when it had to.

However, the one Arab nationalist cause that Qaddafi remained true to throughout his rule was that of the Palestinians. That he latched onto this cause was hardly surprising: Palestine has always been the great *cause célèbre* of the Arab world, with nationalist regimes and opposition elements alike competing to demonstrate their commitment to it as a means of securing domestic legitimacy. Qaddafi's positing himself as the champion of the Palestinian cause was therefore predictable enough for a nationalist leader of his ilk.

Yet there was nothing ordinary or straightforward about Qaddafi's approach to the Palestinian issue. The Colonel not only wanted to champion the cause; he wanted to *be* the cause – and, more importantly, to control it. To this end, he employed a typically scattergun approach, supporting a host of competing liberation groups, playing one off against the other as it suited him. Among those into which he channelled Libya's oil money were George Habbash's Popular Front for the Liberation of Palestine (PFLP) and Ahmed Jibril's Popular Front for the Liberation of Palestine – General Command. He also backed the notorious Abu Nidal, leader of the Fateh – Revolutionary Council, who was accused of being behind a string of terrorist atrocities, including the bombing of Vienna and Rome airports in December 1985. His support for these more militant groups was not coincidental. While he backed factions across the board, he and his fellow revolutionaries favoured those elements that took a more radical stance, which dovetailed with their own hardline attitude towards the Israeli state. Indeed, so intent was Qaddafi on leading the struggle against the Israelis that he readily opened military camps inside Libya to train Arabs to fight against the Jewish state. He also set up a special Jihad Fund, dedicated to supporting armed struggle in the usurped Palestinian territories. Sometimes the Leader looked as though he was trying to be more Palestinian than the Palestinians.

Qaddafi's backing of these militant factions did not preclude him from providing support to those groups that took a less hardline stance. This included Yassir Arafat's Fateh movement – the most important representative of all the Palestinian bodies. However,

Qaddafi's relationship with Arafat was a turbulent one. The Colonel rejected what he believed to be Arafat's sell-out of the cause, especially following Fateh's 1974 drafting of a Ten-Point Programme that sought a peaceful resolution with Israel. For the Colonel, the Palestinian leader's stance amounted to a betrayal. As if to make his point, Qaddafi consistently supported those factions that broke away from Fateh, such as a group led by Abu Musa, which split from the movement in 1983.

The other reason why Qaddafi came to have such stormy relations with Arafat was that he was unable to control the veteran Palestinian leader. Qaddafi seemed to believe that being paymaster meant he could manipulate the recipients of his largesse, forcing them to comply with his revolutionary vision. But Arafat proved a less than willing lackey. In the late 1970s, the Palestinian leader refused to allow Qaddafi to set up revolutionary committees among Palestinian fighters in Lebanon. A petulant Qaddafi responded by closing down Fateh's offices in Tripoli. The Colonel also expected Fateh's leaders to do his bidding. Arafat's second man, Salah Khalef, known as Abu Ayad, who had a particularly antagonistic relationship with the Colonel (not least because the Libyan leader tried to spread rumours that he was Jewish), complained:

> We have to be the friends of his friends and the enemies of his enemies ... what he wants is a paid revolution and he treats us like paid mercenaries. He never abided by the decisions made at the different Arab summit meetings to give us financial support. He is moody. If you do not satisfy him, you get a kick. He owes us contributions amounting to between $80 million and $90 million.[8]

Yet in spite of Qaddafi's oscillating support for these different factions, he remained unswerving in his commitment to the Palestinian cause. He was genuinely horrified by the Camp David

Accords of 1978 and the Egyptian-Israeli peace treaty of the following year, referring to the US-sponsored agreement as a 'filthy' and 'unholy' alliance.[9] Like his pan-Arab dream, his Palestinian policy was fast becoming a tale of disappointment and failure. He was also becoming somewhat of a joke in the Arab world that he loved so much. For all his efforts to appeal to the Arab masses, he was widely viewed across the region as a figure of ridicule, a madman who was as bizarre as his ludicrous ideas.

As he grew increasingly resentful of his failures in the Arab sphere, Qaddafi cultivated a politics of disdain. He lashed out at his fellow Arab leaders, attacking Arab heads of state, particularly those from the conservative monarchies of the Gulf, scornfully accusing them of doing nothing to support the Palestinian cause. He dismissed the Arab League as a mere talking shop, and, in highly theatrical performances, regularly stormed out of Arab summits, hurling insults at his fellow leaders as he went. This continued until the end of his rule. At a summit in 2003, for example, he insulted Crown Prince Abdullah of Saudi Arabia by declaring that King Fahd had once told him he was willing to cooperate with the Devil to protect his kingdom. The spat between the two became so bad that Qaddafi was even implicated in a plot to assassinate the crown prince. On another memorable occasion, during an Arab League meeting in Tunis in 2004, the feisty Colonel sat back in his chair and lit up a cigarette, challenging all those present with the smoke that curled contemptuously from his lips.

Frustrated by his fellow Arabs, Qaddafi hoped to have more success in sub-Saharan Africa, a part of the continent that he viewed as fertile ground for the spread of his revolutionary ideas. Although Africa did not resonate in the way the Arab world did, it was still Qaddafi's backyard, and it offered countless opportunities for the Colonel to extend his influence. Indeed, this was not about securing domestic legitimacy (Libyans felt no attachment to Africa, viewing themselves first and foremost as part of the Arab world). Rather it was about projecting himself and his revolution beyond the 'gigantic bowl of sand' that was Libya. For Qaddafi, Africa was a huge arena, where Libyan petro-dollars would go far, and where he could play out his quest for power. As one Tunisian politician, Mahmoud Mestiri, shrewdly observed in 1981, 'Libya's strength is not her own power but the weakness of others.'[10]

So it was that the Colonel took to meddling in African states with gay abandon, intervening wherever he saw fit in order to pursue his own objectives, be they anti-imperialism or the promotion of Islam. There was no overarching strategy: the erratic Qaddafi simply jumped in whenever the opportunity arose, throwing Libya's money around in his bid to garner support and to stamp his mark on the continent.

One of the first recipients of Libyan largesse was Ugandan President Idi Amin. In 1972, Qaddafi sent the notorious dictator some four hundred Libyan troops to assist him in his conflict with neighbouring Tanzania. Qaddafi's support for the Ugandan dictator was based largely on the fact that Amin was Muslim, and the Colonel hoped that he would become a force for resurgent Islam in East Africa.[11] Amin, who was attracted by the Libyan leader's supply of cash, had also agreed to renounce his previously close relationship with Israel. This was not a one-off: as soon as he came to power, Qaddafi started channelling huge amounts of diplomatic energy into encouraging African states to break off relations with the Jewish state, and by 1973 had managed to convince almost thirty African countries to do so.[12] Even President Nasser could not have achieved such a triumph.

Yet Qaddafi's support for the increasingly oppressive Amin did little for Libya's international reputation. Moreover, it ended in disaster; in all his greenness, the young Colonel sent a further 2,500 troops to Amin's rescue in 1978, after Tanzania invaded Uganda.

The Libyan troops were no match for the powerful Tanzanian forces, which routed them in a matter of days. One visitor to Kampala described the scene:

> Huge Russian tanks and personnel carriers were sprawled and overturned among the banana groves. The Libyans had manned them … The liberation forces had walked through the groves and plantations, rounded hills, and on foot from each side totally annihilated the large Libyan force … Libyan soldiers trained for desert warfare were not at ease in the rain forests, in the wet season, among peoples in densely populated districts where Swahili, not Arabic, was understood.[13]

Qaddafi had completely misread a situation into which he had rushed headlong.

If Qaddafi's support for Amin raised eyebrows, so, too, did his backing of the infamous leader of the Central African Republic (CAR), Emperor Jean-Bédel Bokassa, whose brutal excesses knew no bounds. Bokassa was desperate for cash – so much so that, after attending the 1 September celebrations in Libya in 1976, he transformed his CAR cabinet into a revolutionary council in imitation of the Libyan system and announced his conversion to Islam. Always on the lookout for compliant friends, this was an opportunity that Qaddafi could not pass up. In October 1976, the Colonel travelled to Bangui, where he presided personally over Bokassa's conversion ceremony – and then handed him $1 million. This 'gift' was just the tip of the iceberg; there was plenty more to come. The following day, Qaddafi was invited to speak at a rally at the Omnisports Stadium in the capital. The Colonel was in his element: playing the role of the gracious and wise benefactor, he held forth on the virtues of Islam and denigrated Christianity, which he described as 'the religion of imperialism'. It was also the religion of more than 80 per cent of the

CAR population, but that did not bother the Colonel. He had precisely what he wanted: a stage and a willing audience. It mattered little that he had had to pay for it.

Bokassa's commitment to Islam did not last long; within three months, the emperor had converted back to Christianity. This provoked no end of amusement among the Arabs and led to the following widely told joke of the time: 'When he converted to Islam, Bokassa underwent the ritual circumcision. On learning that the emperor was planning to convert back to Christianity, Qaddafi informed him that the punishment for leaving the one true faith was beheading. "What kind of religion is it," lamented Bokassa, "that has the end of your penis cut off when you join it and your head cut off when you leave it?" '

However, even this setback did not stop Qaddafi offering the emperor more money when he returned to Tripoli a few years later, even more desperate than before and with his tail between his legs. On this occasion, though still willing to support him, the Colonel made sure that he humiliated the emperor first, obliging him to wait thirty hours before he deigned to see him, and making him grovel for the cash.[14]

On a more serious note, in line with his anti-imperialist ideology, Qaddafi supported a host of African liberation movements that were struggling against colonial or apartheid regimes. These included Robert Mugabe's Zimbabwe African National Union (ZANU), Nelson Mandela's African National Congress, and a range of movements in Angola, Mozambique and Guinea-Bissau. Support for such movements became enshrined as a matter of principle by the General People's Congress in 1981. Qaddafi even supported John Garang's Sudan People's Liberation Army (SPLA) – a Christian force in the south of Sudan – against Muslim Khartoum, although not before he received assurances from Garang that he would not divide the country. While Qaddafi's support for Garang was related to his desire to be seen siding with the oppressed against the oppressor, in typically Qaddafiesque style it was also about revenge. For Qaddafi's relations with Sudanese President Jaffar Numeri had gone from bad to worse, especially after Numeri had sided with Sadat over the Camp David Accords. And so he wanted to make the Sudanese leader pay. As he once told Jalloud, 'I won't bring Numeri down, but I will make him bleed, and when that happens, the opposition forces in the north will bring his regime down.'[15]

Qaddafi's words were symptomatic of how he came to view the continent: Africa was a place where he could make things happen, where he could impose himself and force the outcomes he desired. Africa was also a realm in which the Colonel felt appreciated. It may have been because of his money, but he was taken seriously by some African leaders at least, as well as by a chunk of the African masses, who appreciated not only his interest in the continent – almost unique among Arab leaders – but also his virulent anti-imperialist stance.

Yet Libya's African adventurism prompted serious concerns among other of the continent's players. Senegalese President Léopold Senghor, for example, broke off diplomatic ties with Tripoli in July 1980, accusing Qaddafi of creating a mercenary army aimed at destabilizing Chad, Niger, Mali and Senegal. Indeed, the Libyan leader's penchant for backing rebel movements became increasingly irritating to those on the receiving end of his efforts to move the furniture around to suit his own agenda.

Yet the Leader seemed not to care about the impact of his actions, as he forged vigorously ahead in the service of his revolution. Nowhere was this truer than in Qaddafi's most ill-fated of African adventures – Chad. His meddling in Libya's southern neighbour began in the early 1970s, when the Colonel supported Muslim rebel groups in the north, under the umbrella movement, the Chad National Liberation Front (FROLINAT). This was not a new alliance – even under the monarchy, Libya had backed FROLINAT.

However, the injustice of an impoverished Muslim population in the north, marginalized and mistreated by a Christian government in the south, was like a red rag to Qaddafi's bull; all the more so because the Chadian regime had the backing of the French, who had stepped in to help it against the rebels in 1968. Qaddafi was driven, too, by his claims on the mineral and uranium-rich Aozou Strip in the north of the country, which Libya occupied in 1972, allegedly with the secret agreement of Chadian President N'Garta Tombalbaye.[16]

The complexities of the Chad affair are beyond the scope of this book. However, as the country descended into a long and bloody civil war, which was to last until 1987 and which saw successive regimes of different hues take over the Chadian capital, Qaddafi did not restrict himself to sitting on the sidelines. The Colonel sent thousands of Libyan troops into Chad to support and fight alongside FROLINAT forces. Such was his commitment to the cause that he was not deterred even when it became apparent that such forces were no match for their French and US-backed rivals. In fact, the Colonel proved to be more militant than the factions he was supporting. In the mid-1980s, FROLINAT leader, Goukouni Oueddi, recognized that he could not triumph over his rivals (who were backed by the French and the Americans) and conceded that the time had come to seek reconciliation. But Qaddafi was having none of it. Having launched himself into the conflict, defeat was not an option for him. With characteristic impulsiveness, on 30 October 1986 the Libyan leader arrested Oueddi, who happened to be in Libya at the time. The Chadian was shot in the stomach in the process.

Qaddafi's actions prompted Oueddi to join forces with his rivals, and the various Chadian factions then worked together to oust the troublesome Qaddafi from their land. Yet even this was not enough to deter the Libyan leader: despite defeat after defeat, in which the Chadians totally routed the Libyan forces, Qaddafi kept sending thousands of fresh Libyan recruits into the country. It is estimated that between 8,000 and 10,000 Libyan troops were killed, and over 1,500 captured, in the course of the Chad war.[17] Many of these young soldiers were conscripts or simply students, some of whom had been press-ganged from outside cinemas and football stadiums, or on street corners, and sent off to fight.[18] Most went without any preparation or training, and certainly without any willingness. Yet as far as Qaddafi was concerned, the masses were little more than cannon fodder, and they should be ready to sacrifice themselves for the sake of the revolution.

It was only after Chadian forces moved into Libyan territory in September 1987 that Qaddafi finally admitted defeat, although even that did not stop him from continuing to lay claim to the Aozou Strip. The matter was finally resolved in 1994, when the International Court of Justice ruled in Chad's favour, meaning that the entire disastrous military adventure had brought Qaddafi nothing. The senselessness of the whole episode was not lost on the Libyans, most of whom saw the campaign as a futile loss of life in an arena in which they had no interest. It was not lost either on the Libyan army, which was deeply embittered over a reckless campaign that had resulted in the death of so many soldiers. So disillusioned were they that a good number of troops who had been captured by Chadian forces during the conflict defected and joined the Libyan opposition. The army was also dismayed that it had lost an estimated $3 billion worth of military equipment in the misadventure, severely denting its arsenal.[19] As a result of the international sanctions that were imposed on Libya in the 1990s, the country was never able to recover and rebuild its armed forces.

For Qaddafi, the cost of the Chad conflict seemed to matter little. It certainly did not temper his desire to be an operator in Africa. Wherever there was an arena to play in, Qaddafi was keen to play. Yet his African policy continued to be driven by a reckless opportunism, fuelled by an inflated self-image that often seemed to supersede all else. Thus, while Qaddafi may have scored a few triumphs in Africa, or at least found a more appreciative audience there than he did in the Arab world, overall his African strategy was hardly a resounding success.

Qaddafi versus the West

If Qaddafi's African and Middle Eastern adventures read like a list of disasters, it was his relations with the West, and with the United States in particular, that really landed the Colonel in hot water. America's relations with the revolutionary regime were never going to be good; Qaddafi's anti-imperialist rhetoric, his insistence on breaking the monarchy's pro-Western orientation, and his early steps to evacuate the US bases were all clear signs that the Colonel was hardly going to be on the best of terms with the major Western power. Moreover, the Americans were troubled by the prospect of another nationalist regime in the region.

Yet in the first years after the coup, the two sides rubbed along, largely out of a necessity driven by their shared interest in Libya's energy sector. Libya wanted access to US oil technology and expertise, while the Americans wanted Libya's high-quality low-sulphur crude. Thus the two countries fostered a degree of wary mutual tolerance.

However, this tolerance was to show signs of strain in the early 1970s, after Qaddafi part-nationalized the oil industry and began using oil as a political weapon – Libya took part in the Arab oil embargo, in protest at the US government's support for Israel in the October 1973 war. Libya's virulent stance on the Palestinian question was also a worry. However, it was as the Cold War progressed that the alarm bells really began to ring: Libya's ties to the Soviet Union, and in particular its seemingly unquenchable thirst for Soviet weaponry, were serious cause for concern. The US feared that

Qaddafi was about to fall deep into the pockets of the Soviets, thereby realizing one of their worst nightmares: the USSR would be able to secure a base right in the middle of the Mediterranean.

Such alarm was probably misplaced. Although the new regime in Tripoli rushed to build ties with Moscow and to purchase Russian military equipment, Qaddafi was not about to jump into bed with the Soviets. While he may have had a shared interest in undermining Western interests, he remained deeply ambivalent about his Soviet counterparts. This ambivalence was based partly upon their 'godless communism' that was entirely alien to the devout Bedouin. More importantly, Qaddafi was not about to be swallowed up by a bigger power; having toppled the Western-backed monarchy, he was not going to hand his revolution straight over to a different master. The Colonel viewed the USSR as another imperialist state, once quipping that there was no difference between Russian Premier Alexei Kosygin and US Secretary of State Henry Kissinger. Libya was not about to become the next Soviet satellite.

For their part, the Soviets were keen to woo Libya, as they did want a base in the Mediterranean. They were also in need of a loyal ally in the region, especially given the rupture in relations with Egypt that had followed Sadat's expulsion of Soviet military advisors in 1972. Yet right from the start, Qaddafi and his fellow revolutionaries made it clear that they were their own men. While on a weapons-buying mission to Moscow in the early 1970s, Jalloud did not mince his words, telling President Leonid Brezhnev that the Soviets were not doing enough to support the Arabs and the Palestinians. Qaddafi displayed a similar lack of deference when he travelled to Moscow in April 1981 and insisted that he be permitted to pray in the capital's Grand Mosque, which had been closed up for ideological reasons. He also insisted that the call to prayer be broadcast from the minaret, and quibbled when he was asked to lay a wreath at Lenin's mausoleum in return.[20] Displaying a similar self-importance, he also objected to vodka being served at an official reception he attended in Moscow four years later, when he complained that he was not being treated with the honour due to the head of the Jamahiriyah.[21]

Such assertions were hardly surprising. It was always part of Qaddafi's vision to lead his own camp. In line with his Third Universal Theory, he saw himself as leader of a middle way that would resist imperialist domination from both the capitalist and the communist blocs. His dream was to gather behind him Third World countries that would adopt his Jamahiriyah system, and stand united to take on the big players of the world. It was for this reason that the Colonel took to supporting liberation movements and radical groups, not only in the Middle East and Africa, but the world over. He extended his revolutionary net far and wide.

The breathtakingly long list of groups that received his support over the years represented a wide range of political persuasions. They included the Irish Republican Army (IRA), the Italian and Japanese Red Brigades, the Basque separatist movement ETA, the Moro National Liberation Front of the Philippines and a host of Latin American movements, including the Sandinistas of Nicaragua. He also supported the infamous Carlos the Jackal, the Venezuelan who was behind the 1975 raid on the OPEC headquarters in Vienna, which killed three people and was followed by a string of attacks on Western targets. The political orientation of these groups seemed not to matter; what was important was that they were anti-imperialist. Supporting them fed into Qaddafi's image of himself as patron of the great struggle, leader of the weak against the strong.

Qaddafi's determination to support these groups was too much for America to stomach. By mid-1976, the Ford administration had begun to suggest that Libya supported and financed international terrorism, and was refusing to sell weapons to the Libyan regime. By 1977 the Pentagon had placed Libya, along with Cuba and North

Korea, on a new list of potential enemies, on the grounds of 'irresponsible support for terrorism' and material and political support for Palestinian guerrillas, the IRA and other terrorist groups.[22]

Relations continued to be strained during President Jimmy Carter's time in the White House. Although Qaddafi had hoped that this Democrat and former peanut farmer might provide the opportunity to get relations back on a better footing, he was to be sorely mistaken. The Carter administration continued to refuse to sell military equipment to Tripoli and sided with Egypt in its 1977 skirmish with Libya.[23] Things were to get worse: Carter's sponsoring of the Camp David Accords in September 1978 was anathema to Qaddafi, while Washington, already unhappy with Libya's intervention in Uganda in 1978, accused the Libyan government of not doing enough to protect its embassy in Tripoli, which was sacked and burnt by angry crowds during the Iranian hostage crisis of December 1979.

However, it was under the presidency of Ronald Reagan (whom Qaddafi loved to dismiss as a 'second-rate actor' who read not books, but 'cheap Hollywood scenarios') that US–Libyan relations deteriorated almost to the point of no return. From the outset of his presidency in 1981, the hawkish Reagan was convinced that the man he famously went on to label the 'mad dog of the Middle East' was little more than a Soviet puppet who should be eliminated.[24] Wherever he saw Qaddafi, Reagan saw Soviet hands. This was all the more worrying for the US president, who came to power intent on rebuilding American influence in the Middle East and Africa, where Qaddafi was meddling right, left and centre.

Reagan was also deeply anxious over Qaddafi's backing of revolutionary movements and regimes the world over. Some of this support was getting alarmingly close; in the early 1980s Qaddafi had taken to providing economic and political support to a number of left-wing regimes in Central America, including in El Salvador and Nicaragua.

As far as Reagan was concerned, Qaddafi was working against US interests in every conceivable way.

The president decided to act quickly. Four months after taking office, he closed the Libyan People's Bureau (embassy) in Washington and broke off diplomatic ties with Libya. In November 1981, he ruled that Libyan diplomats to the United Nations were to be restricted to a twenty-five mile radius of the UN headquarters in New York. More seriously, Reagan proved willing to use force against the 'pariah' Qaddafi: in August 1981, the US shot down two Libyan planes in the Gulf of Sirte, following a disagreement over sovereignty of the bay.[25] The provocative assault on what the Colonel deemed to be his own territory outraged Qaddafi, who used the attack as one of the justifications for the mass militarization of Libyan society that began the same year.

The Gulf of Sirte attack, US media reports that Reagan wished to see Qaddafi assassinated, US support for Libyan opposition groups abroad − none of these had the desired effect on the mercurial Libyan leader. He refused to alter the direction of his foreign policy and continued to support whichever groups he believed would further his ambitious objectives of being the champion of revolutions everywhere. The visionary from the desert was not going to kow-tow to anyone, least of all the leader of the Western world. Indeed, the higher the stakes, the more Qaddafi, with his restless revolutionary spirit, seemed to rise to the challenge and to positively revel in his provocative behaviour.

However, Qaddafi did not understand that he was up against a man who was almost as extreme as he was. Reagan became almost as ideological about getting rid of Qaddafi as Qaddafi was about standing up to him, and he singled the Colonel out as the major threat to the Western world, declaring in 1986:'Qaddafi deserves to be treated as a pariah in the world community.'[26] The US president also accused the Libyans of complicity in a host of terrorist attacks, including the seizure of an Egypt Air jet in November 1985, in which fifty-nine people were killed, and the December 1985 attacks on Vienna and Rome airports by the Abu Nidal group. Although Qaddafi certainly had ties with the extremist Abu Nidal group, there was no concrete evidence at the time of actual Libyan involvement in the attacks. However, by this point there was a growing body of opinion within the Reagan administration – including Secretary of State George Shultz – that the only way to deal with this rogue state was by military force.

Although force was not yet an option for Reagan, he was determined to make Qaddafi pay for his foreign adventurism. In March 1982, the US imposed an embargo on oil imports from Libya and introduced export licence requirements for all US goods destined for the country, except for food, medicine and medical supplies. This was a major blow to Qaddafi, whose revenues were cut by a third overnight. However, the situation was not disastrous: European importers readily stepped in to fill the gap. Indeed, many European countries, which relied heavily on Libyan oil supplies, favoured a more pragmatic approach towards the unpredictable colonel and criticized Reagan's dogged determination to corner him at any cost.

Such criticism was not limited to Europe; Reagan had his fair share of critics in the US, who accused him of picking on Libya because it was a soft target. As one observer wrote,

> The despicable Qaddafi was a perfect target, a cartoon character Americans loved to hate ... Libya was neither strategically nor militarily formidable. Taking Qaddafi on was the counterterrorism equivalent of invading Grenada – popular, relatively safe, and theatrically satisfying.[27]

Furthermore, in many ways Reagan was helping to build the myth of the Colonel, propelling his influence and importance far beyond what he could ever have achieved himself. It is surely ironic that the man who put Qaddafi on the map was the man who sought to bring him down.

Such criticisms had little impact on this most hawkish of presidents. In November 1985, his administration banned all imports of Libyan petroleum products; the following year it froze Libyan assets in the US and stopped providing loans and credits to the country. It also prohibited all financial transactions between US and Libyan citizens. However, it was in 1986 that Reagan found his justification for teaching Qaddafi a lesson he would not forget. In the early hours of the morning of 5 April, a bomb placed under a table near the disc jockey's booth exploded at the La Belle disco in West Berlin. The club was popular with US servicemen posted nearby, and the attack killed two US personnel and one Turkish woman, and injured scores more. The US rushed to blame Libya, asserting that intercepted messages between Tripoli and agents in Europe made it clear that Qaddafi had been the brains behind the attack. Just ten days later, Reagan took his revenge.

At 2 a.m. on 15 April 1986, eighteen US F-111 bombers that had taken off from bases in the UK dropped sixty tons of munitions on a range of Libyan targets, including a Tripoli airfield, a naval academy and Qaddafi's Bab Al-Aziziya compound. Some of the bombs missed their targets, hitting residential areas, a centre for the disabled, and some foreign embassies. A number of civilians were killed in the attack – supposedly including Qaddafi's four-year-old adopted daughter, Hana, although there have been repeated alleged sightings of Hana in recent years.

The Colonel himself narrowly escaped death. Although Jalloud maintains that Qaddafi was hiding out in one of his underground bunkers, the Leader claimed to have been at home in bed at the time of the attack. The Libyans had, in fact, been warned of the attacks one or two days in advance by Italian Prime Minister Bettino Craxi, who had sent word via the Libyan embassy in Rome. However, the bombing still seems to have taken the Colonel by surprise. He asked a US reporter after the raids: 'Why didn't you tell me they were going to bomb my home?'[28] Qaddafi's son, Saif Al-Islam, who was fourteen years old at the time of the attack, remembered the close call the family had had:

> It was a very difficult night. I was asleep; the bombing started approximately 40 km away from us. I went quickly to my sister Aisha and then hastened to wake everyone up and I took them, one by one to the shelter. After that the bombing reached where we lived. If I hadn't done what I did, I don't know what would have happened.[29]

The bombing was a sharp wake-up call for Qaddafi in more ways than one. For all his provocations, the Libyan leader never believed the Americans would go so far as actually to strike Libya, yet alone to hit his own Bab Al-Aziziya compound. More importantly, the raids demonstrated to the Colonel that, despite the massive military arsenal he had been building up since the start of the revolution, when it came to it, he was unable to defend himself. His military, already destroyed and disheartened by the failed adventures in Chad, proved useless: Libyan guns opened fire ten minutes after the raid had started, when most of the planes were already on their way home, and terrified military officers fled their posts at the crucial hour.[30] Even more humiliating was the desperate attempt at retaliation: fifteen hours after the attacks, the Libyans launched two Soviet-built missiles at the tiny Italian island of Lampedusa, 290 kilometres north of Libya. The missiles both failed to hit their target – a US Coast Guard radar navigation installation on the island – dropping pathetically into the sea.

To make matters worse, there were rumours of power struggles being played out in the immediate aftermath of the bombings, with speculation about prolonged gun battles and possible coup attempts. Although much of this appears to have been overplayed, not least by the Americans, who were jubilantly announcing to the world that elements of an army battalion had attempted a mutiny, there certainly appears to have been, in the words of one Western diplomat, 'a manoeuvring and testing after the US attack'.[31]

Of greater note was the fact that the US raid also highlighted just how far the Colonel had isolated himself. No one rushed to his defence. It was as if all Qaddafi's foreign policy exploits of the previous decade and a half had come back to haunt him at one fell swoop. Even at this time of crisis, his fellow Arab leaders stood back. Although there were popular demonstrations against the attacks in some Arab capitals, and although a handful of Arab leaders issued condemnations of the bombing, there was no unified response, nor any hint of practical measures being taken against the West. Worse for the Brother Leader, there was no real mobilization against the attacks inside Libya itself. The Colonel must have hoped for some outpourings of popular support for the revolution, but these never materialized. In fact, in the days following the attacks, state television was forced to air reruns of a 1977 rally in Derna, although this was eventually replaced by broadcasts of a defiant and upbeat Qaddafi, sporting a white suit and clutching a handful of pink flowers, as he visited the injured in hospital.

Two months later, when the immediate panic had died down, there were still no signs of public support for the Leader in his time of adversity. Jalloud recounts how, on the anniversary of the expulsion of US forces in June 1986, he and Qaddafi went by car to the celebrations that had been organized at the former US airbase, just outside Tripoli: 'We found no large crowd at the celebrations. There were [the Palestinian leaders] Abu Musa and Ahmed Jibril, but the number of Libyans attending was very small.'[32]

Yet if Reagan hoped that the raids would precipitate the end of the Qaddafi era, he was to be sorely disappointed. The Leader responded to the challenge like a wounded lion whose roar would not be silenced. He stepped up his verbal assaults against the US. In September 1986, for example, while attending the Non-Aligned Movement Summit in Harare, the Colonel lambasted the US in the most strident of tones. Cutting a dashing figure in his red high-necked shirt and flowing robes, he declared that he would form an international army of tens of thousands of troops, which he would 'spread all over the continents of the world to put fire under the feet of the United States'.[33] In a similar vein, in a speech to the General People's Congress in 1987, he threatened that he would unleash freedom fighters, who would become martyrs in the struggle against the US and Britain. At the same time he proclaimed: 'The Yankees have no morals; they have no conscience. They should not be treated as humans. They constitute a threat to the future of mankind.'[34] He called on every Libyan to help defend their nation by spending LYD 200 ($600) on a Kalashnikov. This was the Colonel at his theatrical best.

Somewhat ironically, what the US did through the bombings was to hand Qaddafi a symbol that he could draw on time and time again, as proof of his long-held insistence that the West was out to humiliate, subjugate and crush the Arabs. Qaddafi routinely took journalists and visitors to the bombsite at Bab Al-Aziziya, where he erected a grotesque statue of an enormous gold fist crushing a US fighter plane. It is no coincidence that when the NATO raids began in 2011, Qaddafi delivered a number of speeches from the highly symbolic site. After Tripoli fell, rebel forces from Misarata carted the great gold fist off to their hometown, erecting it there as a war trophy.

Bravado aside, the 1986 attacks were a sobering reflection on what seventeen years of foreign policy Qaddafi-style had reaped. Libya was held up to the world as the ultimate example of a pariah state, and the country was left more isolated than ever. For all Qaddafi's cherished dreams of unity and greatness, by the mid-1980s he had locked the country into a seemingly never-ending downward spiral. As ever, it was the ordinary Libyans who were to carry the burden.

CHAPTER 6

Jamahiriyah in Crisis

Two months after the US raid of 1986, an already unnerved Qaddafi had another startling experience. He and Jalloud travelled to the tiny village of Harawa, in the scrubby deserts near the Colonel's birthplace of Sirte. The two revolutionaries sat with the sheikhs of the powerful Awlad Suleiman tribal confederation. After sharing a convivial lunch, the sheikhs brought a five-year-old girl to the Colonel. Plucking up all her courage, the girl stepped forward to tell the Brother Leader: 'Uncle Muammar ... for the last five years I haven't eaten a single apple.'[1] More ominously, one of the sheikhs then warned: 'Oh Muammar ... if we told you that ten or fifteen per cent of Libyans are with you, we would be lying to you. So be careful.'[2]

This was shocking stuff for the Colonel, who still believed that his Jamahiriyah was the pinnacle of all human achievement; all the more so because he was on home ground, in staunch pro-Qaddafi territory. Yet Libyans had good reason to be disillusioned. Their leader had transformed Libya into an international pariah, shunned by governments the world over. He had also turned the country upside down with his relentless revolutionary experimentation:

Libya was enveloped by chaos, and all semblance of normality had become little more than a distant memory. Fear and intimidation had also become part of daily life, with Libyans afraid that the scruffy young zealots of the revolutionary committees would emerge out of the shadows at any moment to haul them off to an uncertain fate.

The country was also facing growing economic difficulties: the US sanctions that had been imposed a few years before were beginning to take their toll, as was the fallout from the global decline in oil prices. With prices dropping from $26.92 per barrel in 1985 to $14.44 per barrel in 1986, revenues had dropped significantly, creating serious budget shortfalls.[3] With all their inexperience, Libya's young revolutionaries did not know how to deal with the problem. In a panic, they adopted a series of rash measures: they ran down foreign currency reserves, temporarily suspended the payment of trade debts, slashed imports and tried to swap oil for imported goods.[4]

These short-sighted policies had a direct impact on the Libyans. The decrease in imports was particularly painful – the already sparse state supermarkets now had even fewer goods on display. A journalist visiting in 1986 found that the entire ground-floor food section of one of these surreal monuments to Qaddafi's economic vision stocked only ghee and powdered milk.[5] Another visitor to the country in 1987 found that state supermarkets in Ajdabia and Sirte carried little other than enormous quantities of Dutch milk powder, Italian suits and Chinese tea.[6] Indeed, these state outlets had become as tired as the revolution itself; so much so that illegal traders had taken to setting up shop inside these cavernous symbols of progress. Egyptian traders could be found amidst the dust-caked shelves, broken-down escalators and empty aisles of the local supermarket in Tripoli's Souq Al-Juma district, for example. On sale underneath the portraits of a grinning President Hosni Mubarak were Egyptian-manufactured Philips light-bulbs, air freshener and furniture polish.[7]

Meanwhile, just making ends meet was becoming more difficult for ordinary Libyans; salaries were still low and were regularly paid late, medicines were in short supply and the cost of goods on the black market was rocketing. Things were so bad that some army officers were reduced to hawking onions in hotels in the evenings just to get by.

Qaddafi may have been totally wrapped up in revolutionary fervour, but he was astute enough to feel the tension in the air. Nor could he ignore the sporadic attacks that were being carried out against his security apparatus. These included the killing in 1987 of powerful revolutionary committee stalwart Ahmed Al-Werfelli, who was hated in particular because he routinely prevented vegetables from reaching the inhabitants of Benghazi, as a kind of siege against the population there. The gap between the regime and the masses was getting wider, and Qaddafi knew it. Indeed, even if he believed that the problem was not with his perfect vision, but with its implementation, in his heart of hearts he knew that the sheikh's sobering warning rang true.

Qaddafi was also concerned about the growing cooperation between opposition groups outside the country, and, more importantly, about their links to the United States. In April 1988, a senior army officer, Colonel Khafter, who had defected during the Chad war and who was now receiving a supply of arms from Baghdad, announced that he and his band of loyal followers were joining forces with the NFSL – a movement that had ties to the US intelligence services. Despite all his efforts to silence the opposition abroad, Qaddafi was still unable to tame this beast that ate right into his deeply embedded sense of paranoia.

Faced with this host of challenges, the Colonel had to act. For all his restless revolutionary spirit, Qaddafi was shrewd and practical enough to know that he had to make some concessions to his uncompromising vision, if he was going to ensure the survival of his

Jamahiriyah. Presumably influenced by the *perestroika* that was under way in the Soviet Union, Qaddafi decided to embark upon his first flirtation with reform. It was time for another revolution within his revolution. The first targets of this shake-up were the revolutionary committees. Aware that the brutal excesses of this movement had got completely out of hand, the Colonel sought to rein in its members. Among other things, he dissolved the reviled revolutionary courts that had enabled these ideologues to act with almost total impunity, replacing them with the slightly less ominous 'people's courts'.

More importantly, however, Qaddafi took to distancing himself from the movement. He began publicly criticizing the young ideologues, whom he used to refer to as the new prophets and who had spent the past decade doing his dirty work for him. In May 1988, he acknowledged publicly: 'They deviated in conduct or in ideology. Especially in their conduct … They deviated, harmed, tortured … No one has immunity … at all if he has deviated. The revolutionary does not practice repression.'[8] Unwilling to condemn the philosophy behind the movement, which he declared was still 'one hundred per cent correct', the Colonel laid the blame on the revolutionaries themselves. It was they who, in the words of one senior Libyan official, had 'distorted the revolution'.[9] This way, Qaddafi could portray himself as a paternalistic saviour figure, rescuing the Libyans from the excesses that his Jamahiriyah had unleashed in some of its most ideologically committed followers.

As if to hammer the point home, Qaddafi accompanied the reining in of these forces with a series of highly theatrical gestures. On 3 March 1988, in front of a crowd of diplomats and supporters who had been summoned to Tripoli's Furnash prison, the Colonel climbed onto a bulldozer and began ramming the gaol's iron gate. The demolition job did not go quite to plan and the scene unfolded rather like a farce: the gate would not give way, and so Qaddafi started ramming the prison wall instead. When the barbed wire-topped wall finally collapsed, it did so outwards, forcing the gathered diplomats to beat an unseemly retreat in clouds of dust, and causing a faulty sewage pipe to rupture.[10] Four hundred prisoners clambered out of the prison to freedom, as the Colonel proudly proclaimed: 'Peoples don't triumph through building prisons and raising their walls even higher.'[11]

A few days later, the Brother Leader appeared on state television at the immigration office, personally tearing up the blacklists of people who had been prohibited from travelling abroad. He announced, too, that Libyans would no longer need exit visas to leave the country. To demonstrate the point, he clambered up onto his bulldozer again and set about demolishing a security post at Ras Al-Jadir on the Tunisian border. As if to cement these changes, Qaddafi penned a new treatise, the *Great Green Charter of Human Rights in the Era of the Masses*, which was issued by the General People's Congress in June 1988. While this charter may have contained noble clauses about the sanctity of human rights, in essence it was another meaningless tract, amounting to little more than a reaffirmation of the basic principles of the Jamahiriyah system.

While Qaddafi's changes on the political front consisted primarily of showy gimmicks, the Leader did take more concrete steps in the economic sphere. In a televised speech in March 1987, he introduced a series of new directives that represented a backtracking on the socialist-style economic policies he had implemented in the late 1970s and early 1980s. Among these directives was a new ruling that enabled Libyans to become partners in small businesses through a system of *tasharaqiat* (cooperatives). What this meant was that anyone who owned a small concern, such as a farm, could now hire workers, so long as the profits were shared equally between the owners and the workers. This was a welcome move for many. Even Qaddafi could see the utter ludicrousness of some of his earlier economic directives. In a speech aired on state television in 1987, the

Brother Leader described how, during a two-month stint in the countryside, he had come across a once prosperous farm that had fallen into disrepair when its owners became too old to work.[12] With both sons having left home, the couple had no choice but to let the farm fall into decline because, under the regime's insistence that wages were a form of exploitation, they were prohibited from employing workers who could look after the farm's upkeep. As the farm deteriorated in front of their eyes, the couple had to claim handouts from the state in order to survive. Under the new directives, anyone in the same position as this couple would be able to bring workers in as part of a cooperative – provided they could all share in the rewards.[13]

Qaddafi also understood the pressing need to sort out the problem of consumer shortages. As he rather ineloquently expressed it,

> People queuing for macaroni is something which does not belong to socialism or revolution and there is no benefit in it ... The revolution never says there should be queues for macaroni in Libya. How can one who went to the market say 'I have returned without macaroni?' I have made studies in the past two months. I went to the market and I returned without macaroni ... The Libyans ... have money and cannot find anything to buy.[14]

Qaddafi's solution was to reopen the doors to private trade. Law No. 8 of 1988 abolished the state's monopoly over imports and exports, enabling Libyans to set up shop once again. This was a major U-turn for the Colonel who, just a few years before, had so relentlessly dismantled the country's entire merchant class, although, in typically Qaddafiesque manner, he singled out the elderly, the physically handicapped, widows and divorced women, and those who were on social security or who were unemployed as the most fitting to engage in such activities. Meanwhile, coffee-shops, restaurants and hotels could now be established privately; doctors, lawyers and other professionals were also allowed to practise privately, although the state still set the fees they were allowed to charge.[15]

The Colonel continued, too, to make space for the black market. The parallel economy was an important, albeit expensive, means for Libyans to acquire basic goods that they could not access through state distribution networks. Qaddafi was not about to clamp down on this important outlet. Yet, while turning a blind eye to black-market activities as a vent for public pressure may not have been that unusual for an authoritarian regime facing tough times, Qaddafi went further. The quixotic Colonel actively sought to turn the black market to the service of his revolution. In a speech to the revolutionary committees in 1988, he declared:

> You may think that black-markets are negative. On the contrary. As far as we are concerned as revolutionaries they show that the people spontaneously take a decision and without the government make something which they need; they establish a black-market because they need it ... What are black-markets? They are people's markets.[16]

Those officials in charge of steering Libya's economy must have been left scratching their heads.

On the surface at least, these laws began to change the face of the Jamahiriyah. The rows of small private shops began to raise their regulation green shutters once again, and farming initiatives could now sell direct to the people. Libyans were also able once more to get their hands on consumer goods: razor blades, light-bulbs and other such luxuries reappeared on the market. However, this private sector activity remained limited; Libyans, who had witnessed the large-scale confiscation of businesses in the 1970s, were not about to risk getting their fingers burnt again. Moreover, there was no push by the regime to actually create a more dynamic and sustainable private sector that went beyond the retail, service and import and export sectors. This was hardly surprising: as in the political sphere, the changes were not meant to be truly transformative; the Colonel had simply made space for the private sector to step in and plug the consumer shortages.[17] This whole reformist effort was just the Colonel's way of extricating himself from an immediate socio-economic crisis.

While plastering over the cracks may have been a way for Qaddafi to ease the domestic pressures that were biting at the end of the 1980s, the 1990s were to bring a much more sustained set of challenges, which plunged Libya into the most extreme of circumstances and which were to require more creative responses.

The roots of this crisis go back to 21 December 1988, when a Pan American World Airways (Pan Am) flight on its way from London to New York exploded over the Scottish town of Lockerbie, killing all 259 passengers on board, as well as eleven people on the ground. For the first two years after the bombing, the investigation focused on Iran, which, it was believed, had hired the Syrian-sponsored Popular Front for the Liberation of Palestine (PFLP) to carry out the attack in revenge for the US's downing in July 1988 of a civilian Iranian Airbus over the Strait of Hormuz – an action that had killed 290 passengers. However, attention turned to Libya in 1990, after it was discovered that a computer chip lodged in the bomb's detonator matched parts in ten detonators that had been found on two Libyans who had been arrested in Senegal in 1988. Furthermore, the same type of detonator and the same kind of Samsonite suitcase used in the Lockerbie bombing had also been used in an attack on a French UTA airliner that was brought down over the deserts of Niger on 19 September 1989, purportedly at Libyan hands.

In November 1991, the US and Britain charged two Libyan citizens, Abdelbasset Al-Megrahi and Al-Amin Khalifa Fhimah with the Lockerbie bombing. The former was head of security at the Libyan

1 Italian fascist leader Benito Mussolini, carrying the 'Sword of Islam', presented to him during a visit to Tripoli, March 1937.

2 King Idris arriving to open the BP-Nelson Bunker Hunt oil terminal at Marsa Al Hariga, near Tobruk, February 1967.

3 A young Muammar Qaddafi taking tea in his father's tent in the deserts of Sirte, August 1973.

4 Qaddafi addresses Libyan students, Tripoli, August 1973. On Qaddafi's right is his second in command, Abdelsalam Jalloud, and on his left is fellow RCC member Khweildi Al-Humaidi.

5 Qaddafi poses in yellow robes, 1984.

لا ديمقراطية بدون مؤتمرات شعبية

في الحاجة تكمن الحرية

IN NEED FREEDOM IS LATENT

NO DEMOCRACY WITHOUT POPULAR CONGRESSES

6 State supermarket, with slogans taken from the Green Book on the walls, August 1981.

7 Qaddafi with Soviet president Leonid Brezhnev, at a welcoming ceremony at Moscow's Vnukovo airport, April 1981.

8 Qaddafi with Tunisian president Habib Bourguiba, in Monastir, Tunisia, August 1983.

9 Saif Al-Islam accompanies convicted Lockerbie bomber Abdelbasset Al-Megrahi as the latter returns to Tripoli following his release from Scotland's Barlinnie prison on compassionate grounds, 20 August 2009.

10 Qaddafi stands with French president Nicolas Sarkozy at his Bab Al-Aziziya residence, July 2007. The giant gold fist commemorating the 1986 US attack on Libya can be seen in the background.

11 Qaddafi's Bab Al-Aziziya residence, destroyed after the fall of Tripoli in August 2011.

12 Benghazi residents celebrate the liberation of their city, 25 February 2011.

13 Libyans queue to view the bodies of Qaddafi and his son Moatassim in Misarata, October 2011.

Arab Airlines office at Luqa airport in Malta, and the latter was a security agent. Both men had been identified by a Maltese shop-keeper, Toni Gauci, who claimed he remembered selling them clothes that had been found in the suitcase which contained the bomb. Investigators determined that the device had travelled in the suitcase from Malta to Frankfurt, then onto London, where it was put on the Pan Am flight at Heathrow. London and Washington immediately demanded that the two suspects be handed over for trial in Scotland or the US.

Qaddafi was outraged. He insisted that Libya had had nothing to do with the attack, asserting: 'The evidence against Libya is less than a laughable piece of a fingernail.'[18] He scornfully claimed that the indictment against Al-Megrahi was a case of mistaken identity, while Fhimah was just 'a simple person who has nothing to do with politics or with the secret services'.[19] Predictably enough, this was a position that the Colonel was to hold throughout his time in power. However, he was not the only one to question the allegations against Libya. A full discussion of this issue lies outside the scope of this book; however, there is a body of opinion which contends that there has never been sufficient evidence to conclude that Al-Megrahi – or even Libya – was solely behind the plot.[20] This includes Dr Jim Swire, whose daughter, Flora, died in the attack.

While we will probably never be able to piece together the events that led up to the bombing, if one is to believe Libya's former foreign affairs secretary (minister), Abdelrahman Shalgam, there are serious questions to be raised about Libya's role in it. Following his defec-tion in 2011, Shalgam, who readily acknowledged that the Libyan intelligence services had been behind the UTA bombing, told the *Al-Hayat* newspaper: 'Lockerbie was a complex and complicated process. At the time there was talk about the role of countries and organizations. The Libyan security was party to it but I believe that it wasn't purely Libyan made.'[21] While Shalgam admitted that all his attempts to open an investigation into the affair inside Libya during his time as foreign affairs secretary were met with a stony response from the upper echelons of the regime, he was clear that, even among his closest confidants, Qaddafi always insisted that Libya was not responsible for the atrocity.

Thus, Qaddafi viewed the whole affair as a political move by the imperialist powers to curtail his Jamahiriyah. All the more so as, on 27 November 1991, the British and Americans issued a joint declaration demanding not only that Libya surrender for trial those charged with the crime, but also that it accept responsibility for the actions of Libyan officials, disclose all it knew of the crime, allow full access to the evidence, and pay appropriate compensation. Despite the fact that the trial had not yet taken place, this statement seemed to be a strong assumption of guilt.

Yet for Qaddafi, the issue went far beyond the political; it was personal. The Colonel was utterly convinced that the imperialist powers were out to get him and that they would stop at nothing. As the general secretary of the General People's Committee, Abu Zeid Dorda, announced when the indictment was issued, 'The prime target of the United States is Colonel Gaddafi in person and as a regime because he never accepted to bow to its threats and pressures.'[22]

For all his fears, the Colonel rose to the challenge with typical aplomb; like a cobra rearing up and spreading its neck, Qaddafi unleashed another tide of populist venom against the 'corrupt' Western powers:

The issue is not Pan-Am, Lockerbie or even Kuwait. The West wants to enlist its capabilities to destroy the Arab nation so that the state called Israel, the West's creation, dominates the Arabs, because there is an historic racist attitude towards them from Andalusia, the Roman conquests, the crusades and from Western neo-colonialism and the establishment of Israel.[23]

Indeed, Qaddafi used the Lockerbie issue to portray himself as the wronged victim of Western aggression and the heroic champion of Arabs and oppressed peoples everywhere.

There was no way that the restless revolutionary was going to simply roll over and comply with Western demands to hand the suspects over. Taking the role of defender of the two men, Qaddafi declared: 'the Libyan people would say, "these two men are our compatriots ... You cannot take them and give them to another country ... We are not sheep that he [Qaddafi] would dispose of us in this way, handing two, three or four of us out." '[24] His comments were not far off the mark. For all that Libyans may not have supported Qaddafi, most were deeply uncomfortable with the idea of surrendering two of their countrymen to the US and Britain like lambs to the slaughter. Moreover, Al-Megrahi came from an important Libyan tribe – the Megraha – that had proved a loyal ally of the regime. The Megraha were also the tribe of Qaddafi's right-hand man, Abdelsalam Jalloud – something that only added to the pressures on Qaddafi to resist demands for the men to be handed over.

In the months that followed the November 1991 indictment, Libya, Britain and the US locked horns in a period of intense diplomatic wrangling.[25] As Washington and London tightened the screws and talk of sanctions became increasingly commonplace, a desperate Qaddafi tried to avoid crisis by coming up with face-saving ways of making it look as though Libya was willing to cooperate. First, he proposed that Libya would try the two men itself – a suggestion that was quickly dismissed by Britain and the US. Then, in February 1992, terrified of the prospect of sanctions, the Colonel informed the UN that he would consider handing the two men over for trial in a third country, such as a fellow Arab state or Malta. He also made a series of conciliatory gestures: he announced that Libya would comply with French demands over the UTA affair, and that it would sever relations with terrorist groups that targeted innocent civilians. Tripoli even went as far as to share details of its past support for the IRA with the British government.[26] Who could have imagined that the fiery world revolutionary of the early 1980s would have bent to such a degree?

But at that point Britain and the US were having none of it, and, along with France (which was still trying to get Libya to comply with its demands over the UTA bombing), brought the issue before the UN Security Council. On 31 March 1992, Qaddafi's worst fears were realized: the UN Security Council passed Resolution 748, which instructed member states to impose sanctions on Libya. The embargo covered a host of prohibitions: air links were to be cut, the supply of parts or servicing to Libyan aircraft was to be banned, and the provision of arms-related material, advice and assistance was to be prohibited. Member states were also to reduce levels of Libyan diplomatic representation and to ban all Libyan Arab Airlines offices from operating on their soil. Furthermore, they were to expel or deny entry to all Libyan nationals suspected of terrorist involvement. A special sanctions committee was formed that was tasked with reviewing the measures in the resolution every 120 days. This committee was to prove a special source of anxiety for the Libyans, who, at the end of each review period, feared that the sanctions regime would be tightened. Things got even worse the following November, when the Security Council passed Resolution 883, which provided for the freezing of Libyan assets abroad and banned the export to Libya of selected equipment for downstream operations in the energy sector.

Luckily for Qaddafi, however, the embargo was not as devastating as it could have been. Against the wishes of the US, the sanctions did not prohibit Libya from exporting oil. This was because a number of European states, especially Italy, Spain and Germany – all keen importers of Libyan energy supplies – lobbied hard to ensure that

Tripoli could continue to sell its most valuable resource. Ironically, Libya produced and exported more oil in the 1990s than it did in the decade before. In 1989, for example, it produced 940,000 barrels per day, whereas by 1995 this figure had risen to 1.130 million barrels.[27] Furthermore, although the freezing of its assets was a major setback, Libya had anticipated the move and shrewdly moved many of its liquid assets into safe havens before the UN resolution came into force.[28] Therefore, while the imposition of international sanctions was a serious blow, in financial terms it was not crippling – at least in the early days.

It is perhaps for this reason that Qaddafi took such a 'gung-ho' attitude to the sanctions in the early 1990s, pompously declaring in September 1993:

> The nation should realize and the West must understand that we are not being affected by the blockade, the boycott, the air embargo or anything else. We hope that there won't be any relations at all between us and the West, that none of their goods get here, that we won't buy anything from [them]. What matters is that they spare us their evil and harm, and that the sea is between them and us. Good that we are rid of them as it were.[29]

Yet, while they may not have bitten immediately on the economic front, the sanctions were enormously damaging to Libya on the psychological level. The Jamahiriyah was now almost completely isolated. Once again, the Colonel's fellow Arabs proved unwilling to come to his defence; worse still, they complied with the 'Christian crusader' embargo. This was a crushing blow. Qaddafi's anger was palpable, and almost overnight state newspapers unleashed tirades of vitriolic anti-Arabism. There was little tangible support from elsewhere at this point. For all his dreams of leading a powerful force of oppressed nations, united under the banner of the Jamahiriyah and ready to smash the imperialist powers, Qaddafi had wound up almost completely alone, adrift on a sea of disinterest and disdain.

Internal challenges: tribes and Islam

As the sanctions and the isolation took hold, Qaddafi found himself up against a series of internal challenges, some of which pushed his regime to its limits. The first such test came from within his own ranks, in the form of an attempted coup by a group of disaffected army officers from the influential Werfella tribe. The Werfella, based primarily in Bani Walid in Tripolitania, were always considered one of the tribes most loyal to the Qaddafi regime. They proved ready recruits to Qaddafi's security forces, as well as to the revolutionary committees, and made up one side of the security triangle that comprised the Qaddadfa, the Megraha and the Werfella – the three main tribes that shored up the Jamahiriyah.

However, in 1993, a handful of rather green army officers from the Werfella got themselves embroiled with the exiled opposition group, the NFSL, which was keen to capitalize on Qaddafi's weakness in the face of the newly imposed international sanctions. Having come into contact with some members of the Werfella, and having sensed their unhappiness with the way things were going inside Libya, the NFSL set up a series of meetings in Zurich. At these meetings, which went on long into the night in the rooms of the Ambassador Hotel, the NFSL outlined its ambitious and highly risky plan to the nervous young officers: it wanted them to go back to Libya and to recruit a network of rebels from inside the armed forces, who could eventually stage a coup against Qaddafi.

To the young officers' surprise, there was another, riskier, dimension to the plot. At the first of these Zurich meetings in February 1993, the NFSL also arranged for the Werfella officers to meet an American. One of the officers, Khalil Jedek, described the scene:

The American waited for us in the gardens ... the American introduced himself saying that his name was John. Of course he worked
for US intelligence ... We began to talk. The American was asking
about a number of points. He asked about chemical weapons, the
rocket development programme, the effect of the embargo on Libya
and the Russian experts; were they still in the Jamahiriyah or not?[30]

Upon their return to Libya, the intrepid Werfella officers set
about recruiting from within the trusted circles of their own tribe
in Bani Walid. However, the regime was way ahead of the plotters.
On the morning of 11 October, the security services, which had
been monitoring the men for a while, arrested all the officers
involved as they made their way to work, finishing off the conspiracy
at a single blow. A week after the arrests, the foreign media carried
reports of an armed mutiny at the military base in Bani Walid, as
well as of major uprisings elsewhere in the country. The whole affair
was portrayed as a serious tribal revolt among parts of the Werfella,
prompting speculation that Qaddafi was at risk of losing the support
of one of the country's most important tribes. This version of events
has remained largely unchallenged, and the Bani Walid uprising has
been built into Libya's historical narrative.

However, the reality of the Bani Walid affair was nowhere near as
dramatic. Given the difficulty of accessing information from inside
the country at the time, the press relied almost exclusively on NFSL
sources, which were based outside Libya. It is not clear whether the
NFSL intentionally misled the press, whipping the story up into
something bigger than it was in the hope of encouraging unrest, or
whether it was simply a case of wishful thinking on its part. However,
according to a former NFSL member, there was no such rebellion or
uprising by the Werfella and no movement of regime forces.[31]
Rather, the regime had moved quickly to nip in the bud a nascent
plot, orchestrated mainly from outside.

Yet the plot was still a serious matter for the Colonel, and the fact that a number of military officers from one of the most loyal tribes had got as far as starting to recruit inside the country, right under the regime's nose, was deeply troubling. Qaddafi believed he had already purged the rogue elements from within his armed forces following the end of the Chad war. What made things far worse and amplified the conspiracy in the Colonel's mind was the American component. Once again, the Americans had succeeded in extending their reach all the way into Libya, and into one of the most loyal of areas at that. The Colonel's worst nightmare was coming ever closer.

The punishment could only be extreme. Qaddafi was going to make examples of these young officers, and they and their families were to pay a terrifying price. The men were hauled off for the regulation interrogation, which was broadcast repeatedly on Libyan television. The petrified young men were forced to confess to their crimes and were portrayed as little more than humiliated stooges of the US who had sold themselves and their country cheaply. They were then convicted of espionage by a military court.

However, Qaddafi could not afford to give the impression that there was a crack in relations between the state and one of its most loyal tribes. Cunningly, therefore, he made the Werfella mete out a punishment of its own: he called on loyal Werfella elements to wreak revenge upon their cousins. In line with tribal norms, in which those who bring dishonour are disowned, the Werfella had to demonstrate that the officers were little more than rogue elements who could be dispensed with as traitors both to the state and to the tribe. Revolutionary committee members from the tribe set about bulldozing the houses and land of the families of those who had erred. Family members of those involved were also forced to go on television and denounce the 'traitors' that had been in their midst. In August 1995, revolutionary committee members forced the local population of Bani Walid to attend a meeting where they were made to sign a petition calling for the execution of those who had been involved in the affair.[32] In January 1997, the show was finally over: six officers were executed by firing squad, while two civilians who were also accused of involvement in the affair were put to death by hanging.

While Qaddafi came out of the affair with the loyalty of the Werfella intact, the whole episode demonstrated that, for all he had sought to get rid of tribalism, viewing it as the antithesis of what it meant to be modern, it was still a powerful tool that he could draw on in times of trouble. Unlike the revolutionary committees, the tribes were, in his own words, 'a natural social structure', and an important element in the country's social fabric. It was dawning on the wily Colonel that harnessing the tribes in a more formalized way could assist him in this difficult period.

That is not to say that the Leader had ignored the tribes until this point. While denouncing tribalism as backward, the Bedouin from the desert had skilfully played the tribal field, pitting different tribes (or elements within tribes) against each other and buying tribal loyalties as he saw fit. He regularly courted tribal sheikhs, handing out money, privileges or positions in return for support. Indeed, the Leader allowed the tribal elites to get involved in the 'farcical fighting for posts', while he sat 'laughing his head off in his tent'.[33] In this way the power of each tribe rested only in its relationship to the Leader, and he managed to create a situation in which the tribes were left competing for his favour. Tribal elders regularly visited Qaddafi to pledge their allegiance to him, taking with them gifts of expensive textiles, pedigree horses, camels and land in a bid to seek his approval, as he lorded it over them like a king.[34] Moreover, he had shored up his regime with the Qaddadfa, as well as the Megraha and the Werfella, turning the state into a kind of overarching tribe, with him, his family and his tent at its pinnacle. Thus, Qaddafi succeeded in neutralizing the tribes, subordinating them to his revolution.

Yet with the mounting pressures of the 1990s, Qaddafi came to realize that he could use the country's complex tribal tapestry in a more constructive way: the tribes could become another tool of mobilization to shore up his regime. To this end, the Colonel expanded his revolution by setting up yet another institution, the 'social people's leaderships', which he described as an 'engine' that would propel his revolution ever forward. These social people's leaderships comprised 'respected natural leaders' of local communities, namely tribal elders, who were tasked with mobilizing the masses and with resolving local conflicts and problems. From now on, these tribal elders were to be held responsible for everything that happened in their own areas. As he explained to them in 1994, 'The commune will be responsible for everything: even car number plates will be the responsibility of the commune ... Then, if something happens in the commune you will be held responsible, even for price rises.'[35]

What this meant in practice was that the tribes were turned into another mechanism of social control. As in the Bani Walid affair, they were given the special task of weeding out disloyal elements, and were charged with avenging tribal honour if anyone strayed from the straight and narrow. To get the point across, Qaddafi began visiting tribal notables and impressing upon them the need to defend their honour by uncovering the 'traitors' in their midst. He instructed a gathering of tribal elders in Zintan in 1994:

... look for treason, detect it and contain it and disown any of its clans which are involved in treason and say to the Libyan people: we are not traitors, we have washed our hands of such-and-such a clan which has traitors ... Every clan should expel the families containing traitors until those very families disown the members who are traitors.[36]

Thus Qaddafi skilfully clouded the country's most trusted social units with the heavy weight of suspicion. He also brought them directly under the stewardship not only of the regime, but of his own family: in line with his growing preference for surrounding himself with members of his own family and tribe, he appointed his cousin, Sayyid Qaddaf Al-Dam, as the 'general coordinator' of this new body. Indeed, as the world around him became more insecure, so Qaddafi retreated into the security of his roots.

However, his skilful manipulation of Libya's tribal system was not to save him from a far more formidable foe, which came in the form of a wave of Islamist activism and which caught him almost completely unawares. The discovery in the mid-1990s of a series of armed Islamist groups, intent on bringing down his regime and replacing it with an Islamist state, was to shake the Colonel to the core. This prophet of the desert was not as invincible as he thought. He found himself up against an ideology that was stronger than his own and that inspired a devotion that would stop at nothing to achieve its objectives. Despite the terrifying array of security measures that the Colonel had put in place to protect his Jamahiriyah, here were young men, brimming over with righteousness and willing to risk their lives to bring down his cherished creation. This was all the more difficult for the Leader to stomach given that he had invested so much in building Islam into his revolution. Why should any Libyan need to follow the 'reactionary' forces of political Islam when he had already shown them the way?

This challenge was all the more concerning for the Colonel because the Islamist current was rooted in a wider ideological shift that went far beyond Libya's borders. From the late 1970s, and spurred on in particular by the Iranian revolution of 1979, the entire region had experienced an Islamic awakening that had shaken the foundations of the post-independence regimes. Islamist opposition groups – both moderate and militant – had sprung up across the region, and by the 1980s they had proved successful at tapping into popular grievances. Islam had come to be seen by those seeking change as 'the solution' and as the alternative to the 'corrupted' elites that had taken power at independence and that had promised so much, but delivered so little. From Egypt to Tunisia, from Algeria to Sudan – in whichever direction the Colonel looked, Islamism had reared its head. While all the neighbouring leaders had struggled against the Islamist tide, it was in Algeria that the effects had proved most devastating. From 1992, when the army cancelled elections that the Islamists looked set to win, the country was plunged into a brutal civil war, with Islamist militants fighting it out against the state. The contagion effect was on everybody's mind. As if that were not enough for Qaddafi to contend with, Sudan had become a veritable hub of Islamist militancy, with the Islamist government there hosting an array of jihadists, including Osama Bin Ladin. Islamism was all round.

Given Islamism's momentum, Libya was not going to remain immune from the tide. The Islamist message, reassuringly rooted in tradition, was always going to hold more sway for the Libyans than Qaddafi's hare-brained 'new gospel'. It is not surprising, therefore, that, in the early 1980s, groups of young men, many of them students, who were 'searching for something'[37] began to gather in each other's houses to share their interest in Islam. While Qaddafi was filling the air with revolutionary slogans, these young men would huddle together to listen to cassettes of sermons or to read pamphlets by radical Islamist scholars, who preached that it was a religious duty to fight against un-Islamic rulers. It was a risky business; anyone caught engaging in such activities would face the severest of penalties. But for many of these young men, frustrated with what they saw around them, this was their way of tapping into the new and exciting ideas that breathed of a new way.

As the 1980s progressed, it was not only these new ideas, but also the jihad in Afghanistan that came to capture the imagination of many of these young idealists. In 1979, Soviet tanks had rolled into Afghanistan, prompting Arabs from far and wide to join the local Afghans in their struggle against the 'godless' communist forces. For these young Libyans, living in a land in which everything had been subjugated to the suffocating and emasculating ideology of the Jamahiriyah, the idea of fighting jihad in the name of Islam was both heroic and noble. It was also exciting. The appearance of smuggled cassettes by key fighters and sheikhs in the Afghan struggle only added to this sense of adventure and of a 'new dawn'.

So it was that a steady stream of young Libyans, fired up by romantic notions of jihad, went to join the ranks of the mujahideen. It was not long before the Libyans had established their own guest-house in the Abu Sayaf camp at Babi in Pakistan, near the border with Afghanistan. It was here that the more seasoned among them would welcome fresh new arrivals and arrange for them to be trans-ferred to the front lines. Although there are no official statistics of the numbers who went, some of those involved have estimated that there were between 800 and 1,000 Libyans who joined the Afghani jihad during the 1980s.[38]

Back in Libya, meanwhile, there was a growing sensibility among the population at large to the Islamist message. Signs of increased religiosity were appearing everywhere: the *hijab* (Islamic veil) – something Qaddafi once described as the 'act of the devil', which forced women to 'sit at home' – began appearing with greater frequency, especially on university campuses.[39] Long beards – another symbol of religiosity – also became more common, despite the fact that growing one brought its own risks. One former militant recounted how his brother, an electricity ministry employee in Benghazi, was hauled off a public bus on his way to work one day by a member of the security services, who promptly set his beard alight.[40] There were stories of scuffles breaking out on univer-sity campuses between Islamist-leaning students and those who were loyal to the revolution; and in 1989, demonstrations that erupted in protest at Libya's cancellation of the World Cup qualifying match between Libya and Algeria took on an Islamist hue. Protesters turned their wrath against the regime, and chants of 'Allah is great. Qaddafi is the enemy of Allah' rang through the air.

Such manifestations of Islamist sentiment were deeply concerning to Qaddafi. For all his efforts, the masses were not only proving resistant to his ideology, but they were now actively adopting one of their own. What was more shocking, however, was Qaddafi's realization that he was up against something far more sinister. In 1989, the regime uncovered armed militant Islamist cells in Ajdabia and Misarata.[41] Another was discovered in Benghazi after its leader, a fiery imam, Sheikh Mohamed Fahkih, embarked upon a suicidal mission to launch his own jihad against Qaddafi. Given the cell's pitiful lack of training and expertise, the security services were able to finish it off in record time, killing Fahkih in the process. However, the imam's rashness was to have bitter consequences: the discovery 'made the security services and the government wake up'.[42] The regime launched a mass arrest campaign, hunting down hundreds of suspected Islamists and their sympathizers. Indeed, Qaddafi cast the net wide and arrested anyone with the slightest connection to the Islamist movement. The message was clear: Qaddafi was not going to let Libya become another Algeria.

Indeed, while the other North African regimes all flirted (to varying degrees) with strategies of 'accommodationism' towards the Islamist opposition, Qaddafi left no space whatsoever for those of an Islamist persuasion. He spelled this message out in no uncertain terms: 'From now on', he declared, 'the sentence ... for everyone who is found guilty of not knowing God properly will be to crush him immediately.'[43] He also threatened:

If you are told that one member of your family was found in this [religious] movement, it is as if you have been told that he has

AIDS, and that he is finished. You cannot possibly plead on his behalf. His is a religious hypocrite and must be crushed [*sic*].[44]

In fact, Qaddafi came to display an almost personal hatred for his Islamist enemies. He labelled them heretics, intent on destroying progress. He also accused them of being hashish smokers, and sought to ridicule them at every turn. As he wrote in one of his short stories,

> If we were to believe in what the parties of the God coalition say, there is no need for our children to go to schools, higher technical institutes or the Bright Star University of Technology ... rather, let them out in the open air on sidewalks selling cigarettes and cakes to adults ... the only important thing to do is to learn the prayer.[45]

Yet for all his tough talk, Islamism turned out to be a phenomenon that even the canny Qaddafi could not contain. While the 1989 arrests may have temporarily quashed militant activity inside Libya, there were still scores of young Libyan militants in Afghanistan waiting for the opportunity to get back into Libya to destroy his regime. It was among these militants that Qaddafi's fiercest enemy was to be born. Buoyed up by victory following the Soviet withdrawal from Afghanistan in 1989, a group of Libyan fighters formed the Seraya Al-Mujahideen (the Mujahideen Brigades), later to be renamed the Libyan Islamic Fighting Group (LIFG). The group sought to bring Libyan jihadists under their wing, in order to prepare to return to Libya to overthrow the 'Pharaoh' Qaddafi and to bring Islamic rule to Libya.

Getting back into Libya to execute this plan proved much more difficult than these hardened militants had anticipated. Nevertheless, a number of fighters did manage to smuggle themselves into the country, where they worked to spread the LIFG's message, mainly tapping into the remnants of the jihadist structures that had escaped the cull of 1989.[46] They established small cells across the country, appointing emirs to lead each region. They adopted a cautious approach and focused on gathering recruits, weaponry and ammunition. By 1994, the group had tripled its numbers to some 300.[47] Their caution paid off; the regime was unable to detect the growing current of militant opposition that was developing once again right under its nose. Moreover, the LIFG was not the only militant organization on the scene. Other groups, including the Islamic Martyrs' Movement, which was more localized in nature (emerging in, and recruiting almost exclusively from, Benghazi), had also emerged on the scene.

Meanwhile, more moderate currents were also operating. Although Qaddafi believed he had stamped out the Libyan branch of the international Muslim Brotherhood, having clamped down on the movement immediately after taking power, the group had been able to take advantage of the regime's weaknesses in the late 1980s and early 1990s, and had started rebuilding its presence in the country. Although limited, it succeeded in developing a base in a number of mosques, where its members sought to spread the Islamic message.[48]

Indeed, the early 1990s were the heyday for all these groups, as they sought to take advantage of the vulnerability of the Qaddafi machine and to challenge its overwhelming physical and ideological hegemony. However, in 1995, a naïve error on the part of one LIFG cell resulted in calamity for all the Islamist currents. The cell had been tasked with freeing two of its members – one from hospital and the other from a detention centre in Benghazi. However, it botched the operation: a handful of fighters, disguised as members of the security services, went to the hospital and carted their man out, raising the regime's suspicions. It was not long before the security services had uncovered a network of cells intent on overthrowing the regime.

The hunt for the LIFG was on. The regime unleashed its full force on the militants, mopping up as many as it could and throwing them into the Abu Slim prison without a backwards glance. The LIFG and the other militant groups on the scene at the time fled to the Jebel Akhdar (Green Mountains) in the east, from where they fought back as best they could. From their hideouts, where they came under attack from ground and air strikes, they launched a string of attacks against the regime, mostly against high-ranking figures in the security services. They even tried to assassinate Qaddafi, most famously in November 1996, when LIFG member Mohamed Abdullah Al-Ghrew, threw a grenade at the Leader while he was visiting the desert town of Brak.

Qaddafi hit back hard. Never one for half measures, the Leader set out to teach the Libyans a lesson they would not forget. Scores of suspected Islamists were arrested; so, too, was anyone suspected of having the slightest sympathy with the cause. The revolutionary committees were given free rein to eliminate suspected Islamists, and triumphantly paraded the corpses of those they had 'liquidated' through the streets. The regime also moved to intimidate entire families and towns. The families of suspected militants were forced to join the security services in combing whole areas in a bid to hunt down their relatives. Indeed, the east of the country was turned into a kind of security zone, with the whole region placed under siege in a bid to flush out anyone with suspected Islamist tendencies.

The Colonel also sought to deter tribes from even thinking about protecting Islamist elements. In March 1997, he introduced a collective punishment law, the Charter of Honour, which ruled that anyone who concealed, sympathized with or failed to disavow and hand over criminals would be considered to be 'involved in the collective crime which requires the imposition of a collective punishment'.[49] This punishment was to take the form of denying whole families or tribes access to services, such as water or electricity. Meanwhile, the regime had engaged in an even more sinister elimination of its Islamist foes. In June 1996, after a rebellion by some Islamists who were detained in the Abu Slim prison, the regime engaged in a wholesale massacre of prison inmates. An estimated 1,286 prisoners were mown down in the prison yard and buried in mass graves. This was to be one of the most notorious crimes of the Qaddafi era.

By 1998, the LIFG knew it was beaten. The group's leadership called an end to the struggle and ordered its shattered members to leave the country, prompting those who could to flee abroad, many to Afghanistan and others to Europe, where they remained an organization in exile. That year also saw an end to the Muslim Brotherhood's presence in the country, after the regime launched a mass arrest campaign, picking up 152 members of the movement, including its leadership. By the late 1990s, therefore, it was all but over for the Islamist current, and Qaddafi had triumphed over adversity.

However, deeply shaken by the experience, the Colonel was not going to let the matter rest there. It had not gone unnoticed that it was the east of the country that had provided the core of the Islamist opposition. It was in this socially conservative region, still closely linked to its tribal and Bedouin roots, that the message of political Islam had had a greater hold. Although the Islamist movement had found support in the west, and while much of its leadership had originated in Tripolitania, the rank and file came predominantly from Cyrenaica. Indeed, its head may have been in the west, but its heart was anchored firmly in the east. The whole Islamist episode, therefore, confirmed Qaddafi's sense that the east was a troublesome and recalcitrant region that would require extra vigilance to be kept in check; the assault was to continue.

Not only was security maintained at the highest levels, but the east was to be punished. It was kept in a permanent state of underdevelopment and near isolation. Benghazi was allowed to fall into a shocking state of disrepair, so starved of investment that parts of the city came to resemble a post-conflict zone that time had forgotten. The city and its inhabitants were made to feel, more than ever, as though they were Tripoli's poor relation. The east was never to be allowed to forget what it meant to challenge the regime. Yet while this hardline approach may have calmed the storm, it did not quell it altogether. The brutality that the Colonel had employed against the east fostered an extreme resentment that became more bitter with each year that passed. This festering anger was to bubble away under the surface, rearing its head sporadically in public protests that were speedily put down, until it exploded so spectacularly in February 2011, when the east finally took its revenge.

The end of the decade

Although Qaddafi had managed to navigate his way through the various challenges with his Jamahiriyah intact, by the end of the 1990s the Brother Leader and his regime still were not out of the woods. Falling oil revenues and the effects of decades of economic and administrative mismanagement were taking their toll, and chaos ruled. Libya was in a pitiful state and, as the rest of the world was careering into the globalized age, isolated Libya was looking more anachronistic than ever. Still clinging obstinately to his Cold War rhetoric and socialist-style vision, Qaddafi came increasingly to resemble a relic from a bygone age.

The regime was also feeling the effects of the international embargo. Although oil exports were not included in the embargo, the inability to get hold of spare parts and the ban on international travel were cumbersome restrictions that were making life increasingly difficult. The sanctions were also starting to have a negative effect on Libya's energy sector, still the mainstay of the economy. As the then head of Libya's National Oil Corporation (NOC), Hammouda Al-Aswad explained,

The Americans knew our equipment, and they placed every item on the sanctions list. Then, when the UN embargo was imposed in 1992, the problem became even more complicated because we couldn't buy on the open market. Some machinery has been smuggled in, but we've now used up all our stores. We've had to go to junkyards to recondition our discarded parts, and we've even attempted to manufacture our own parts, but we haven't been successful.[50]

The sanctions were also making life even more difficult for ordinary Libyans, who were already exhausted by the years of revolutionary experimentation. Prices went up, as the cost of importing goods rocketed and the domestic market declined due to problems over importing spare parts. From 1993 to 1997 inflation averaged a breathtaking 35 per cent.[51] For Libyans, whose salaries remained frozen at 1981 levels, life became tougher than ever. Even getting married became a challenge in its own right due to the rise in the price of gold, an essential component of a woman's dowry; a gram of gold that was worth 12 dinars before the sanctions cost four times as much in 1994.[52]

Although the state ensured that people did not go hungry by expanding the rationing system, under which families were entitled to subsidized goods, simply getting by became more difficult.[53] Moreover, for many families, depending on subsidies was a humiliating experience, made all the worse by the fact that the subsidy system became a victim of corruption. Those controlling the system were accused of selling only a fraction of the subsidized goods, flogging the rest on the black market for a substantial profit.[54]

Indeed, the sanctions regime created a whole class of 'new rich' who were able to exploit the crisis to their advantage. This class comprised not only officials who had been able to profit from the situation, but also private traders who were fortunate enough to have international contacts, access to foreign currency and the right connections to officials in the regime. These individuals were able to import goods and sell them at vastly inflated prices.[55] By the mid-1990s, luxury goods such as French mustard, Italian chocolates, Italian suits and electronic equipment from Asia began to fill the shelves of private shops in Tripoli and Benghazi. Yet the vastly inflated prices only added insult to injury for most Libyans, who could only dream of affording such extravagances. In 1998, mobile telephones were being sold for around LYD 3,000 – five times the monthly salary of a senior academic.[56] Similarly, Libyans eyed the swanky new villas that were springing up in the Gargarish and Janzour suburbs of Tripoli and the Al-Fuwayyat district of Benghazi (nicknamed Hay Al-Dollar, or the 'Dollar Neighbourhood') and that were way beyond their means. This growing gap between rich and poor created a surly resentment among those who were left struggling to make ends meet.

This resentment hardened on account of the fact that vital public services were still being eroded. Schools and universities found themselves starved of funds and unable to buy the basics, such as textbooks, despite the fact that the numbers of pupils and students enrolling were rising dramatically.[57] Teachers were in short supply, and school and university buildings became increasingly dilapidated as they were left to fall into disrepair. Hospitals also became increasingly decrepit; medical equipment that broke was not replaced, and it became harder to acquire medicines through the public sector. The lack of public funds, combined with administrative ineptitude, resulted in general deterioration; roads went unrepaired and rotting rubbish piled up in the streets.

Despite the difficulties, Qaddafi continued to indulge himself in his pet project. Begun in the early 1980s, the Great Man Made River (GMMR) scheme – the Colonel's plan to bring drinking water from beneath the deserts of the south of Libya to the populated coastal areas through enormous underground pipes – was not going to be sacrificed. Qaddafi, who had once declared that there was no great people that did not have a great river, saw the GMMR as his great showcase project, and nothing was going to stop it. The project continued to soak up some 15 per cent of government expenditure during the toughest years of the 1990s.

Not that Qaddafi shunned all efforts to appease the population. However, more often than not these were little more than empty gestures aimed at bolstering the Colonel's own popularity. In September 1996, the Leader announced a new wealth distribution scheme, under which each needy family was to receive US$5,000. However, in December 1996, Qaddafi imposed certain conditions on the scheme, announcing: 'You are not allowed to get your money and spend it on something which is not beneficial to society or to yourself.'[58] By March 1997, the policy had changed again: the regime decided instead to give each family twenty sheep, rather than the cash![59]

Equally ludicrous was the regime's attempt to bolster Libya's economy through tourism. In 1994, the country established a tourism secretariat and announced that it was turning its coastline over to tourism. While Libya certainly had a lot to offer foreign visitors, the idea of a country that was under international embargo, that prohibited alcohol and that was sorely lacking in real service provision turning itself into a Mediterranean tourist hotspot was delusional, to say the very least. Even the director of Libya's national tourist agency, Fawzi Ghnedi, struggled desperately when, in 1992, he was asked by a journalist what kind of people might like to take their holidays in the Jamahiriyah: 'Perhaps reformed alcoholics ... You know, we don't allow alcohol. And then there are those who like adventure.'[60]

Clearly such gestures were not going to go far in quelling the mounting public anger and frustration. Libyans were becoming

increasingly fed up with the suffocating situation they found themselves in. As one twenty-five-year old economics graduate exclaimed
in 1995, 'Today, it is very difficult being a Libyan. Before we used to
travel freely to Europe, America, anywhere. Today if they see a
Libyan passport, they immediately brand us as terrorists ... I am sick
and tired of it all.'[61] Yet Libyans were not only angry with the West,
which had imposed the sanctions: they were also becoming increasingly frustrated with the Qaddafi regime.

All these pressures that were bearing down on Qaddafi like an
enormous weight led him to conclude that something had to give.
The Brother Leader knew that if he and his Jamahiriyah were to
survive into the next century, he needed to put his heady ideology
slightly to one side and take decisive action to pull Libya out of the
crisis.

CHAPTER 7

The Chimera of Reform

Qaddafi was faced with a dilemma. Libya was deep in crisis and the Colonel desperately needed a way out. Everywhere he looked, the pressures were building and he feared the country might slip out of his hands. His cherished Jamahiriyah was on shakier ground than ever before. If his regime was going to live, he was going to have to do something drastic. The exhausted Colonel knew that the key to extricating himself from this mess was to hand over the Lockerbie suspects, thereby securing the lifting of the international embargo that was strangling the country and grinding down the all-important energy sector, which was crying out for US technical expertise.[1] Yet the idea of surrendering the two suspects was still anathema to the Brother Leader. How could this proud Bedouin, who had invested a lifetime in spouting anti-imperialist rhetoric, simply bow down to Western demands? Moreover, beyond the issue of personal pride, the Leader had domestic concerns to think about. For all that Libyans may not have liked the Qaddafi regime, most viewed Western demands to give up the suspects as a further example of imperialist bullying. Most important of all, however, the Colonel feared that, if he handed the men over, imperialist powers would use the trial to incriminate the Libyan state – and him personally.

Yet the cornered Qaddafi knew he had to find a way of navigating himself out of the crisis. His chance came in August 1998, when Washington and London put forward a new proposal: the Lockerbie suspects could be tried in a specially convened court in The Hague, under Scottish law and in front of a panel of three Scottish judges.[2] This proposal was not, in essence, very different from one that the Libyans had put forward themselves in 1994. Back then, keen to be seen to be making some concessions that would nevertheless not look as though the two men were simply being relinquished to the Americans and the British, Libya had suggested that Al-Megrahi and Fhimah could be tried at the International Court of Justice (ICJ) in The Hague. Tripoli had also conceded at the time that the men could be tried under Scottish law, before a tribunal of Scottish judges.

However, back in 1994 the idea was not acceptable in Washington or London, where the Clinton administration and John Major's government were unwilling to give in to what they considered to be yet another example of Qaddafi's political manoeuvring. By 1998, however, the US and Britain had good reason to change their tune. Tripoli's willingness to be flexible had won it some support on the international scene. The Arab League supported its stance, as did the Organization of African Unity (OAU), which, in 1998, threatened that its member countries would stop applying the sanctions unless Britain and the US agreed to trial in a neutral country. To Qaddafi's delight, a number of individual African states had already broken the sanctions. Meanwhile, countries such as Egypt, Morocco and Tunisia – all key US allies – also began to question the legality of the embargo.[3] Libya's position was strengthened further when Russia and China waded into the debate and began criticizing British and US intransigence. Indeed, Qaddafi's shrewd willingness to hand the men over for trial in a neutral country gave him a kind of moral authority in the eyes of many in the developing world and beyond, bringing him the international support that his ideological visions had always failed to elicit.

In the face of this international backing, and with the embargo at risk of being undermined, the US and British governments were forced to think again. The coming to power of the New Labour government in Britain in May 1997 also heralded a new approach on the part of the British. The Blair government was keen to resolve the stand-off with Libya, and proved willing to take a more flexible approach than had its predecessor.[4] And so the Blair government invested efforts in lobbying to get the Americans to support the proposal of a trial in The Hague.

Ever the opportunist, Qaddafi knew a chance when he saw one: Tripoli formally accepted the proposal just one day after it was put forward.[5] Predictably enough, however, the handover was not going to be so straightforward. The Libyan leader began flapping about 'procedural issues' that needed to be ironed out before he would allow the suspects – who, he reminded the world, were human beings and 'not tins of fruit' – to be handed over.[6] These procedural issues concerned matters that were highly sensitive in Libya, such as where the men would be held if convicted, and under what conditions. The Colonel's insistence on imposing his own set of conditions was partly related to his desire to challenge the perception that he had simply rolled over in meek submission to the Western powers. However, it was also about prevarication; with his heightened sense of paranoia, the Leader, who still believed the Americans were out to get him, was convinced that the proposal was an elaborate political trap. In spite of the long list of assurances he was given by the British, the most important of which was that they would not seek to implicate anyone in the trial other than the two defendants, Qaddafi was so mired in his own worldview that he was unable to shed his suspicions.[7]

It took the intervention of outside intermediaries to finally reassure the Colonel that he could hand the two men over without risking his entire regime. The most important of these intermediaries was South African President Nelson Mandela, who entered the fray after Tony Blair appealed to him for assistance.[8] Mandela's involvement was crucial for the Leader in more ways than one. Not only did it provide him with a sense of assurance, but it also gave him some much-needed legitimacy. If the leader of South Africa's anti-apartheid struggle was supporting the handover of the two suspects, then Libya need not fear giving the men up. So keen was the Colonel to get the point across that, in March 1999, he got Mandela to address the General People's Congress and to reassure the delegates that all the necessary guarantees for the trial were in place.

Having cloaked himself in this all-important international legitimacy, Qaddafi stopped prevaricating. Proving that pragmatism could win out over the ideology that had underpinned his regime for so many years, in April 1999 Libya handed the two men over for trial. On 5 April, Al-Megrahi and Fhimah boarded the specially chartered UN plane, gesturing with victory signs as they entered the aircraft, and were flown to the bleak Valkenburg airbase in the Netherlands. Two days later, decked out in tweed jackets and ties, the men appeared in the makeshift court at Camp Zeist, where they were formally charged with murder and conspiracy to murder. In return, the UN suspended the sanctions that had tied Qaddafi's hands for almost a decade.

The trial, which began on 4 February 2000, lasted until January 2001, when Fhimah was acquitted and his co-defendant Al-Megrahi was found guilty of murder. Al-Megrahi was given a mandatory life sentence, passed with the recommendation that he spend twenty years in prison. His conviction came as a shock to many, including his defence team, which had chosen not to call any witnesses, in part because it considered that there was insufficient evidence to convict the men. Indeed, there was a growing belief in some quarters that a verdict of 'not proven' – possible under Scottish law – would be handed down.[9]

The guilty verdict came as a particularly heavy blow to Qaddafi. The conviction confirmed his suspicions that the trial had been politicized and that he had stupidly walked into the political trap he had so feared. The furious Colonel railed against the decision, announcing that he would produce evidence of Al-Megrahi's innocence 'within days'. He also declared that the judges had three options: to admit the truth, to resign or to commit suicide![10]

The Libyan people were equally outraged: angry demonstrations erupted in Tripoli, with thousands gathering in Green Square and outside the British embassy to protest about the verdict. Some of the protesters marched to the United Nations office, where, in grisly scenes, three young men produced knives and tried to commit suicide by slashing their throats. One of the men succeeded and died at the scene, while others were rushed to hospital with serious injuries. Given the nature of the Jamahiriyah, such public protest can only have occurred with the blessing of the regime, which had bussed in groups of young men from around the country to take part. The regime even mobilized the country's imams to whip up popular sentiment; the imam of Tripoli's Moulay Mohamed Mosque, Ahmed Al-Balaz, proclaimed: 'The verdict was a political decision taken under the pressure of the big powers, the United States of America and Great Britain.'[11] Yet while this outpouring of anger may have been orchestrated by the regime, it also reflected a very real sense inside Libya that Al-Megrahi had been made a scapegoat and that he was the victim of a politically motivated show trial. This was an affront to Libyan nationalism, and it became a matter of national honour to bring Al-Megrahi home. While probably most British and Americans put the affair to the back of their minds after the trial, the Libyans did not. It was for this reason that the Libyan regime continued to lobby the British government so hard to bring its man home.

Despite the anger at Al-Megrahi's conviction, there was at least some relief in Tripoli that the country could now start to put the whole Lockerbie saga behind it. However, the Libyans soon discovered that their wish to turn a new page was not going to come so easily. They found themselves forced to jump through a seemingly ever-increasing set of hoops in a bid to secure full rehabilitation. These hoops were largely the work of the Americans, who still could not shake their suspicion of Qaddafi. The US also wanted to make the Colonel pay for the Lockerbie bombing, not least because the families of the American victims had become an influential lobby group in the US. Washington imposed another set of conditions on Tripoli: Libya should pay compensation to the victims' families, should renounce terrorism, should reveal all it knew about the Lockerbie affair, and should publicly accept responsibility for its officials.

Qaddafi was apoplectic. For all his desperation to restore relations with the US, its repeated raising of the bar was too much for the ever-proud Bedouin, who perceived it as another Western attempt to humiliate and subjugate him. However, while the Colonel fumed, some parts of the Libyan regime were more circumspect. Determined not to lose the gains that had been made by the handover of the Lockerbie suspects, a group of high-ranking officials – including the Libyan ambassador to Italy, Abdel Ati Al-Obeidi; chief of external security, Musa Kusa; Foreign Affairs Secretary, Abdelrahman Shalgam; and the ambassador to London, Mohamed Zwai – concluded that Libya had no choice but to comply with the demands. This group, which was to sow the seeds of what later became known as the 'reformist faction', knew that the country could not afford another period of isolation, and that working with the US was the only way to rehabilitation. Its members struggled hard to convince the Colonel;

according to Shalgam, they went to Qaddafi some fifty times to try to persuade him to agree to pay compensation.[12] Each time Qaddafi refused, insisting that an injustice had been done to Libya, and that it should not be forced to pay for a crime it did not commit.

However, in the face of US obstinacy, the Leader was finally persuaded that cooperation was the only option. He reluctantly gave the go-ahead for the establishment of a special compensation committee, headed by businessman Mohamed Abdel Jawad, that was to negotiate the compensation package. After several rounds of knotty secret negotiations with the US and the UK, a deal was finally thrashed out in August 2003. Libya was to pay US$10 million to each of the victims' families. This was to be paid in three tranches: the first $4 million was to be paid after UN sanctions were removed; a further $4 million was to be paid when US unilateral sanctions were removed; and the final $2 million was to be forthcoming when Libya was removed from the State Department's State Sponsors of Terrorism list.

The Colonel grudgingly agreed to the deal. He also agreed to provide a letter denouncing terrorism. But accepting responsibility for the bombing was a far thornier issue. Qaddafi feared that accepting any kind of responsibility would mean falling victim to yet another trap aimed at destroying his regime. Straight after the trial, Shalgam had made it clear that Libya would not countenance any acceptance of responsibility for the bombing. Yet the regime was shrewd enough to understand that it had to come up with something to appease the Americans. So it was that Tripoli finally agreed to the wording of a letter in which it admitted responsibility for the actions of its officials, but not for the bombing itself. This letter was not what the US or Britain would have liked. However, with their 2003 invasion of Iraq weighing down heavily on them, they were keener than ever to come to a resolution with Libya, in order to create a success story in the Middle East.

Libya's fulfilment of these criteria paved the way for the lifting of UN sanctions the following month. Yet that did not stop the Qaddafi regime from continuing to protest its innocence. Tripoli viewed the whole compensation issue as an unpalatable and hugely unjust obstacle that had to be overcome in order for the country to move on. Libyan officials were not shy to declare that they had purchased the lifting of the sanctions; the general secretary of the General People's Committee, Shukri Ghanem, prompted outrage when, in February 2004, he told the BBC: 'We thought it was easier for us to buy peace.'[13]

While Qaddafi believed that he had made major and humiliating concessions over the Lockerbie affair, it was not enough to get Libya out of its crisis: the Americans wanted more. There had long been anxiety in US policy-making circles, and beyond, about Libya's capability to acquire and produce non-conventional weapons, including nuclear ones. Despite his repeated insistence that Libya's nuclear programme was purely peaceful, on several occasions from the 1970s onwards the Leader had mentioned the desirability of acquiring an 'Arab' bomb. While much of this talk was bravado, from the early 1980s Libya began to take practical steps to try to acquire the fissile material required for nuclear weapons.[14] Although it was repeatedly thwarted in its bid to legitimately acquire sensitive technology and expertise from overseas, Tripoli's efforts set the alarm bells ringing in Western capitals. The late 1990s opened up new opportunities in this respect: Libya made contact with the illicit A.Q. Khan network, headed by Pakistani nuclear scientist, Abdel Qader Khan, and was able to purchase a significant number of centrifuges, as well as nuclear weapon designs. The network also provided overseas training opportunities for Libyan personnel. Although Libya had not got to the point where it could figure out how to put a nuclear weapon together, it certainly had the equipment and the desire to do so.

As such, it became increasingly important for the Americans that the quixotic colonel should be reined in; they began to link normalization not only to compliance over Lockerbie, but also to cooperation over weapons of mass destruction (WMD). The Clinton administration, which had opened a secret dialogue with Tripoli in 1999, made it clear to Libya then that the US would only normalize relations fully and lift unilateral sanctions if the Qaddafi regime agreed to put a halt to its efforts to acquire WMD. While the Bush administration (which came to power in January 2001) took an equally tough line on the WMD issue as its predecessor, the new president was reluctant to start his own secret talks with Libya, primarily because he feared that the Lockerbie victims' families would react badly if they discovered that Washington was engaging with the Qaddafi regime.[15]

However, the 9/11 attacks on the US in 2001 were to bring about a dramatic shift in the way in which Washington dealt with Qaddafi, and also with regimes across the Middle East and North Africa. The US – and the West more widely – were suddenly in desperate need of all the friends they could muster in the Arab world, as they sought to get as much information as they could about potential terrorist suspects. Libya was no exception in this respect. The 9/11 attacks gave a new urgency to resolving relations with the Qaddafi regime.

Qaddafi was quick to seize on this opportunity to improve his relations with the West. The Libyan leader, who took great pleasure in reminding the world that it was he who had warned them against Osama Bin Ladin as early as 1995, was happy that the West had finally woken up to the problem of Islamist terrorism. Qaddafi had long condemned Western countries for giving political asylum to Libyan Islamists, taking particular umbrage at the British. In a treatise on terrorism posted on his personal website shortly after the 9/11 attacks, Qaddafi commented: 'If we believe that youths that trained in Peshawar, who entered Afghanistan, accompanied Bin

Laden, and who spread across the four corners of the earth are members of the so called Qa'ida organization, then Britain has the lion's share.'[16] The attacks of 9/11 were therefore a kind of vindication for Qaddafi and other leaders in the region: they had been right all along to castigate their own Islamist opposition movements as terrorists.

With typical theatrical aplomb, the Colonel made a very public show of condemning the 9/11 attacks and offering the US his support, organizing a high-profile 'blood drive' to help the victims. Even more surprisingly for a man who had thrived on anti-Americanism, he described Washington's invasion of Afghanistan in November 2001 as a justified act of self-defence.[17] Yet Qaddafi was determined to capitalize on this chance to further his mission to restore relations with the US and to pull Libya out of crisis. To prove his seriousness, the Leader willingly shared counter-terrorism intelligence with the US and the UK. Just one month after the 9/11 attacks, his security chief, Musa Kusa, who had been expelled from the UK in disgrace in 1980, hurried to London, armed with files containing the details of Libyan Islamists dotted across the globe.

But if Libya hoped that, by sharing intelligence over terrorist suspects, the US would take a softer line over issues such as WMD, it was sorely mistaken. While this new cooperation helped to build trust between the parties and to put Libya in a slightly better bargaining position, there was no way the US or the British were going to let Tripoli off the hook. President Bush did not mince his words; in 2001, after Qaddafi had instructed Shalgam to enlist the help of Algerian President Abdulaziz Bouteflika in his efforts to normalize relations with Washington, Bouteflika reported back that Bush's message to the Libyans was either that they must give up on WMD or he would destroy the weapons and everything else besides.[18] When a concerned Shalgam relayed this message to Qaddafi, the Leader accused his foreign minister of being a coward.

Yet for all Qaddafi's swagger, the message had been received loud and clear. In response, Libya signed the Comprehensive Test Ban Treaty (CTBT) in November 2001, and the following month Qaddafi informed diplomats in The Hague that Libya was willing to sign the Chemical Weapons Convention (CWC).[19] Despite these efforts, the US continued to take a hawkish stance. In March 2002, the Pentagon's Nuclear Posture Review listed Libya – along with Iran, Iraq, North Korea and Syria – as a potential adversary, due to its history of hostility toward the West, links to terrorism and non-conventional weapons programmes.[20] Yet this did not deter Qaddafi, who displayed a dogged determination to restore his tattered relations with Washington in the bid to give himself the new lease of life he and his regime so desperately needed.

In August 2002, the UK Foreign Office minister responsible for relations with North Africa, Mike O'Brien, paid a visit to Libya, where he discussed the subject of WMD with Qaddafi and was given 'positive assurances of co-operation over the weapons issue'.[21] Three months later, Libya signed the International Code of Conduct against Ballistic Missile Proliferation. However, it was in 2003 that progress really accelerated. Much of the push came from the Libyan side; in March 2003, the Libyans contacted the British intelligence services to initiate talks aimed specifically at dismantling its WMD programmes. It was also at this juncture that Qaddafi's son, Saif Al-Islam, entered the fray. The young Qaddafi, who contacted MI6 and left a message saying 'I am Saif Al-Islam, the son of Muammar Qaddafi and I want to talk with you about WMD',[22] had now become an important lynchpin in the regime. His involvement in the issue demonstrated Libya's seriousness in resolving the matter. What followed was a nine-month secret dialogue between British, American and Libyan representatives that resulted in the final agreement of December 2003, by which Tripoli pledged to dismantle its WMD programmes and to open the country to 'immediate and comprehensive verification inspections'.[23]

It is notable that progress on the WMD front occurred at the same time as the US and British invasion of Iraq. This has led certain political figures and analysts to observe that it was America and Britain's tough stance against Saddam Hussein that frightened Qaddafi into giving up his WMD programmes. Former US Secretary of State Colin Powell made a direct link between the invasion of Iraq and the Libyan decision to relinquish WMD, remarking in 2004:

> And then he [Qaddafi] takes a further look around and sees that the Bush administration comes in with a strong foreign policy and with a determination to respond to the threats. And so he watches that a little bit, and then he sees what happens in Afghanistan and Iraq. And he says to himself, you know, it's time to get out of this.[24]

This connection to Iraq was furiously denied by the Qaddafi regime. Shalgam claimed that any suggestion that Libya had been scared into making concessions by the Iraq invasion had been put about by malevolent journalists.[25] The regime also insisted that it had been working to build relations with the US for at least a decade. Few could argue with the fact that Libya had demonstrated a willingness to engage on the WMD issue prior to 2003, and that its decision to abandon its non-conventional weapons programmes was the culmination of longstanding efforts to normalize relations with Washington, dating back to 1992.

However, one cannot discount the impact of the Iraq war altogether. For a man who displayed such obvious paranoia about the US, the invasion of Iraq must have served as serious food for thought. Just before Libya made its March 2003 overture to the US and the UK on the WMD issue, Qaddafi warned Shalgam: 'They [the US and the UK] will laugh at us and document that we have WMD. They implicated Saddam Hussein and they want to implicate us too.'[26] Moreover, there was an unmistakable mood of anxious anticipation in Tripoli at the time of the Iraq invasion, as Libyans quietly wondered whether their leader might end up sharing the same fate as Saddam Hussein. Graffiti appeared in Tripoli warning 'Today, Saddam. Tomorrow, Qaddafi', and a boisterous crowd at a football match taunted Qaddafi's football-mad son, Saadi, chanting 'Saadi, don't think you are a big guy ... Your destiny will be like Uday's' – a reference to Saddam Hussein's son, who was killed following the US and British invasion.[27] While Libyans had no desire to see American or British boots on their soil, these sentiments reflected the population's utter desperation for change, as well as their deterministic sense that Qaddafi's hold on the country was so completely overwhelming that they would never find a way to oust him themselves.

In such a climate, it is perhaps unsurprising that Qaddafi should continue to fear that the whole WMD agreement was yet another political trap. Such was the Colonel's paranoia that even once the agreement had been made, working out how to announce it to the rest of the world proved torturous. On 18 December 2003, after the Americans and British proposed that he should publicly renounce the country's WMD programmes, after which Blair and Bush would offer their thanks and praise for his decision, the Leader declared: 'I refuse that totally. They will laugh at us. I will speak and they won't speak after me. This is a trick and a conspiracy.'[28] The following day, the usual suspects – Shalgam, Musa Kusa, Mohamed Zwai and Abdel Ati Al-Obeidi – gathered in Shalgam's office to try to figure out how to announce the news in a way that would be acceptable to both sides. It was a long day: discussions dragged on from 9.00 a.m. until 8.30 p.m. and involved more than fifty phone calls to MI6 and the CIA, and countless others to Qaddafi and Saif Al-Islam. Things were so tense that Musa Kusa almost passed out.

With pressure mounting, the Libyan team eventually persuaded the US and the British, who were more desperate than ever for a good-news story from the Arab world, that Shalgam, rather than

Qaddafi, would make the crucial statement. For all his desire to get the matter sorted, Qaddafi could not bear to humiliate himself by having to announce publicly what he knew would be seen across the Arab world as a demeaning climb-down. In the end, Shalgam made a statement, following which a statement in Qaddafi's name, supporting what his minister had said, was broadcast by the Libyan news agency, JANA; after that, Blair and Bush duly came out and offered their messages of thanks and support.

For all that the announcement was toe-curling for Qaddafi, it marked a momentous occasion for Libya. This was the beginning of the country's real rehabilitation into the international community. In March 2004, British prime minister Tony Blair visited Libya, memorably shaking hands with the Brother Leader in his tent. The meeting was later dubbed the 'deal in the desert', as it was announced at the same time as the Anglo-Dutch oil firm Royal Dutch Shell signed a major gas exploration deal with Tripoli. In June 2004, the US and Libya re-established diplomatic relations, and an American diplomatic team set itself up in Tripoli's towering Corinthia Hotel. Three months later, the US lifted its unilateral sanctions, and finally removed Libya from its State Sponsors of Terrorism list in June 2006. By the time of the uprising, in 2011, the two sides had developed their relations to such an extent that they had signed a number of bilateral agreements on a range of issues, including trade and investment, economic development, defence and counter-terrorism. In an indication of just how far relations had moved on, the two countries signed a Defence Contacts and Cooperation Memorandum of Understanding in January 2009. A few months later, Qaddafi's son Moatassim made a visit to Washington in his guise as National Security Commissioner, and there he met US Secretary of State Hillary Clinton. Even more surprising, in September 2009, Qaddafi visited the US for the first time to participate in the UN General Assembly in New York. As a young revolutionary, hell-bent on standing up to the West, this simple Bedouin of the desert can hardly have imagined that one day he would find himself in the heart of the 'viper's nest'. While the visit inevitably caused controversy – not only over where he should pitch his trademark tent, but also over the fact that he used the UN platform to deliver a rambling speech that was full to bursting with his trademark rhetoric – the fact that he was there at all was proof that, for all the lingering suspicions, Tripoli and Washington were cautiously entering an era of new relations.

Looking inwards

Libya's rehabilitation and its bleary-eyed emergence from the years of isolation prompted speculation in Western capitals and beyond that the eccentric Qaddafi would seize this opportunity to turn the country into something more akin to a conventional state. Normalization created expectations inside Libya, too, that the Colonel would finally get down to the serious business of reform. After UN sanctions were suspended in April 1999, there were high hopes that the Leader would use his annual speech at the 1 September anniversary of the revolution celebrations to announce a raft of reforms that would herald a new era. There was even talk that the Colonel would move to transform his unique Jamahiriyah into some kind of 'presidential republic'. The stage was set for a big announcement; the Libyan capital was decked out with flags, lights and victory arches, and Green Square sported enormous white electric candles to mark what was to be the revolution's thirtieth birthday.

Yet, as anticipation filled the air and regime loyalists filled the public squares, Libyans were to be bitterly disappointed. There was no talk of reform. Rather, Libyans were treated to yet another outpouring of revolutionary rhetoric. The main event of the anniversary was the unveiling of Qaddafi's latest invention – the Jamahiriyah Rocket, a rocket-shaped car designed to minimize road accidents. The sleek-looking vehicle was launched at a summit of the Organization of African Union that had been specially convened for the thirtieth-anniversary celebrations. Dukhali Al-Meghareff, chairman of Libya's domestic investment company, which produced the prototype of the car, declared: 'The Leader spent so many hours of his valuable time thinking of an effective solution. It is the safest car produced anywhere ... the invention of the safest car in the world is proof that the Libyan revolution is built on the happiness of man.'[29] The Colonel seemed to be playing a cruel trick on the Libyans, who had suffered so heavily over the past decade and more from the repercussions of his revolutionary misadventures. Such insulting triviality at this crucial juncture in the country's history was a stark reminder to Libyans of just how far their Leader was removed from everyday reality, and of how much he was wrapped up in his own bizarre world.

Hopes for change were dashed further in late September 1999, when Qaddafi stated categorically to a meeting of People's Committee representatives that there would be no political change in Libya. The Colonel was still talking about the need for 'permanent revolution', as if the Cold War had never ended. As if to make the point, in March 2000 he dissolved the entire General People's Committee (cabinet) overnight, transferring some ministerial functions to local people's committees and abolishing others altogether.[30] The following year, he tried to initiate a revolutionary revival in the universities, announcing that he needed a new inner team of young revolutionaries who would reinvigorate the ideas in his *Green Book*.[31] This was 'reform' Qaddafi style, sending Libya into a spin with chaos-inducing arbitrary decisions sold as 'furthering the revolution'. It was becoming clear that, as far as the Leader was concerned, Libya's rehabilitation was not going to be accompanied by an overhaul of his Jamahiriyah system, and that the country would continue to be hostage to his eccentric political vision.

However, Qaddafi knew he had to put on some sort of show. If Libya was going to achieve full rehabilitation in the international arena, it had to demonstrate to the rest of the world that it was serious about opening up. It had to do something to bring its grinding economy into the twenty-first century. With international sanctions suspended, Qaddafi could no longer hide behind the international embargo as an excuse for the country's crumbling infrastructure and poor living standards. Something had to change. While he continued to lambast international investors, dismissing them as 'a handful of speculators and traders',[32] the Colonel adopted a parallel discourse aimed at convincing the rest of the world that Libya was open for business. In September 1999, he told a group of foreign businessmen attending a symposium on Prospects for International Investment and Trade in Libya: 'If you want to invest in Libya, you are welcome.'[33] He reiterated these sentiments at another investment conference in 2000, when he noted: 'Libya wants to encourage foreign capital investment and partnership ... We will create the right atmosphere for the investor.'[34] Qaddafi also repeatedly spoke of the need to diversify Libya's economy away from its reliance on the energy sector. While there was an ambiguity about his discourse, the Leader wanted to send a message to the West that its money would be more than welcome in the Jamahiriyah.

Qaddafi's talk was accompanied by some action, and Libya took several important steps towards bringing its economy into line with international standards. In June 2003, in a bid to encourage foreign investment, the Central Bank unified the dual-rate exchange system, under which individuals requiring foreign currency used a 'commercial rate', while transactions undertaken by state companies were at an official rate.[35] That same year, Libya showed itself willing to be part of the global economic system, when it accepted its obligations under Article VIII of the International Monetary Fund's Articles of Agreement; in October 2003, it released the details of the IMF's first

Article IV consultations that called for wide-ranging structural reforms, improved macroeconomic management and the removal of trade barriers and price subsidies.[36] Accepting a role for the IMF was a major step for a regime that had so fiercely rejected any hint of foreign, yet alone Western, interference and that had stood by its socialist-style economic principles for so many years.

There was reform, too, in the energy sector. In August 2004, the National Oil Corporation (NOC) announced a licensing round, in which exploration and production agreements were to be awarded under a transparent bidding process. The licensing round proved popular with international energy firms, which were champing at the bit to get back into the country. January 2005 saw the return to the Libyan market of many US firms in particular: eleven out of the fifteen blocks on offer went to US companies, including Occidental, Marathon, ConocoPhillips and Hess. This was a triumph for the Libyans, not only because the terms of the contracts they awarded were on the tough side, but also because the upgrading of its energy sector could begin in earnest.

Perhaps the greatest indication that Libya intended to reform its economy came in June 2003, when a little-known oil economist, Shukri Ghanem, was parachuted into the post of general secretary of the (reconstituted) General People's Committee (effectively, prime minister). Ghanem was a friend and ally of Saif Al-Islam, who had taken on the mantle of being the user-friendly reformist face of the regime. This slick son of Qaddafi's had completed an MBA in Austria, was a keen advocate of free-market economics, and spoke a new language that seemed light years away from the anachronistic rhetoric of his father. 'The old times are finished', he proclaimed to the Davos summit in January 2005, 'and Libya is ready to move onto a new stage of modernization ... [which will] be conducted in a well organized manner that ensures new ownership and ownership by the people of Libya, not just a small class of oligarchs like Russia or Egypt.'[37]

This breath of fresh air managed to persuade his father that Ghanem, another proponent of liberal economics, was the hand that Libya needed on the tiller to steer the country in the direction of reform. Ghanem's appointment was not uncontroversial. It ruffled feathers among those of a more traditionalist bent, who viewed the westernized technocrat, who had headed the OPEC Secretariat in Vienna, as an outsider whose new-fangled ideas might threaten their own privilege and position. Indeed, Ghanem was something of an unknown quantity. His appointment was all the more unusual because the Jamahiriyah's formal political structures had always been dominated by the narrowest of elites. For the first thirty years of the revolution, Libya had had a total of only 112 secretaries (ministers) in the General People's Committee, some of whom stayed in their posts for only one or two years.[38] The same few faces were simply shuffled around the pack ad infinitum.

Anticipating the stir (and likely hostility) that the appointment of this newcomer would elicit, Qaddafi delivered a special address to the General People's Congress, telling it that Ghanem had been brought in to transform the economy and to sort out the country's economic difficulties. The economist, Qaddafi proclaimed, did not 'need' Libya thanks to his international reputation; the Colonel also told the Congress that Ghanem was 'worth his weight in gold' – although he also quipped that unfortunately Ghanem did not weigh very much!

The Colonel's overt backing of Ghanem certainly gave the impression that Libya was serious about change, and the technocrat set about trying to shake up the country's archaic and dysfunctional economy. However, he soon learned that the path to change was to be beset with obstacles. One of his first tasks was to try to pare down the unwieldy state sector. The public sector employed more than 800,000 Libyans, out of a population of almost 6 million, and was a serious drain on the public purse.[39] Ghanem sought to draft employees out of this sector. He also vowed to tackle the problem of 'ghost employees' – those who drew salaries, yet never turned up to work – as well as to weed out those salaries that were being paid to workers who did not exist or who had died.[40]

However, turning these ambitions into reality was fraught with difficulty. Despite having supported Ghanem so publicly, the Leader openly contradicted his efforts through his repeated insistence on expanding the country's administrative bodies at whim. In March 2005, for example, he suddenly announced that an additional 100,000–200,000 Libyans should be drafted into the security services. More importantly, however, attempts to reduce the public sector were hampered by the fact that there were no real opportunities opening up in the private sector.[41] There was strong resistance both inside and outside the regime to pushing people out of their jobs while there was no private sector alternative. On top of this, Ghanem also had to deal with the fact that the regime's insistence on acting as a distributive state over the past three decades had spawned a culture of reliance: Libyans had come to look on a public sector job as a rite of passage and as a source of income for which they generally did very little in return. As Ghanem summarized matters,

> The first and the most important requirement of reform is to work strongly in order to change the thinking, the mentality and the culture of the people which could be summarized in their general feeling that the state is their father and it is their guarantor that has to pay everything for them and provide them with housing, [medical] treatment, work and everything else.[42]

Ghanem's efforts to lift state subsidies on basic goods were hardly more successful. While he managed to remove subsidies on some goods, his doing so angered many Libyans, who felt they were being robbed of their much-needed entitlements. Ghanem soon earned the nickname 'Shukri Tomato Paste', for his efforts to lift the subsidies on tins of the same. He was also blamed for the sharp increases in utility bills that took effect in 2005; these were all the more galling to the many Libyans who lived in blocks of flats that were regularly without water and other basic utilities. Ghanem's efforts to lift the subsidies also brought him into conflict with what came to be referred to as the 'old guard' – regime loyalists, many of them members of the revolutionary committees, who saw it as their duty to uphold the ideology of the revolution.

Yet while some of the resistance of this old guard, which had lived on a diet of Qaddafi's revolutionary slogans, was related to ideology, much of it was associated with the desire to protect its privileges. The members of this group had been the great beneficiaries of the Jamahiriyah system that Qaddafi had set up, and they all had their various wheezes to siphon money off from the state. State subsidies were one area where they had been able to profit, and they were not about to let this newcomer take that away – even if he was backed by the Leader's son.

This group was equally determined not to let Ghanem make headway with his privatization programmes. The new general secretary came to power with the plan to privatize 360 companies, completely transforming the Libyan economy. However, the hardliners were determined to put the brakes on the plan. In 2005, for example, Qaddafi's cousin, the much-feared Ahmed Ibrahim, who was then deputy secretary of the General People's Congress, annulled Ghanem's resolution to privatize a marine transportation company that was under the control of Qaddafi's son Hannibal. A furious Ghanem engaged in a very public spat with Ibrahim during a session of the General People's Congress in January 2005 and complained of 'invisible forces' that were working against the policies of his government. The upshot was that Ghanem was left with the dregs: while he managed to oversee the transfer of forty state-owned companies to the private sector, many of those companies were small firms, and their

privatization had negligible impact. As one member of the privatization board, Abdullah Badri, complained, many of the companies that
Ghanem had planned to privatize were already dead in the water.[43]

That is not to say that there were not some privatization success
stories. Libya made some advances in privatizing its primitive
banking sector.[44] Libya's rehabilitation was also accompanied by a
mushrooming of private shops, hotels, internet cafés and restaurants,
as well as a growing real estate market, all of which changed the face
of Tripoli dramatically. However, these businesses were, for the
most part, small-scale affairs. Dr Fathi Al-Ba'aja, who became a
member of the National Transitional Council following the 2011
revolution, despairingly commented in 2007:

> The private sector doesn't mean these shops that are open now as
> a way for people to bring in income. These are just small places
> that consist of brooms, two canisters and some tins of tomato paste
> … of course this is not what is meant by the private sector. Earning
> ten, twenty or thirty dinars a day means nothing other than the
> fact that you managed to continue living.[45]

Those private concerns that did take off were generally owned by
individuals who had the right connections to the upper echelons of
the regime. One of the country's security brigades was behind a
string of internet cafés that opened in Tripoli, while some of the
smart new cafés and restaurants that sprang up in the centre of the
city belonged to the offspring of senior members of the regime,
including Qaddafi's own family.[46] By the late 2000s, a new 'entrepreneurial' class had emerged, to be found rubbing shoulders with the
Western businessmen who filled the swanky cafés of Tripoli's smart
new international hotels. Indeed, the lobbies of the five-star Corinthia
and Radisson Blu hotels became the wheeling and dealing hubs of
the 'new Libya', where those with the right connections could make

their fortunes, while the rest of the population looked on in bitter and distant envy. For all Saif Al-Islam's comments about not creating a group of oligarchs, the new economic opportunities that were accompanying Libya's return to the international community seemed to be concentrated in the hands of a very narrow elite, who were enjoying the bonanza.

All this became too much for Ghanem, and he was genuinely relieved when, in 2006, he was suddenly removed from office without explanation and sent to head up the National Oil Corporation. While Ghanem, an oil man at heart, may have heaved a hefty sigh of relief to be out of the political firing line, his removal from office brought disappointment, and was widely viewed as an indication that Qaddafi's flirtation with economic reform had come to an end. Indeed, Ghanem's failure was not only down to the hardline elements who stood so fiercely in his way; the main problem was that he never had the real backing of the Leader. While the Colonel might have been persuaded by Saif Al-Islam that bringing Ghanem in was a good idea, Qaddafi never channelled any real political will behind the general secretary's reform agenda. He was content to sit back and let Ghanem and the old guard battle it out, while he continued doing what he had always done. Moreover, the more the country's energy sector got back on its feet, the less the pressure was to reform. Ghanem had served his purpose. He had done his bit to convince the world that Libya was changing, and now that oil revenues were flowing back into the public purse, he could be shunted out of the way and the reformist agenda put on the back burner.

Jamahiriyah for ever

If economic reform was piecemeal and mostly ineffective, political reform was to prove even more disappointing. Reforming a system that was believed by its creator to be the pinnacle of human achievement was always going to be a Sisyphean task. But, as in the economic sphere, Qaddafi knew that, for his revolution to live on, he needed to create at least the impression of change.

As soon as the UN sanctions were suspended in 1999, reformist-minded officials began to speak of a new era, openly condemning the excesses of the past. The dark decades of the 1980s and 1990s were conveniently attributed to the zealousness of the revolutionary committees, as if to exonerate the regime of the brutalities that were committed in its name. Qaddafi also came forward with a number of pronouncements about how it was time to set aside the 'revolutionary phase' and adapt to the new realities facing the country. As if to substantiate these assertions, the regime made a number of gestures. In 2004, Qaddafi announced the abolition of the people's courts. Not that this meant the end of political trials, as these courts were quietly replaced by the equally ominous State Security Appeals Court, which held sessions inside a prison belonging to the Internal Security Agency; but the abolition of the courts provided Libya with some positive publicity. So, too, did its claims that it was going to amend the penal code; although a draft penal code was drawn up, it never got to see the light of day.

However, it was through the figure of Saif Al-Islam that the whole political reform debate came to be articulated most forcefully. The irony of the Leader's own flesh and blood spearheading the reform process was not lost on the Libyans. Yet given the intensely personalized nature of the regime, and the fact that the Colonel did not allow the slightest space for anything outside his Jamahiriyah, the push for reform could only come from within the regime itself. And where better than from within the family? By the end of the 1990s, as they came of age, Qaddafi's children had all begun to make their presence felt in public life, carving out their own spheres of influence. Of all of them, Saif Al-Islam was the most obvious choice to take on the mantle of change-maker.

Saif Al-Islam was Qaddafi's eldest son by his second wife, Safiyya, and this gave him a natural authority over his brothers. (Although the Colonel had a son, Mohammed, with his first wife, he was generally not inclined to politics.) More importantly, perhaps, Saif Al-Islam cut a different figure from his brothers. As with all Qaddafi's children, his childhood had been far from normal: he, his brothers and his one sister had been largely brought up at the hands of senior figures within the regime and had rarely seen their father. As Saif Al-Islam recalled,

> I never felt that I had a father who shared my problems at school. I did not feel that I had a father with whom I could go to the movies or the theatre, or anywhere else, or even play with us as fathers play with their sons. I hardly saw him as he had difficult circumstances, he leads a whole nation.[47]

However, while many of his brothers took the obvious route, following their father down the military path, the more sensitive Saif Al-Islam sought out a different course in life.

After studying architecture at Tripoli University and working for an architectural firm in Libya, he set his sights on continuing his studies in the West, enrolling in 1998 for an MBA at the IMADEC University in Vienna. The Colonel's son cut a rather immature figure at this point, drawing attention to himself by insisting that his beloved pet tigers, Barney and Fredo, accompany him to Austria, where they were placed in Vienna's zoo so that he could visit them regularly. As he explained, 'I love playing with my tigers, although they can sometimes be a little rough!'[48]

However, for all that he may have been immature, Saif Al-Islam was not entirely frivolous. Far from it: by the late 1990s, the young Qaddafi was steadily increasing his influence at home. In 1997, he set up a charity, the Gaddafi International Foundation for Charitable

Associations.[49] Although Saif Al-Islam repeatedly claimed that, as head of this charity, he was no more than the representative of Libya's civil society, the organization became a vehicle for his political and economic ambitions. It was through the foundation, for example, that he brokered a series of high-profile deals (such as securing the release of the Abu Sayaf hostages in the Philippines in 2000) and resolved many of the country's most pressing files including the La Belle disco bombing compensation and the eventual release of Lockerbie bomber Abdelbasset Al-Megrahi on compassionate grounds in 2009. Indeed, Saif Al-Islam used the charity to bypass the formal mechanisms of the state and, despite having no official position, became the country's key negotiator, brokering deals that would enable Libya to restore its place in the international community.

Meanwhile, the sharply dressed son began to give interviews to the international media, projecting a very different image of Libya to the one the world had come to know. He began extolling the virtues of democracy and employing the latest buzzwords, like 'transparency' and 'rule of law'. In 2002, he told one foreign news outlet: 'I would like Libya to be strongly linked to the developed world and to be a safe oasis for foreign investment and democracy, respecting human rights and the environment.'[50] He even joked about the situation in Libya, telling a US congressional aide who asked him at a dinner whether Libya needed more democracy: 'More democracy would imply that we had some.'[51] Such language was unheard of in the Libyan context. Yet Libya was out to impress, and the softly spoken Saif Al-Islam, with his easy smile, was the regime's most potent weapon in its charm offensive on the West.

To some, this Jamahiriyah protégé cut a convincing figure; some Western policy-makers and commentators seized on Saif Al-Islam as if he were the hope of the future. For anyone who knew Libya, such talk of democracy was a million miles away from the reality on the ground. Qaddafi was not going to step aside and allow his Jamahiriyah to be swept away and replaced with something he had been railing against for over three decades. Yet while installing a modern democracy was off limits, Saif Al-Islam and his father knew that they had to do something to release some of the pressure that had been building in the country and that was threatening to blow.

They concluded that the best means of doing this was through the issue of human rights. Taking on the role of 'champion of the people', the young Qaddafi set about tackling some of the country's most sensitive files. In 2003, through his charity, he instigated an anti-torture campaign. Posters appeared overnight on the streets of the capital, condemning torture and encouraging Libyans who had suffered to come forward and register their grievances.[52] Libyans had never seen anything like it. The Leader's son also began making overtures to Libyan exiles abroad, putting out feelers to dissidents and listening to their demands in a bid to convince them to make their peace with the regime and return home. As one regime opponent, Ashur Shamis, who met Saif Al-Islam for the first time in 2002, says, 'Nobody had ever come to us from the Gaddafi side talking in these terms.'[53]

More controversially, Saif Al-Islam began talking about bringing those who had committed human rights abuses to justice and shedding light on some of the darker events of the past. He was careful not to implicate his father or the upper echelons of the regime in any of the human rights abuses he was uncovering; the blame was still to be placed squarely on the shoulders of the revolutionary committees, which were getting increasingly fed up with having to take all the flak. However, discussing such issues in an open way was something truly new in the Libyan context. This did not mean that human rights abuses became a thing of the past – the grim fate that continued to meet individuals such as Fathi Al-Jahemi, who dared to speak out against the regime, was testimony to that.[54] However, Saif Al-Islam had at least enabled those with serious grievances to express their anger and to feel as though someone in the regime was listening.[55] What was really important about these moves, however, was that they worked to absorb some of the popular anger that the Colonel knew was threatening to undermine his regime, particularly in the east, where there was hardly a family that had been left untouched by the regime's brutality.

Yet Saif Al-Islam's most extraordinary achievement was his 'Reform and Repent' programme to rehabilitate the country's Islamist prisoners. Under this initiative, his charity entered first into a dialogue with prisoners from the outlawed Muslim Brotherhood. After protracted negotiations, a hundred or so Muslim Brotherhood prisoners were freed in March 2006, after they agreed not to enter into any political activity outside the framework of the Jamahiriyah.[56] Even more astonishing was what came next: in 2007, Saif Al-Islam embarked upon a similar dialogue with the country's militant Islamist prisoners. In return for their release, these hardened radicals would need to renounce violence and admit the error of their ways. In August 2009, after months of tough negotiations, the LIFG's leadership – including the group's spiritual leader, Said Saaidi, and its emir, Abdelhakim Belhaj,[57] (both of whom had been returned to Libya in 2004 under secret rendition programmes) – finally issued a set of revisions in which they renounced violence. While the revisions were undoubtedly heartfelt by many who signed up to them, the pressure on the prisoners was enormous. So desperate was Saif Al-Islam to score a success that he employed tactics of coercion to get them to sign up, bringing the families of some of the militants into the prison to pressurize them, and also offering to provide their children with educational opportunities and other perks.[58]

Yet once the revisions were agreed, Saif Al-Islam kept his word: accompanied by scenes of emotion, hundreds of prisoners, dressed in white, were freed from the Abu Slim prison, some of them having been incarcerated for two decades.⁵⁹ This was a remarkable achievement, especially given that many within the security services were dead set against releasing these militants back into society. Indeed, many of Saif Al-Islam's schemes were to come up against the old guard, which, fearing the loss of privilege and way of life, tried to scupper his plans. Yet this hostility on the part of the regime loyalists had its uses: it enabled the Leader's son to posit himself as defender of human rights and champion of the Libyan people – as a lone man struggling against the state. He became what one Libyan observer described as 'the oppressed oppressor'.⁶⁰ Even in a land so saturated with slogans, gestures and promises, the young Qaddafi came to be regarded in some quarters as a saviour of sorts, and whenever anyone had even the slightest problem, it was to him that they went to get it resolved.

But Saif Al-Islam knew that, if Libya was going to transform itself into something approaching a modern state, he had to go beyond the human rights realm. And so he turned his reformist attentions to the media. Libya's state-run newspapers, with their sycophantic revolutionary outpourings, had long been considered a joke, with the regime only bothering to print some 3,000 copies a day, most of which went unread. Even senior officials in the regime used to jest about how they never bothered to read them.⁶¹ Saif Al-Islam decided it was time to shake things up. He established the Al-Ghad media company, to be run by Suleiman Dogha, a former dissident whom Saif Al-Islam had persuaded to return to Libya; launched titles, such as *Corina* and *Oea*; and, in keeping with his savvy image, established some internet news outlets. While this new 'independent' press amounted to little more than a mini media empire, its importance was that it provided some space for Libyans to criticize the official mechanisms of the state. People were positively encouraged to let off steam about issues such as corruption or the failings of the government, and these publications became the focus of some of the liveliest debate during this period. They were like a breath of fresh air in what had been an utterly stale environment.

Buoyed up by his success, Saif Al-Islam even went so far as to start tinkering with the political system itself. By the early 2000s, the favoured son had managed to attract a coterie of reformist-minded officials and academics, who saw in him the country's best hope for change in an otherwise bleak landscape. In 2004, he tasked a group of these supporters with forming a committee to draw up a constitution that would not simply enshrine the *Green Book*, but that would shake up Libya's political structures.[62] This was the first real sniff that the regime might be considering a serious shift in the country's political establishment.

However, these hopes were soon dashed. It was not long before it became apparent that, for all his initial enthusiasm, Saif Al-Islam's commitment to the nuts and bolts of the project was fading fast. As one member of the committee recalled, 'He was always busy. He never responded to us, not once. Saif Al-Islam wasn't interested in details, problems or challenges.'[63] Moreover, the young Qaddafi seemed to have no clear vision as to what this constitution should contain. He relied heavily on outside expertise, and his head was easily turned. After any visit abroad, where he revelled in mixing with Western intellectuals, Saif Al-Islam went back to the committee with new ideas that he wanted incorporated into the draft.[64] He would first demand one thing, and then at the next opportunity would demand the very opposite. The committee became so disillusioned that in summer 2008 it handed over the draft it was working on and washed its hands of the discussions. Unsurprisingly the draft was never to see the light of day.

One of the reasons for the failure of this project was Saif Al-Islam's inability to get his act together. Indeed, he was beginning to look like his father, in so far as he had a habit of championing causes that he did not follow through. Moreover, Libyans became suspicious that the whole project had been about Saif Al-Islam looking for a way to legitimize himself, rather than about any genuine commitment to political change.

However, the failure over the new constitutional draft was also related to a far bigger problem – that of Qaddafi senior. The Colonel was not amused by his son's efforts to make changes to his already perfect Jamahiriyah. Such was his hostility to the project that he exploded with rage when Saif Al-Islam leaked a copy of the draft to the media in 2008. Although the document was not particularly radical – its main thrust was the establishment of a council of representatives from the social people's leaderships that would sit on top of the existing political system – it was enough to make the Colonel see red. After a serious fight, Saif Al-Islam announced that he was withdrawing from public life and stormed off abroad.

Such arguments between father and son were not unusual. As Saif Al-Islam explained, even from his childhood, 'If I were to upset him [Qaddafi], he would not speak to me or see me for a full month. That is why his psychological punishment was more severe than physical punishment.'[65] Yet the constitution episode reflected the fact that, regardless of his ambitions, Saif Al-Islam's reformist project was always going to be constrained by his father. As he acknowledged in August 2007, there were four lines in Libya that could not be crossed: Islam and the application of sharia law; the security and stability of Libya; national unity; and, most importantly, Muammar Qaddafi. While Qaddafi senior was willing for Saif Al-Islam to be the reformist face of the regime, he was not about to give him free rein to do as he pleased. So long as there was Qaddafi, there would be a Jamahiriyah.

Yet the big unknown that was increasingly coming to preoccupy those inside and outside Libya was for how long there would be a Qaddafi. Although he was not yet old – and though he may have believed himself to be immortal – even the Brother Leader could not go on forever. The Colonel never spelled out what he wanted to happen after he died or was forced into retirement. However, it was clear to all and sundry that the stage was being set for some kind of hereditary hand-down of power. It was also clear that Saif Al-Islam was the most likely candidate to take over. Though that is not to say that some of his brothers were not vying for the position of heir apparent; Moatassim, in particular, who had become the darling of the old guard on account of his hardline stance, was keen to muscle in on the scene. However, it was generally presumed that Saif Al-Islam was being groomed to take up the reins when his father eventually gave up the ghost. The favoured son already had large sections of the country in his hands, both in the political and economic sphere. It was he, for example, who had brought Baghdadi Mahmoudi to the post of general secretary in 2006, and according to his brother Saadi, by the time of the uprisings of 2011, he was all but 'running the country'.[66]

Saif Al-Islam always rejected the suggestion that he was being groomed to take over, repeatedly condemning other states, such as Syria, for going down the dynastic route. Yet one could not help noticing that Saif Al-Islam seemed to be preparing himself for power. He was making a concerted effort to consolidate his position within the country, courting key tribal leaders and members of the security services, while simultaneously trying to sideline the revolutionary committees and regime ideologues. As one Libyan who worked with him closely explained, 'Saif was obsessed by the desire to shake up the traditional balance of power and to put an end to the mobilization of the revolutionary committees.'[67] He even made special efforts to court the east, reaching out a hand to try to heal the decades of bad blood, including by announcing the establishment of a large eco-tourism project in the Green Mountains – another project that failed to get off the ground.

What was noticeable, too, was that Saif Al-Islam increasingly came to replicate his father. As he grew in confidence, the Leader's son moved to create a personality cult of his own. He took to holding his own annual celebration on 20 August, and, just as his father insisted that he had no formal position and was merely the leader of the revolution, so Saif Al-Islam kept repeating that he was simply leader of Libya's civil society. For all his talk of democracy, like his father he held no official position that could render him accountable, yet he was moving everything behind the scenes. Furthermore, just as the Jamahiriyah revolved around one man, so the whole reformist initiative revolved around Saif Al-Islam; without him it had no momentum of its own.

This personality cult became all the more pronounced when Saif Al-Islam triumphantly brought home the convicted Lockerbie bomber, Abdelbasset Al-Megrahi, from the UK on 20 August 2009. This gave the impression that the Leader's son was able to move mountains. Saif Al-Islam seems to have interpreted the whole event as some kind of divine intervention, declaring: 'I told them that I would get Abdelbasset out on 20 August and I told them that if he left the prison on 20 August this would be a sign from Allah that I am walking on the right and correct path ... Even this date is a message from Allah.'[68]

Saif Al-Islam also seemed to share his father's desire to be seen as something more than simply a politician. The young Qaddafi, who listed painting as one of his hobbies, took his 'works of art' on a prolonged global touring exhibition. Despite the comments of one art critic, who acerbically observed that Saif Al-Islam's 'sentimentality is only exceeded by his technical incapacity',[69] these exhibitions were extravagant affairs, at which no expense was spared. The opening of the London exhibition in 2002, held in an enormous tent in the grounds of the Albert Hall, was a spectacle to behold: the pink cham-pagne flowed all evening, guests were entertained with traditional

Libyan music and dancing, and a white-suited Saif Al-Islam, sporting gleaming leopard-skin shoes, gave a guided tour of his works.

However, one way in which father and son differed was that Qaddafi senior retained a kind of purity until the very end. Qaddafi was always the Bedouin of the desert, true to his roots, who shunned ostentatious wealth and the trappings of the westernized life. Perpetual revolution was his enduring passion. Even as he grew older, his appetite for extending his revolution showed no signs of diminishing, as he expended more and more effort on promoting himself and his ideas. The Colonel could be found presiding over enormous 'conversion to Islam' ceremonies in Africa, where he also took to courting traditional leaders – unlike the governments of the continent, these people gave him the respect and adoration he had always craved. In 2008, two hundred traditional leaders gathered to crown the Colonel 'King of Kings'.

In contrast, Saif Al-Islam, like the rest of his siblings, increasingly indulged in amassing wealth. The Leader's children all used Libya's new relative openness to the West to build enormous financial empires of their own. Despite his populist calls to clamp down on the country's 'fat cats', Saif Al-Islam was behind a mind-boggling array of business ventures – from the health sector to the aviation industry to the energy sector. In the early days, much of the business was channelled through his One Nine Investment company. He was also the driver of many of the ambitious development projects that the regime embarked upon in its last years – several of them totally unsuited to Libya's needs. Mohamed Zeidan, who was transport minister under Qaddafi, described how Saif Al-Islam and his ally, General Secretary Baghdadi Mahmoudi, were behind plans to build a new airport in Tripoli that would have a capacity of 20 million passengers a year and would cost some $2 billion. When Zeidan suggested that this was excessive and that a capacity of 8 million passengers would be sufficient, the project was promptly taken away from him and handed to a specially created 'Body for Implementing Transport Projects'. The former minister reflected that his suggestions had been rejected because 'the important thing was to sign the contract ... the bigger the contract, the bigger the commission'.[70]

Such stories were typical. It seemed to matter little whether these big contracts were for anything that the Libyan people – who were still struggling to make ends meet – might actually want or need. The population at large had no use for the flashy showcase government buildings or new port that were being planned, or for the towering new hotels that were springing up at breakneck speed (and that would bring yet more Westerners to Libya and further line the pockets of the rich). What Libyans wanted was services, affordable housing and jobs. As one man commented after Saif Al-Islam initiated a highly publicized and ill thought-through scheme to provide a million laptops to schoolchildren, 'I don't think a Libyan needs a mobile or a laptop whilst his feet are wading through sewage.'[71]

But Saif Al-Islam and his siblings were intent on carving up the whole country between themselves, with little thought for the consequences. Qaddafi's eldest son from his first marriage, Mohamed, had the entire communications sector in his pocket, controlling Libya's two mobile telephone companies and a host of other businesses. As Shalgam noted, 'Mohamed was specialized in making lots of money. He was one of the richest men in Libya.'[72] Hannibal (famous for getting Libya embroiled in a major diplomatic spat with Switzerland after he and his Lebanese model wife were accused of abusing two members of their domestic staff) controlled the maritime transport sector. Saadi, who was head of Special Forces, controlled the sports sector, but also had a raft of business interests, especially in the construction and car hire sectors. Moatassim and Khamis – both army men – also made small fortunes in their own way. Qaddafi's only daughter, Aisha, was also engaged in a series of business ventures, some of them through her Watasimu charity. Wherever there was a business in Libya, nine times out of ten it was a safe bet that one of the Qaddafi children had a hand in it somewhere.

In acquiring these businesses, they often ran roughshod over senior officials. Moatassim was appointed Libya's national security commissioner in the mid-2000s. This entitled him to be present at meetings of the General People's Committee, where he would regularly insult the ministers present. He also used to demand that NOC head Shukri Ghanem should give him oil fields,[73] and on one occasion he even sought to take over the NOC building for himself. Ghanem bravely rejected his demand, declaring that he would cut off his own hand before giving up the building. Moatassim is also believed to have assaulted Musa Kusa after the two clashed over some aspect of the security portfolio.

Saif Al-Islam likewise had a habit of insulting officials when it suited him. Shalgam complained how, on one occasion, the favoured son openly attacked one of Libya's ambassadors, dismissing him as a 'backwards child'.[74] Yet there was little these officials could do beyond complaining to the father – the Colonel himself.

As if dividing up the country in this way was not enough of an insult, the children took to frittering away Libya's money on vulgar displays of wealth and on lifestyles that were completely alien to the socially conservative Libyan population. Libyans were horrified at the stories and photos that appeared on the internet of wild, alcohol-fuelled parties in the Caribbean or other such destinations, where the Qaddafi boys could be seen cavorting with women on luxury yachts, or paying top Western stars (such as Beyonce, or the rapper 50 Cent) vast sums of money to perform for them. Even Aisha's engagement party was far removed from the simple Bedouin life-style that her father had always lauded: dressed in an expensive white suit, she and her fiancé sipped champagne and canoodled to

Western-style pop music. The children's spouses were at it, too: Hannibal's wife even chartered a private jet for her dog, so that it could be brought back to Libya from Beirut.[75]

While Qaddafi did not like his children's behaviour (and often backed his officials when they complained to him about it), he seemed unable to control them. This revolutionary, who had come to power so full of self-righteous purity and anti-Westernism, had ended up creating what many Libyans viewed as little more than monsters, whose primary passion was making money and indulging themselves in the westernized pleasures he so abhorred.

All this was too much for ordinary Libyans, who became increasingly repelled by the antics of Qaddafi's offspring. As far as they could see, all that the country's rehabilitation had done was to concentrate even more wealth and power in the hands of the Qaddafi family. For all the regime's talk of change, it was clear that the entire reformist project had amounted to little more than a series of showy stunts and cosmetic changes, aimed at proving to the world that Libya was open for business. Reform, it turned out, meant fiddling around the edges while the Jamahiriyah ground on, edging ever closer to disaster. Ordinary Libyans remained as burdened as ever by the heavy yoke of the chaos-inducing Jamahiriyah. People were feeling angrier and more cheated than ever before. As Qaddafi was soon to discover, it would only take a spark for this anger to ignite into something that even he could not control.

CHAPTER 8

A New Dawn

At 3.30p.m. on 15 February 2011, seven cars from the general security directorate drew up outside the modest home of Fathi Terbil, a
young and unassuming lawyer from Benghazi. Some twenty security
personnel entered the building and set about ransacking the place,
destroying Terbil's possessions and assaulting his mother. They then
arrested the young lawyer and carted him off to the general security
directorate in Benghazi. Little did Terbil know it, but his arrest was
to be the spark that ignited Libya's revolution.

The softly spoken Terbil was a well-known face in Libya's second
city. He had been representing the families of the victims of the Abu
Slim prison massacre of 1996, an atrocity in which he had lost his
brother, cousin and brother-in-law. Emboldened by Saif Al-Islam's
reformist project, the victims' families had taken to demanding that
the regime come clean and provide them with details of how
their loved ones had died. They had also started protesting in
Benghazi on a weekly basis, and the case had become something of a
cause célèbre in the city. For the regime, the families were proving a
major source of irritation and a headache it could well do without.
By choosing to represent these families, therefore, Terbil was

pushing the boundaries of what was acceptable in the new era of 'reform' and 'openness'.

Yet it was not Terbil's involvement with the Abu Slim families that prompted his arrest. His crime had been that he, along with a group of young Libyans, had been in the process of organizing a 'Day of Rage', planned for 17 February. This Day of Rage was to comprise a mass demonstration, in which Libyans were to take to the streets to call for reforms, including the introduction of a constitution. The date of this planned day of protest was not insignificant: it was on 17 February 2006 that fourteen Libyans had been killed when popular protests erupted in Benghazi. These protests had started out as a demonstration against the Italian MP Roberto Calderoli, who had incited outrage by announcing that he intended to print T-shirts bearing reproductions of the cartoons of the Prophet Mohamed that had appeared in the Danish *Jyllands-Posten* newspaper and that had sparked such fury across the Muslim world. Indignant Libyans had descended on the Italian consulate in Benghazi and begun hurling stones and bottles at the building in disgust. However, it was not long before the protesters turned their wrath against the regime. Angry youths began attacking state buildings, including the tent-like *math-abas* of the hated revolutionary committees. In their panic, the security services opened fire on the crowd, killing eleven and injuring scores more. Other protesters were arrested and summarily carted off to Tripoli.

Although the security services were able to put down the unrest easily enough, it still represented the largest and most serious outbreak of public protest that Libya had witnessed in decades, and it shook Qaddafi and his regime to the core. This was not what rehabilitation was supposed to be about. The situation was made all the worse for the regime, as images of the violence were broadcast around the world in moments, bringing Libya's claims to have reformed its ways into serious doubt. The 17 February, therefore, was a deeply significant date for Libyans, particularly those in the east, and a highly sensitive one for the regime.

Although the planned Day of Rage was not intended as a call for the overthrow of Qaddafi, recent events in the region were on everyone's mind. In January 2011, the Tunisians stunned the world when, seemingly out of nowhere, they succeeded in ousting ageing President Ben Ali from power in a popular revolution. A few weeks later, the Egyptians followed suit, with popular protests forcing an utterly bewildered President Hosni Mubarak to step down from office. These revolutions brought about an entirely new mood in the region; it was dawning on people that these all-powerful tyrants who had held their countries to ransom for so many decades were not invincible after all. Bit by bit, 'people power' was breaking the fear that had reigned – in many cases since independence. The Arabs were on the march.

Libyans proved no exception. Despite the fact that they were living under what was arguably one of the most repressive regimes in the Arab world, the Libyans were not going to be left out of this blossoming Arab Spring. Indeed, Libyans had tried to become a part of it as soon as Ben Ali was unceremoniously forced into exile. In what now looks to have been a kind of dress rehearsal for the real thing, immediately after Tunisia's 'Jasmine Revolution', Libyans began posting messages on the internet and on social networking sites calling on people to take to the streets. Some heeded these calls: protesters in certain eastern cities attacked government buildings and private companies, and there was even some rioting. One young Libyan, Ahmed Lebderi, went so far as to emulate the Tunisian stall-holder Mohamed Buazizi, who had unleashed the Tunisian uprising by setting himself alight.

What was more worrying for the regime, however, was that in unprecedented scenes Libyans went in their thousands to occupy empty and half-finished blocks of flats in government housing projects across the country.¹ The protesters vented their anger and frustration not only at the general housing shortages, but also at the regime's failure to allocate the units in these projects in a fair or timely manner. As with other schemes that were supposed to help the poor, those with the right connections had been given the flats in the new blocks, leaving ordinary Libyans to carry on camping out with their extended families. The new flats became yet another source of bitterness: Tripolitanians regularly grumbled that the only ones who could even dream of living in them were the 'desert people' from Sirte, a reference to Qaddafi's family and tribe.

While the regime succeeded in containing these demonstrations, it was utterly stunned by this mass demonstration of public disobedience. It should not have been: protests were becoming an increasingly common occurrence in the rehabilitated Jamahiriyah. These spontaneous expressions of public discontent were mainly localized affairs, related to specific matters (such as the non-payment of salaries or the taking over of public land by those linked to the regime) and, as such, were easily containable. However, they were symptomatic of the burning anger and seething resentment that had been building in the country for decades, but that had worsened in recent years. All the more so in the east, which continued to be made to feel as though it was Tripoli's poor relation. Indeed, the years of systematic neglect meant that, by the time the Arab Spring arrived, Benghazi was on a knife-edge, ready to explode.

Qaddafi was certainly aware of the dangers posed by the tumultuous events in Tunisia and Egypt. He felt all too keenly that he was suddenly outflanked, exposed on both sides. He also knew that the grievances affecting the Libyans were not that dissimilar to those of their neighbours. The possibility of the 'domino effect' was something the now ageing Colonel could not ignore. He moved quickly to condemn the events in Tunisia, declaring: 'There is none better than Zine [El Abedine Ben Ali] to govern Tunisia.' He also dismissed the Tunisian protests as the criminal actions of a minority, asserting: 'Tunisia now lives in fear … families could be raided and slaughtered in their bedrooms and the citizens in the street killed as if it was the Bolshevik or the American revolution … And for what? In order for someone to become president instead of Ben Ali?'[2] His words put him completely at odds with the masses in the Arab world. Here was someone who had championed the people and anti-imperialism all his life, defending one of the most reactionary and pro-Western regimes of the region. Yet he had no choice.

In typical 'Qaddafiesque' style, the Colonel also pontificated that the turmoil in Tunisia would be justified if it resulted in its adoption of the Jamahiriyah system! However, the message was clear: Qaddafi was going to do his utmost to ensure that what had happened in Tunisia was not going to happen in Libya.

To this end he employed a two-pronged approach. On the one hand, he did his utmost to convince Libyans that he was taking their concerns and demands seriously. Following the Tunisian revolution, he embarked upon a series of showy public consultations, holding meetings with Libyans from all walks of life, in which he played the part of the magnanimous listener, keen to get to the bottom of what was upsetting the people. In Derna, for example, he met with a cross-section of residents, who complained about unemployment, housing, the lack of infrastructure, low salaries and administrative corruption. The Colonel responded with noble promises, insisting that the state was on the verge of solving these very problems. Predictably enough, these meetings were not all smiles and niceties: Qaddafi peppered his promises with stern warnings, threatening journalists and social networking activists not to take part in rioting, and making it clear that their tribes would bear full responsibility if they did anything to destabilize the country.[3]

As part of his charm offensive, Qaddafi also courted the country's tribal leaders, hosting them in lavish ceremonies in specially erected tents. He even went so far as to invite the families of the victims of the 17 February 2006 riots to Tripoli, where he honoured them by giving them medals. In a particular sop to the east, the Colonel sent his son Saadi to Benghazi to try to convince local inhabitants that the regime was serious about tackling development problems in the region. Choosing Saadi for this task was a curious move. Saadi had a particularly antagonistic relationship with the eastern city that dated back to the late 1990s. Residents had not forgotten how the Leader's son had arrogantly bulldozed their football stadium and relegated their much-loved football team, Al-Ahli – Benghazi. He had done so as punishment for their having sent a donkey into the street wearing a football shirt bearing his number, in protest at his repeated rigging of matches to ensure that his favoured team, Al-Ahli – Tripoli, won. Sending Saadi to Benghazi, therefore, was hardly going to calm tensions. Saadi's approach was even more bizarre. He told the local radio station: 'I have taken permission from my father, so he can give me Benghazi. No one will come near it, I am coming to live there. I am even bringing my clothes.'[4] Saadi's efforts clearly were not cutting it, and he soon found himself trapped and under siege in Benghazi's Ozo Hotel, from where he had to be rescued by security forces and spirited out of the city.[5]

On a more practical note, the regime also began talking about raising salaries, hoping that it could deter the Arab Spring's arrival in Libya by buying people off. There were hints, too, that at long last there was going to be some political reform. It was mooted that the hugely unpopular General People's Committee was about to be sacked.[6] However, such gestures were fairly inconsequential to a population saturated with endless promises of change. The Libyans were in no mood for more talk of reform.

These 'sweeteners' dovetailed with the regime's tried and tested method of raw intimidation. Expecting trouble to arise first in the east, the Colonel bolstered his security presence in the eastern regions, posting top security chiefs, such as Abdullah Sanussi, to Benghazi and moving members of the revolutionary committees to the 7 April military camp there. The regime also tried to stop the Day of Rage from taking place; it was in this context that Fathi Terbil was arrested. The dangers of the Day of Rage were serious enough for the young lawyer to be questioned by Abdullah Sanussi himself. Sanussi tried to intimidate Terbil into calling off the day of protest. Yet the brave Terbil remained defiant. He told the feared security chief that the Day of Rage was out of his hands, and that the regime's best bet would be to pull its security forces from the streets and leave people to demonstrate peacefully. Sanussi, who was in the company of several major figures in the regime, including Qaddafi's cousin Omar Ishkal and key revolutionary committee stalwart Tayib Saafi, retorted: 'We won't submit and we are capable of confronting people.'[7]

Yet the most memorable effort by the regime to pre-empt the Day of Rage was Qaddafi's bid to arrange mass public demonstrations of his own. Pro-regime rallies were organized in all the major cities, and sports clubs were all issued with instructions to hold special celebratory festivals to mark the anniversary of the Prophet's birthday, which fell on 15 February. Qaddafi went on a special glory tour of Tripoli. Who could forget the scenes of the grinning Leader waving to the crowds from an open-top limousine, as he was driven through the streets of the capital? Demonstrating his lack of under-standing of the seriousness of the situation, the Colonel even quipped that, because they were part of the 'state of the masses', the Libyan people had no need to revolt; they could not rise up against them-selves. It would not be long before his cruel joke would be turned against him to devastating effect.

Indeed, the regime's efforts to stop the Day of Rage were a case of too little too late. As news of Terbil's detention reverberated through Benghazi, the families he was representing began gathering at the gate of the general security directorate in Benghazi to demand his release. They were joined by lawyers and other professionals, who added their voices to the calls for Terbil to be freed. The Day of Rage was kicking off a day early. To make matters worse, these seeds of protest were soon catapulted into the international arena. A Benghazi-based writer, Dr Idris Mismari, took the brave decision to give a telephone interview to the Al-Jazeera satellite television channel, in order to tell the world what was going on in the country's second city. As he talked, Mismari found himself being chased by the security services. In dramatic scenes, a breathless Mismari called on the outside world to come and protect the Libyans, before his telephone line was abruptly cut.

Under the glare of the international media, the regime decided to release Terbil. However, he was called back to the security directorate the following day. But by then it was too late, and the citizens of Benghazi had got the bit between their teeth. They knew that this was their chance to break the yoke that had been crushing them for decades, and nothing was going to stop them. The 17 February saw demonstrations erupt at various spots across the city, while the lawyers and families of the victims of the Abu Slim massacre began a full-blown protest in front of the Benghazi courthouse, where they were soon joined by other demonstrators. Some protested outside the revolutionary committee *mathaba* and others outside the offices of the Green Book Studies Centre, while others set fire to police stations. The slogans calling for reforms and a constitution were replaced with far bolder demands: the people wanted an end to the regime. Protesters also began holding up the flag of pre-Qaddafi Libya – a flag that was to become one of the enduring symbols of Libya's new revolution. It was suddenly looking as though the remarkable scenes that had been played out in Tunisia just weeks before were about to be replicated in Libya.

The ruthless Qaddafi determined to do whatever it took to preserve his regime. Showing none of the restraint exercised by his

Tunisian counterpart, the Colonel lashed out hard. Security forces were instructed to put down the unrest by all means necessary, and they began firing on the unarmed protesters. On 17 February, thirteen people were killed and a further two hundred injured in Jamal Abdel Nasser Street alone, while eight were killed in Omar Bin Al-Aas Street. Similar scenes were replicated across the city. The regime's heavy-handed response did not, however, deter the dissent, and things became even more heated on 18 February: in a show of defiance, demonstrators gathered for Friday prayers in front of the Benghazi courthouse, after which they began protesting against the regime. The young and the old, Islamist and liberal, the comfortably off and the poor – all united by the desire for change and all sensing the first, tantalizing taste of freedom – thronged into the streets to call for an end to tyranny.

It was not long before things turned violent. Police and security centres were torched, as were revolutionary committee offices. The situation became especially tense after security forces opened fire on mourners attending the funerals of those already killed in the violence. The bloody-minded brutality of this act set off a spiral of violence, as the regime did its utmost to control a situation that was fast getting out of hand. Indeed, it was not only in Benghazi that people were protesting. Other towns in the east had shed their fear and were rising up in solidarity with those people in Benghazi. The regime employed a similarly heavy-handed response: on 17 February security forces killed thirty people in Al-Baida, six in Derna and ten in Ajdabia.

Yet the more the regime used brute force, the more defiant people became. As Libyan diplomat Ahmed Jibreel, who defected to the opposition, explained,

Qadhafi's guards started shooting people on the second day and they shot two people only. On that day we only had 300 protesters in Al-Baida. When they killed two people, we had more than 5,000 at their funeral, and when they killed 15 people the next day we had more than 50,000 the following day ... This means that the more Qadhafi kills people, the more people go into the streets.[8]

For the residents of the east, it was a terrifying time. As one student blogger who had barricaded herself into her home on the outskirts of Benghazi described it:

I've seen violent movies and video games that are nothing compared to this. I can hear gunshots, helicopters circling overhead, then I hear the voices screaming. I can hear the screeching of four-by-fours in the street. No one has that type of car except his [Qaddafi's] people ... There are even stories here that he [Qaddafi] has poisoned the water, so we dare not drink. If he could cut off the air that we breathe, he would.[9]

Although cutting off the oxygen was one trick that was beyond the Colonel's powers, the regime certainly did its best to isolate the city, cutting off telephone lines and internet connections, and interrupting mobile telephone coverage. However, by this point the citizens of the east were being carried on the crest of a wave. As the young blogger also described, 'It's like a pressure cooker. People are boiling up inside. I'm not even afraid any more. Once I wouldn't have spoken at all by phone. Now I don't care. Now enough is enough.'[10] Even the all-powerful Qaddafi was unable to halt the Arab Spring's arrival in Cyrenaica.

However, it was not only in the rebellious east that Libyans were rising up. Al-Zawiya, in the west of the country, came out against the regime on 19 February. Protesters there carried slogans declaring: 'By our soul, by our blood, we sacrifice ourselves for you, Benghazi.' The next day clashes broke out in Misarata, where rebels took control of the centre of the city. To Qaddafi's utter horror, demonstrations also broke out in the capital. There were uprisings on 18 and 19 February just metres from Qaddafi's Bab Al-Aziziya residence, although protesters dispersed after a rumour began circulating that Qaddafi had escaped the compound and after police started shooting at the crowds.[11] On 18 February, protesters also began gathering at night in Green Square, thinking that this would be the moment they could finally become masters of their own destiny. They were to be bitterly disappointed: the crowds were not big enough to generate any real momentum, and the regime's brutal efforts at putting the protest down were largely successful. Security forces opened fire on the crowd, and speeding vehicles were sent around the square, mowing down protesters, while the regime loyalists in the cars shot into the crowds at close range. Tripoli would have to wait before it could have an Arab Spring of its own.

While the regime may have been able to hold on to the west, by the end of February most of the east was in rebel hands. Reflecting just how little legitimacy Qaddafi and his regime had been able to build in the region, the eastern cities had fallen with breathtaking speed, as Qaddafi's security forces melted away or joined the opposition. It was rapidly dawning on the regime that it stood no real chance against this new-found determination to achieve change on the part of people who, in many cases, had known nothing other than Qaddafi's rule. This realization sent the regime into spiralling panic. Qaddafi was clearly stunned: in a brief and utterly bizarre appearance on state television (made in part to dispel rumours that he had fled to Venezuela), he looked utterly stupefied. The usually verbose Colonel – now unshaven and sporting the most unbecoming deer-hunter hat as he sat in a white golf cart with a large white umbrella – made a speech that lasted for less than twenty seconds. This 'speech' consisted mostly of attacks on the foreign media and journalists, whom he described as 'dogs'. To anyone who knew the Colonel, he looked like a man who had lost it.

Never one to buckle under pressure, Qaddafi fought back. First, he made the strategic decision to focus his efforts on securing Tripoli. He pulled what forces he had left out of the east and turned his attention to bolstering security in the capital. He also did his utmost to brush the trouble off as a regional problem. He made out that this was not a case of the Arab Spring reaching Libya, but was another instance of those bothersome easterners creating trouble. Given the east's reputation as a bastion of Islamism, he also tried to dismiss the rebels as drug-crazed Islamists with ties to Al-Qa'ida.

At this point, the Colonel believed that, if he could just hold onto the capital, it would only be a matter of time before he could reorganize his forces and re-establish control across the rest of the country. His confidence was born partly out of the well-founded assumption that Libya's experience of the Arab Spring was going to be very different from that of its neighbours. This was largely due to the status of the army. Unlike in Tunisia and Egypt, where the army had taken the side of the people and had been pivotal in forcing Ben Ali and Mubarak out of power, the Libyan army was in no position to be able to force anything. The Colonel, who had fomented his own coup from within the armed forces, had long held a deep-rooted suspicion of the army, once asserting that the military was 'always inclined to tyranny and even conspiracy'.[12] He had purposely kept his armed forces weak and divided – to the point where the army was regularly described as more of a 'military club' than a fighting force. When it came to it, therefore, the army proved unable to play any decisive role in the crisis.

Qaddafi also knew that he could rely upon his most important security forces to stick by him. Over the years, he had ensured that his security brigades were dominated by members of his own family and tribe, and, as his sons had come of age, the toughest and most military-minded of them were given their own security battalions. Khamis, in particular, led the much-feared 32 Brigade, which had always had access to the most up-to-date kit. By filling his security battalions with those of his own kith and kin, Qaddafi ensured that their fate was so closely entwined with his own that they were in no position to try to oust him. Similarly, the power of Qaddafi's inner circle of trusted advisors derived almost entirely from their personal connections to him. He knew they were so close to him that they were unlikely to push him out of power, or even to defect. Indeed, the Colonel had crafted a highly personalized ruling system: he sat at the centre of a web of confidants, many of whom he had known since his schooldays and on whose support he could count.

That is not to say that there were no defections. The first major blow to Qaddafi came early on, when General Abdelfatah Younis Al-Obeidi, who had been at the Colonel's side from the very beginning, resigned from his post as public security secretary (minister) and threw in his lot with the opposition. He did so while in the midst of an operation to protect one of the regime's most important bases in Benghazi. Al-Obeidi's defection to the rebel forces was a major coup for the opposition and gave the revolution some serious legitimacy.

A handful of other members of the regime also defected. However, these were mainly figures from the formal institutions of government or from the diplomatic corps, and, while indeed a setback, the defections were not life threatening to the regime. What was more serious for Qaddafi, however, was the high-profile defection of his trusted intelligence chief, Musa Kusa, who fled to Britain in March. Although Kusa did not join the rebels, the decision by one of the most powerful Qaddafi loyalists to leave what was widely being viewed as a sinking ship did little for the regime's confidence.

Yet, aside from these figures, almost all of Qaddafi's inner circle remained loyal until the bitter end. So, too, did the tribes that had traditionally supported his regime: not only the Qaddadfa, but the

Werfella and the Megraha also remained steadfast. While some elements within these tribes did defect, the tribes themselves were so bound up with the regime that they stuck by their Leader until the death. Secure in these elements, the Colonel felt he could carry on and fight back.

Yet for all his confidence, Qaddafi had to factor another element into his calculations about how to respond to the crisis on the ground. How would the West react and would it intervene to assist the uprising? For a man who had been paranoid for almost all his life that the West was out to get him, this was a difficult thing to weigh up. However, according to those close to the frantic discussions going on in Tripoli at the time, Qaddafi ultimately concluded that it would be difficult for Western nations to embark upon any kind of military action against his Jamahiriyah. With Western troops bogged down in the complexities of Afghanistan, and with the bitter experience of Iraq not far from the surface, the Colonel assumed that Western governments were in no position to launch an assault against his regime. With this in mind, he determined that it was safe for him to go on the counter-offensive. Indeed, the Leader believed that Libyans needed to be shown an iron fist again, and that it was time to deal the rebel forces in the east a crushing blow they would never forget.[13]

Such an approach was not unexpected; Qaddafi was not Mubarak or Ben Ali. With his unstinting Bedouin pride and uncompromising self-belief, there was no way the Colonel was going to step aside and walk away from power gracefully – let alone flee the country. He was not simply a head of state – he was the very embodiment of the Jamahiriyah. He *was* Libya. The Colonel was going to play it tough until the end. He repeatedly declared that he would die in Libya, and few had cause to doubt him.

More unexpected, however, was Saif Al-Islam's response to the crisis. As the man who had almost single-handedly promoted reform and who had presented himself as the champion of change, this favoured son was expected by many Libyans to step up and take charge of the situation. The reformist camp, in particular, believed that this was Saif Al-Islam's moment and his chance to turn his well-worn promises into reality. As one of those around him at the time explained, 'We were all waiting for Saif.'[14]

Saif Al-Islam was certainly more prepared for events than was his father. Having picked up on the warning signs of the Tunisian experience, he had tried to persuade his father that it was time to wake up to reality. His entreaties did not go down well and resulted in yet another clash between father and son. The fight was sufficiently serious to prompt Saif Al-Islam to storm off to Austria.[15] Not that Qaddafi senior was completely unaware of the difficulties: two months prior to the uprisings, the Leader had sent his sons Saadi and Moatassim to visit Abdelsalam Jalloud, who was staying in Paris at the time. According to Jalloud, the Qaddafi boys told him that the government and the revolutionary committees were getting anxious, and that their father wanted him to return to the country to play an important role in what would become the Second Jamahiriyah.[16] Indeed, the Colonel seems to have been ruminating over announcing some major changes to his eccentric political system. However, in true Qaddafi style, rather than come up with any real reform that would appease the increasingly restive population, the Leader had taken refuge in yet another reinvention of his revolutionary system.

While his father was too wrapped up in his own world to fully appreciate the impending dangers, Saif Al-Islam returned from Austria and began holding crisis meetings with his advisors. Seeing their chance, these advisors tried to convince the young Qaddafi that now was the time to act on the promises he had been making for so long. They suggested that he make a speech announcing a raft of reforms that would convince the country that this time he was serious about change.[17] However, the young Qaddafi knew what he was up against, and his frustration was palpable. In one such meeting on 16 February, the Leader's son hit the table three times, declaring: 'My dad doesn't want any reform. He doesn't want to give any concession to the people.'[18]

As Saif Al-Islam dithered, events overtook him. While he deliberated over reform, Benghazi was on the march. The young Qaddafi clearly had none of his father's steely will; one of his closest advisors, Abdelmoutleb Al-Houni, recalled going to the young Qaddafi's house on the day Benghazi fell: 'I found him collapsed.'[19] Al-Houni sat with Saif Al-Islam from four in the afternoon until four the following morning, trying to find a way out of the crisis. Eventually Al-Houni convinced the Leader's son that his only option was to make a speech that would be powerful enough to halt the unrest. Quite what Saif Al-Islam could have come up with that would have placated the crowds in the east at this stage is unclear. While the Leader's son had a degree of legitimacy, things had gone way beyond anything he could offer. Change was under way, and in their own minds the people of the east had already moved into the post-Qaddafi era. Yet with no obvious alternative and with the situation in Benghazi worsening by the hour, the Leader's son agreed to make a ground-breaking speech. The next day Al-Houni sat down at home with the NOC chief, Shukri Ghanem, to compose the speech that was to save the day.

But in the heat of the unfolding events, blood proved thicker than water. Libyans were dumbfounded when, on 20 February, the young Qaddafi went on state television and delivered a blood-curdling address. With a hawkishness not previously seen in the young reformer, an exhausted Saif Al-Islam, dressed in a dark suit, declared: 'We will fight to the last man and woman and bullet. We will not lose Libya ... We will live in Libya and die in Libya.'[20] These were words that one might have expected from the Brother Leader, not from the man who had made it his business to champion the people against the excesses of the state. But Saif Al-Islam went on to dismiss the protesters in the most disparaging of tones, accusing them of threatening national unity and of being little more than deranged Islamist militants, bent on establishing Islamic emirates in the east. Given the young Qaddafi's efforts to rehabilitate Islamist prisoners in recent years, these accusations were truly staggering to many Libyans. The people were also stunned by Saif Al-Islam's bid to blame outside forces for the unrest, and by his warnings that the trouble would lead to Western occupation, civil war and the break-up of Libya. The image of the urbane reformer melted away in a single instant, leaving those who had supported Saif Al-Islam feeling wholly cheated. As one of his advisors ruefully acknowledged, the speech was 'the final chapter in the comedy that was reform'.[21] Indeed, it was with this speech that Saif Al-Islam condemned himself to being part of the problem rather than part of the solution to Libya's crisis.[22]

It still is not clear exactly what prompted Saif Al-Islam to change course at the last minute and to close ranks with his father. Some of those who were close to him at the time believe that his change of heart was a bid to prove himself to his family. He was coming under sustained attack at this time from his father and his brothers, who accused him of being directly responsible for the crisis.[23] His brother Moatassim, the hardnosed younger sibling, had long railed against Saif Al-Islam's reformist ideas, and particularly his bid to rehabilitate Islamist prisoners. As far as Moatassim and (to a lesser extent) his father were concerned, Saif Al-Islam had upset the balance with his 'Western' ideas, and now Libya was paying the price. They may have had a point: all those whom Saif Al-Islam had supported in recent years were now leading the charge against the regime. From the families of the Abu Slim massacre victims who had sparked the protests, to the Islamists who had repented, been released and were now among the front lines of the rebel forces, to the reformist technocrats who had surrounded Saif Al-Islam and who were now busy trying to form a government in waiting – they had all come back to haunt the regime with an unrestrained vengeance. Moreover, it was Saif Al-Islam who had encouraged an atmosphere of openness in recent years, giving people the space to express themselves – something that had fostered a certain boldness among the people. Rather than dish out more reform, therefore, Saif Al-Islam was told to forget his ideas and to stand alongside his family and fight to the end. The young Qaddafi chose to obey, pinning his destiny on his family rather than on his country.

So it was that the Qaddafi family united and focused their efforts on securing the capital. Though a challenge, this was not impossible: the capital was Qaddafi's main power base and it was where many of his security battalions were located. The Colonel ramped up security measures across the city, erecting blockades and supplying weapons to those who were loyal to his regime. He also tasked his regime stalwarts with arming allied tribes, especially the Qaddadfa, ten thousand of whom were reportedly brought to the capital to help protect it.[24] Qaddafi also sought to frighten Tripoli residents into submission, instilling a climate of terror across the city, arresting those suspected of disloyalty and anyone who dared to speak to the international media. The city was on a knife-edge. As one Tripoli resident described matters:

It was Tripoli like we had never known before – checkpoints, grim faces everywhere, armed kids with green flags around their necks roaming the streets in four-wheel-drive cars with Qaddafi's photos on the doors and windows ... Only the extremely brave dared to go out after sunset. Businesses were closed most of the day. At night, silence falls, only the eruption of gunfire can be heard or loud songs glorifying Qaddafi coming from specially equipped vehicles roaming [the] streets.[25]

The policy certainly worked. As the east burned with rebellion, residents of the west could only look with a deep sense of uncertainty and foreboding.

As the regime entrenched itself in the capital, opposition forces in the east set about the daunting task of organizing themselves. The first thing was to set up some kind of interim ruling body. The rebels established the National Transitional Council (NTC), a body of thirty-one members, representing different areas, that was to oversee the country until full liberation was achieved. Below the NTC was a series of local councils set up to run day-to-day affairs in each of the liberated areas. For a country with no real political experience, no properly functioning institutions and no genuine civil society organizations, the speed with which the rebels set up the NTC and went about arranging affairs at the local level was a remarkable achievement. It was all the more extraordinary given that the revolution had not been born out of any organized revolutionary movement or ideological current. This was new territory for all those involved.

At the helm of the NTC was a group of technocrats who had defected from the regime when the uprising broke out. They included the former justice secretary, Mustafa Abdeljalil, who was appointed head of the NTC; former chief of the National Planning Council, Mahmoud Jibril, who was put in charge of crisis management; and former economy minister, Ali Issawi, who was made responsible for foreign affairs. Given their connections to the Qaddafi regime, this group appeared a curious choice as leaders of the opposition. However, many of them had been part of the reformist current and had, in their own way, tried to challenge the regime from inside. They also had a reputation for not having indulged in the kind of corrupt practices that had made other members of the regime so notorious. For example, Mustafa Abdeljalil, who had been appointed justice secretary by Saif Al-Islam in 2007, memorably (and bravely) offered his resignation at a meeting of the General People's Congress in January 2010, in protest at the security services' continued detention of three hundred 'rehabilitated' Islamist prisoners, despite a judicial ruling ordering their release. This move earned him no small degree of respect among Libyans.

More importantly, however, Abdeljalil was a well-known and well-liked figure in the east. With a reputation for piety and humility, he was appreciated for the fact that he had always resisted the trappings of power, continuing to live in his judge's guesthouse rather than relocating to a villa, and insisting on driving his own modest car even after he was made minister. Like Abdeljalil, Mahmoud Jibril was brought into the political arena by Saif Al-Islam, who, in 2007, appointed him head of the National Planning Council. However, Jibril came to blows with many figures in the regime who considered his reformist ideas too progressive for the likes of Libya. He even clashed with Saif Al-Islam and was removed from his post in 2010. While these figures were certainly part of the system, they had distanced themselves from the excesses of the Qaddafi regime.

But the main reason why these former regime figures ended up leading the opposition was that there were few other choices. Given the eccentricities of the Jamahiriyah system and the fact that it had been run along the lines of an 'old boys' club' for so many years, the pool of qualified personnel with any experience of politics – let alone of governing – was extremely limited. In a land without political parties (to say nothing of trades unions or independent professional bodies), there had been nowhere for budding politicians to cut their teeth. It was for this reason that the NTC ended up being composed mainly of technocrats and professionals, most of whom had been orbiting around Saif Al-Islam's reformist circles.[26]

The most pressing – and by far the most daunting – task facing this new body was finishing off the revolution. Hopes that

Tripolitanians would take courage and rise up as their eastern counterparts had done were becoming more distant by the day. The
rebels were going to have to try to topple the regime themselves.
They had little choice but to try to conquer the rest of the country,
town by town, until they reached the capital. Yet, for all its enthusiasm, the opposition was militarily weak and its lack of experience
was painfully clear. Young men without any military training
suddenly found themselves on the front lines in makeshift militias,
many holding a gun for the first time. The rebels were also sorely
lacking in arms. As one colonel explained, 'Our problem is weapons.
We need them, but we don't have them ... Half my men go into
battle without a gun.'[27] The weapons the rebels did have had largely
been raided from military depots or snatched from regime forces and
were, for the most part, in a pitiful state.

Proving the old adage that necessity is the mother of invention,
the rebel forces did what they could. DIY weapons workshops sprang
up all over the place, and innovative Libyans put their minds to
modifying weapons. Pickup trucks were transformed into armoured
vehicles, and portable launchers for firing old Russian surface-to-air
missiles were cobbled together out of old pieces of drainpipe, the
triggers being made from hair dryers.[28]

However, this inventiveness was not sufficient to give opposition
forces the advantage they needed. Things looked desperate. By mid-
March, regime forces had been able to reverse many of the gains
made by the opposition. In the east of the country, they had taken
back the strategically important oil towns of Ras Lanuf and Brega,
and had made progress against Ajdabia. The regime had also recon-
quered Zawiya and Zawara in the west. Qaddafi and his forces were
marching their way back to victory. Worst of all, the regime was on
its way to launching a major counter-offensive against Benghazi.
Regime forces had got as far as the outskirts of the city and, as they
began to close in, it was clear that a major bloodbath was in the offing.

On the night of 17 March, Qaddafi gave a chilling radio address: 'I will finish the battle of Benghazi tonight. I will chase you flat by flat.'[29]

Turning the tables

Qaddafi's confidence was soon to be shattered. Once again, he was to be tripped up by the West. On the night he was poised to retake Benghazi, the United Nations Security Council defied all expectations and voted for the imposition of a no-fly zone over Libya. The Council also voted to authorize the use of military action – including against tanks and heavy artillery on the ground – in order to protect civilians.

The news came as a shattering blow to the Leader, who had clearly misjudged the West's willingness to intervene. Yet there had been a growing disquiet in some Western capitals about what was unfolding in Libya. For all that the West feared getting itself mired in another part of the Islamic world, there was a sense that something had to be done to prevent Qaddafi from butchering his own in his bid to put down the 'rats' that had dared to challenge his Jamahiriyah. Paris and London were particularly keen for the international community to act, seeing an opportunity to support the Arab Spring (and, in the case of the UK's Conservative government, to distance itself from its predecessor's policy of engagement with the Libyan regime). Britain and France, therefore, called on the international community to act by imposing a no-fly zone. They were supported in this by the US, although the Obama administration made it clear from the outset that, while it would take the lead initially, it wanted only a limited role in the campaign.

Surprisingly enough, the Arab League backed the calls of these Western nations, and on 12 March nine of the League's twenty-two members called on the UN Security Council to impose a no-fly zone in order to protect civilians from air attack. The support of the Arab

League was deeply significant for Western nations, which were acutely concerned that an intervention in Libya would be perceived as yet another attempt by neo-colonialist forces to meddle in the Muslim world. The Arab League's decision was significant for Qaddafi, too: could there be a more potent example of the dismal failure of his life-long policy of pan-Arabism? Here were the Colonel's fellow Arab states signing up to what would prove to be his ultimate undoing.

On 19 March, two days after the UN Security Council voted to impose the no-fly zone, the attacks began. Under the leadership of the United States, French and British planes, supported by other countries in the coalition, flew sorties over Libya. Then, at the end of March, NATO took over responsibility from the US for the enforcement of the no-fly zone and the arms embargo. The opposition was jubilant – the tables had been turned most definitely against the Colonel once again.

Yet anyone who believed that the threat of international action would force Qaddafi to back down clearly did not know him. Admitting defeat, especially at the hands of his most reviled enemies, was not an option for the proud Bedouin of the desert, who remained as defiant as ever. In some ways, finding himself the West's target once again suited the Leader. After the rapprochement of Libya's rehabilitation, he was able once again to do what he loved best – to rail against Western perfidiousness, but this time with a new urgency. The Colonel certainly made the most of the propaganda opportunities: he warned that the no-fly zone was little more than a prelude to full-scale military intervention, and that Western boots would soon be landing on Libyan soil. Scenes of Qaddafi surrounded by adoring supporters next to the giant golden fist at Bab Al-Aziziya, erected to commemorate the US attacks of 1986, were shown repeatedly on state television. Once again, the message was clear: the Leader was not going anywhere.

Qaddafi's confidence was not entirely misplaced. While NATO intervention tipped the balance back in the rebels' favour, it was not immediately sufficient to enable them to achieve victory. They were still lacking in weapons and experience, making the possibility of a march on Tripoli still little more than a distant dream. What followed NATO's entry to the Arab Spring was a bloody stalemate, in which a vicious cat-and-mouse game was played out between opposing sides. Towns were taken and then lost and then retaken again, with countless lives sacrificed on both sides. Perhaps the most dramatic battle was for the strategically important coastal city of Misarata in the west. At the start of the uprising, rebels succeeded in taking the city – the third largest in the country and its main commercial port. However, regime forces made a bid to retake it in March, putting the city under siege in their attempt to make it submit. Troops loyal to Qaddafi pulverized whole neighbourhoods, launching mortar attacks on residential areas and sending tanks into the city centre. Snipers were also posted on rooftops along the city's main thoroughfare, Tripoli Street. The residents' only link with the outside world was through the port, and supplies became increasingly hard to come by. People were queuing for hours just to get bread, and fresh food became a rarity. The regime even went so far as to cut off the town's water supplies. The battle for Misarata lasted until the middle of May, when, with the assistance of NATO air strikes, rebel forces were finally able to retake the city.

Losing Misarata was a serious blow to Qaddafi. It also made holding onto Tripoli all the more essential. The capital and its suburbs became a city suspended in time and paralysed by fear. Although some young activists continued to engage in highly risky acts, such as hanging pro-revolutionary banners from public buildings, and while rebel forces periodically launched ambushes on government checkpoints, 'people power' was nowhere to be seen. This is hardly surprising, as snipers were placed all around the city to intimidate anyone from even thinking about taking action. Young men were taken away in the middle of the night and were never seen again. Regime forces regularly came out at night to daub marks on the houses of those they suspected of supporting the opposition. Local residents cleaned these marks off in the morning, but they would generally reappear the following night. The city's streets also rang with the shouts of regime supporters, who were paid around ten dinars a day to go around the city brandishing weapons and declaring their undying loyalty to the Jamahiriyah. Added to this there was the ominous sound of NATO night-time air attacks. These attacks did not always hit their intended targets: in June a bomb went astray, hitting a residential building and killing nine people.

Terrified residents were left sitting it out at home, only venturing beyond the confines of their buildings to get essential supplies. All they could do was to try to follow events as best they could on the satellite television channels, although many feared that tuning into such channels could be used as evidence against them. To make matters worse, food supplies were getting low and the banks were running out of cash. There were fuel shortages, too, as well as regular power cuts. Life was getting tougher by the day. Yet even these strains were not sufficient for Tripolitanians to lose the fear that had bound them for decades and to rise up against the regime.

But, deep in his heart, Qaddafi knew that repression would not be enough to save the day, especially as his forces were slowly but surely being degraded by NATO strikes. He began frantically reaching out to different constituencies, in the hope of bolstering his support base. The regime made a number of unsuccessful appeals to influential Islamic scholars in Saudi Arabia, for instance. These included Sheikh Salman Al-Awda and Sheikh Aaidh Ibn Abdullah Al-Qarni, who were asked to use their religious authority to impress upon the Libyans that it was Islamically unacceptable to rise up against their rulers. For a man who had spent a lifetime shunning the

Saudi religious establishment, this was a desperate move indeed.*
The regime also played the tribal card, organizing a major gathering
of some 2,000 tribal leaders in Tripoli to get them to call for national
unity and for the rebels to disarm.

Yet the greatest sign of Qaddafi's desperation were the overtures
that the regime began making to the West. At the end of March, Saif
Al-Islam sent one of his closest aides, Mohamed Ismail, to London
to put a plan to the British authorities in which the Leader's son
would oversee Libya's transformation into a democratic state, while
his father and the rest of his family would be granted immunity from
prosecution. The following month, former Foreign Affairs Secretary
Abdel Ati Al-Obeidi told the international media that, if the rebels
agreed to a ceasefire, Libya would hold free elections within a six-
month transition period. Al-Obeidi went so far as to state that discussions about reform could include 'whether the Leader should stay
and in what role, and whether he should retire ... Everything will be
on the table.'[30] Such gestures were clearly major concessions on
Qaddafi's part. Yet Libyans were used to the Colonel's endless
promises and tricks. Given that he had based his entire rule on the
false premise that, with no official position, he had nothing to do
with running the country, Libyans were hardly going to accept any
solution that involved him or his family. Moreover, the opposition
had not risked everything and sacrificed so many lives only to end
up with some sort of continuation of the Qaddafi dynasty.

There was little appetite in the West either for the regime's
proposals. For all that Qaddafi had accepted rehabilitation, he was
still viewed as an unpredictable irritant who would be best out of the
way. That is not to say that there were not serious concerns about

---

* The regime even wheeled out Saadi Qaddafi in a bid to appeal to people's religious sensi-
bilities. Dressed in a long white *jalaba* and sporting a beard, Saadi, who was shown
surrounded by religious books, explained to Libyans that it was *haram* (religiously prohibited) to revolt against the state.

the number of Islamist militants and former militants who were swelling the opposition's ranks, some of whom had fought against US personnel in Iraq. Who or what might succeed the man from the desert was certainly unclear and not without its anxieties. Yet getting rid of Qaddafi had become the clear policy objective for almost all involved, and Western leaders stated in no uncertain terms that Qaddafi had to go.

Moreover, for all the concerns about what might come next, the NTC was proving a credible bunch. Its members were, for the most part, liberal technocrats who spoke a language that was comforting to the West. In March, they published a kind of manifesto – 'A Vision of a Democratic Libya' – an inclusive and sophisticated document that evoked a modern liberal democracy. Although the NTC's repeated calls for weapons fell on deaf ears, its members skilfully lobbied the international community and began to make serious headway. The council was coming to be recognized as the sole legitimate representative of the Libyan people. France was the first to grant it such recognition, in March. Other countries soon followed suit: Italy recognized the council in April, while a host of other countries, including Canada and Germany, did so in June.[31] Most importantly, however, in July 2011 the Libya Contact Group, a body set up by the international community to support the rebels, announced its participants' agreement to deal with the NTC as the sole legitimate governing authority in Libya. At the same time, the US also moved to recognize the council – something that opened up the possibility of the NTC getting its hands on the millions of dollars of Libyan assets that had been frozen in the US.

With all this international recognition, the NTC was looking increasingly like a government in waiting. There was little that Qaddafi could do, other than lash out at the council and portray it as the lackey of the colonialist powers. In an audio speech on 7 June, the Colonel declared 'I will choose death before surrender', referred to the NTC as the 'tail of the colonisers' and instructed the citizens of Benghazi to 'explode against those bisexuals who are fighting under the cross and under the American, French and British flags. Libyans will defeat them and the traitors will retreat.'[32] Showing that he had lost none of his flair for the absurd, Qaddafi also announced that Spain's recognition of the NTC gave Libyans the right to support the Basque separatist movement, as well as other independence movements around the world.[33] Indeed, as things were falling apart around his ears, the Leader proved bizarre until the end. In what surely must go down as one of the more surreal moments of the conflict, in June the Colonel had himself filmed calmly playing a game of chess against the World Chess Federation president, Kirsan Ilyumzhinov, in the lobby of a Tripoli hotel.

However, it was not long before the Colonel was to find himself facing another form of checkmate. By August, rebel forces had captured a number of key strategic towns in the west of the country, including Zawiya, Sabratha, Tarhouna and Gharyan. They had done so thanks to greatly improved coordination with NATO and noticeably better organization. The capture of these towns left Tripoli effectively encircled, enabling rebel forces to carry out their plan, which had been refined with the help of British MI6 officers based in Benghazi. As part of this plan, the rebels had been smuggling weapons, communication equipment and fighters into Tripoli over the past few months. So once the city was encircled, those rebels inside Tripoli were ready to rise up. Meanwhile, as NATO forces carried out heavy bombing raids on key strategic targets, including Qaddafi's Bab Al-Aziziya compound, rebel forces from outside the city began advancing on the capital. Fighters swept into Tripoli from Zawiya in the west and, meeting with almost no resistance, were easily able to take the headquarters of Khamis Qaddafi's feared 32 Brigade. Another group entered from Gharyan in the south, and a third came from Tajoura in the east. Meanwhile, two hundred fighters from Misarata who had come by boat disembarked at Tripoli's port. Rebels who had seized control of the Ben Nabi mosque in Sarim Street, near the city centre, used the mosque's loudspeaker system to begin anti-Qaddafi chants and to bring people out into the street.

The rebels had been expecting heavy fighting. However, at the crucial moment Qaddafi's forces simply melted away. Some, knowing they were beaten, dumped their uniforms and fled; others defected. Crucially this latter group included Brigadier Barani Ishkal, Qaddafi's cousin and head of the powerful Mohamed Al-Magarief brigade, which was responsible for Qaddafi's security and for the protection of Tripoli. Ishkal, who had been in secret contact with the NTC, agreed that when the uprising began, his brigade would join the revolution. It was this that opened the way for Tripoli's fall.

At last, six months after the fall of Benghazi, Tripolitanians began to come out into the streets. Tears of joy, of sadness and of pain streamed down their incredulous faces as the 'Bride of the Mediterranean' was finally liberated from the tyrant who had held it in his iron grip for so long. Thousands gathered in the public squares, discharging their guns into the hot night air in celebration. Prisons were unlocked and prisoners freed. Libyans tore down the meaning-less revolutionary banners and the enormous pictures of Qaddafi, and proceeded to punch, kick and stamp on them with jubilant abandon. Rebel fighters broke into the Colonel's Bab Al-Aziziya compound, a place that had always been full of forbidding mystery. They set fire to his famous tent, tore the golden face off a statue he had had made of himself, and pulled down the symbols of his rule. Some even got their hands on his now famous white golf buggy, and they drove it through the streets of the capital to the sound of car horns. It was not just the Colonel's residence that was raided: the plush villas and homes of his family were also ransacked. Libyans streamed into the residence of Qaddafi's daughter, Aisha. Among her possessions they found an enormous, mermaid-shaped sofa made of gold and bearing her own likeness.

Yet for all the jubilation that Libya was finally free, the struggle was not over. The big question preoccupying Libyans was what had become of Qaddafi. Although the fall of Tripoli marked the end of the struggle, for as long as the Leader was still at large, an enormous cloud hung over the country. Having been such an overwhelming figure for the past four decades, Qaddafi had to be caught for Libyans to feel that their revolution was complete. Moreover, all the time the Colonel was still out there, there was a danger that he could regroup his loyalists and become a vicious irritant to the new Libya.

Speculation grew that the Leader was hiding out in the southern deserts; but all the while the Colonel was, in fact, holed up in his hometown. When rebel forces entered Tripoli, he, along with his son Moatassim and other trusted members of his regime, had travelled in a small convoy across the unforgiving deserts until they reached Sirte. It had been Moatassim's idea. The young Qaddafi believed that his father's hometown was such an obvious destination that it would be the last place anyone would think to look.[34] Meanwhile, Saif Al-Islam fled to Bani Walid, the home of the Werfella tribe, which was happy to provide him with protection; Saadi escaped to Niger, where he was granted political asylum; and a heavily pregnant Aisha fled with her mother and her brothers Mohamed and Hannibal to Algeria.[35]

As if seeking out Qaddafi was not enough, the rebels were also faced with capturing the two regime strongholds of Sirte and Bani Walid, which continued to put up fierce resistance to the rebel forces. The fight was a brutal one – not least because, in an ominous sign of things to come, rebel forces unleashed their full revenge against these bastions of Qaddafi loyalism. Both cities were completely ransacked by revolutionary fighters, who went on the rampage, looting and destroying whatever was in their way and committing gross human rights abuses against local residents as they went. When Bani Walid finally fell on 17 October and revolutionary forces entered the city, they destroyed everything in sight. One inhabitant described what happened:

> When the *thwar* (revolutionary fighters) failed to find the Kadhafi [Qaddafi] brigades they had been expecting, they were furious. They shot at dogs, at houses, they looted and burned apartments and public buildings ... Now the whole town is angry. The *thwar* punished everyone, by destroying their homes, stealing their cars and killing their relatives.[36]

The battle for Sirte was no less pitiless. As revolutionary troops encircled the city, those regime loyalists who were still fighting it out were pushed into a tiny neighbourhood of less than one square kilometre. The rebels pounded this area with rockets, forcing its residents to flee in terror. Yet still the city held out. The rebels knew that the reason for this fierce resistance was that there were a number of senior figures from the regime in the neighbourhood. Having tied themselves so tightly to Qaddafi and his regime, the members of this group knew that, if they were caught, the rebels would show them no mercy; they therefore had nothing to lose by fighting it out to the death.

But what the rebels did not know was that one of the senior figures hiding out in Sirte was Qaddafi himself. The Leader was living out his last days hiding in an ever decreasing area, surviving on a diet of rice and pasta that had been scavenged from the deserted flats of those who had fled the city. The life of a fugitive did not suit him. According to his aide, Mansour Dhaw, who was with him at the time, the Leader spent his time reading the Qu'ran and making desperate phone calls on his satellite telephone. As the city's resistance crumbled around him, he nevertheless refused to surrender, insisting: 'This is my country. I handed over power [to the people] in 1977.'[37] In fact, the Colonel seemed to be out of touch with reality and kept asking: 'Why is there no electricity? Why is there no water?'[38]

When they could hold on no longer, the group decided to leave the city and flee to a house near the village where Qaddafi was born. On 20 October, at 8 a.m., some five hours after they had intended to leave, the party set off in a convoy of about forty cars. Qaddafi, who was travelling with his chief of security, a relative and Mansour Dhaw in a Toyota Land Cruiser, said little during the drive. It was not long before disaster struck. NATO had spotted the convoy outside the city and launched two strikes, shattering the windscreen of the Leader's vehicle and injuring him in both legs. Qaddafi and a small group of loyalists then made their way through trees and tried to hide in two concrete sewage pipes that ran beneath a major road. What bitter irony that a man who had referred to those who had started the uprising as 'rats', should have spent his last moments crouched in a filthy sewage pipe.

Qaddafi and his bodyguards were soon spotted by rebel forces, who dragged the beleaguered Colonel from his hiding place out onto the litter-strewn sand. The terrified Qaddafi remained deluded until the end, asking 'What did I do to you?' as his captors dragged him to the bonnet of a car, where they rained blows on him. The excited group of fighters shouted, '*Allah u'akhbar*' ('God is great') and fired their weapons into the air as the petrified dictator begged for mercy, his face covered with blood and his hair caked with dust. However, his pleas fell on deaf ears. Although a couple of the rebels shouted that the Colonel was needed alive, the crowd was baying for his blood. One young fighter delivered a final blow and then shot the Colonel at close range. According to his teenage killer: 'We grabbed him ... I hit him in the face. Some fighters wanted to take him away and that's when I shot him – twice – in the face and in the chest.'[39]

For all the self-imagined glories of his forty-year reign, this was the most ignominious and ignoble of deaths.

Qaddafi's battered body was dragged through the streets of Sirte and then bundled into an ambulance and taken to Misarata. It was rebels from Misarata who had finished him off, and they were not going to let an opportunity like this slip by. They wanted Qaddafi's head and, like victors in an age-old tribal conflict, they wanted to take the spoils of war back home. Despite the NTC's pleas for the body to be handed over for burial, the Misaratans insisted on wrapping the rotting and bloodied corpse in an old blanket and putting it on display in a local meat freezer, like a war trophy. Next to it they put their other big prize catch – Moatassim, who had also been captured in Sirte and who was now laid alongside his father. He, too, had had the most inglorious ending. Videos appeared on the internet of Moatassim's last moments: the skinny, agile son with his long hair and unkempt beard, smoking his last cigarette in a dismal room furnished only with a plastic chair and a mattress on the floor, as his captors repeatedly called him a dog. Like his father, Moatassim was summarily executed by a bullet fired at close range.

The NTC's inability to get the Misaratans to hand the bodies over was an ominous sign of things to come. How could the NTC, secure in its offices in Benghazi, compete for legitimacy with those who had rolled up their sleeves and fought on the front lines? It was the Misaratans – people who had suffered so much when their city was being pulverized by regime forces – who had cut off the head of the snake. They were not going to listen to a group of technocrats and academics – least of all a group whose leadership was linked to the former regime! And they certainly were not going to allow the NTC (which was under pressure from international opinion, outraged at the images of Qaddafi's brutal murder that had been broadcast around the world) to bring the Colonel's killer to justice.

Moreover, the Misaratans refusal to hand over the corpse suited the popular mood. Libyans began queuing up to catch a glimpse of the reeking corpses, many taking photographs of themselves next to the rotting bodies. While this may have appeared a grisly spectacle to the outside world, to many Libyans it was part of a necessary process. Seeing Qaddafi dead was confirmation that this utterly overpowering character, whose personality had filled every space in the country, and whose eccentric ideas had intruded upon and dominated every aspect of life, was no more than a man after all.

Being laid out in a meat freezer certainly was not the way the Colonel had envisaged his own end. During his last days, Qaddafi had written a will. It was almost touching:

> Should I be killed, I would like to be buried, according to Muslim rituals, in the clothes I was wearing at the time of my death and my body unwashed, in the cemetery of Sirte, next to my family and relatives ... I would like that my family, especially women and children, be treated well after my death ... I call on my supporters to continue the resistance, and fight any foreign aggressor against Libya, today, tomorrow and always ... Let the free people of the world know that we could have bargained over and sold out our cause in return for a personal secure and stable life. We received many offers to this effect but we chose to be at the vanguard of the confrontation as a badge of duty and honour.[40]

How far the reality was from this imagined noble ending, which reflected Qaddafi's simple Bedouin roots. Not only was he not buried within twenty-four hours, as is dictated by Muslim tradition, but his body was finally laid to rest in an unmarked grave in the desert. It was the end that many Libyans believed he deserved. As one Libyan who had waited to view his body said: 'God made the pharaoh as an example to the others ... If he had been a good man, we would have buried him. But he chose this destiny for himself.'[41] Indeed, Qaddafi had chosen his own fate right from those early years, when he had marked himself out as different, as a man with a vision – a man who was willing to stake his entire being on the country he had come to lead. There was no option for the prophet from the desert but to die fighting in the defence of his Jamahiriyah.

Qaddafi had once declared 'my successor will be the people'. He surely did not imagine that this was how the people would finally succeed him. Indeed, perhaps the cruellest irony of all in this very public death was that after years of the Colonel calling on the masses to 'rise up' in the service of his revolution, when they eventually did heed his call, they did so in order to destroy him and all that he had created. The sun had finally set on the era of Qaddafism.

Conclusion

One year on from the start of the revolution, Libya was still writhing in crisis. Qaddafi may have gone, but things were not panning out quite the way that those who had risked their lives for change had dreamed of. The country was up against a barrage of challenges, and the jubilation that had accompanied the Colonel's demise was fast being replaced by a profound sense of unease at the direction in which this 'gigantic dust bowl of sand' was heading. The 'Pharaoh' may have been slain, but his death had unleashed a thousand lesser pharaohs, all jostling for power in the new Libya. The revolutionary brigades that had formed during the struggle against the old regime had not disbanded with the fall of Qaddafi, and the chiefs of these brigades, each linked to a city or region, had become the country's new power brokers. Misarata, Zintan and other cities that had been kept down at the hands of Qaddafi's repressive security apparatus had all taken advantage of the enormous power vacuum that had developed in the wake of the conflict to assert themselves. Libya was fast beginning to look like a collection of city states, and the periphery was taking its revenge on the centre.

There was little that the country's new leaders could do to claw back control. The authorities that had emerged from the conflict were doing their best, but the NTC and its affiliated bodies were struggling to garner any real legitimacy on the ground. They were certainly no match for the powerful brigade leaders, who had cut their teeth on the front lines and who had no intention of submitting – yet alone of handing over their weapons – to this group of 'pampered' technocrats, many of whom had links to the former regime. The new authorities were not helped either by the fact that they were so overwhelmed by their efforts to deal with the security situation that they struggled to manage the day-to-day affairs of state. Libyans were getting agitated once again as the promised jobs, improved services and raised living standards failed to materialize.

Such was the frustration that, by the start of 2012, protests, sit-ins and strikes had become an almost daily occurrence, as Libyans began accusing the new authorities of having sold their revolution down the river. Sometimes events took a more sinister turn: in January 2012, angry protesters stormed the NTC offices in Benghazi, throwing homemade grenades and hurling plastic bottles at the council's head, Mustafa Abdeljalil, who was forced to beat a hasty retreat out of the back door. The following month, the interim prime minister, Abdelraheem Al-Keib, was attacked by knife-wielding crowds. Libya's new leaders were learning the hard way the truth of the old cliché that managing the peace is much harder than winning the war. While neighbouring Tunisia pressed steadily ahead with its transition from dictatorship to democracy, Libya found itself limping along, dragging its past behind it.

That things should have taken such an extreme turn is unsurprising. Libya was always going to have a tougher time pulling itself through its Arab Spring than was Tunisia. Qaddafi's refusal to step aside when the people rose up meant that Libya had been through what amounted to almost twelve months of wretched civil war. More importantly, perhaps, though the Tunisian regime had been as brutal and repressive as Qaddafi's, it had built a state. President Ben Ali left behind a strong institutional framework and an entire political tradition that the country's new leaders could at least use as a springboard for change. Qaddafi, on the other hand, left nothing in his wake. For all his big ideas, all that the Colonel left was a country utterly shattered by forty years of Qaddafism.

Indeed, the radical nature of the challenges facing Libya as it moved into the post-Qaddafi era was a bitter reflection of the extreme (often senseless) policies of a man driven by his own vain obsessions. Qaddafi was a leader more preoccupied with self-aggrandizing schemes to project himself beyond the country's borders than with tackling the needs of a nation. State-building always came second. Moreover, in his reckless bid to impose his Jamahiriyah, the Brother Leader razed everything to the ground, destroying the country's institutions, or rendering them impotent. Aside from the energy and security sectors – both essential to the maintenance of his regime – little in Libya functioned in any meaningful way. Virtually every formal body in the state was little more than a façade – an expression of the Leader's vanity – behind which real power was focused almost entirely in the hands of Qaddafi, his coterie of loyal informal advisors, and, as they came of age, his sons.

Thus Qaddafi's left the country's new leaders with the heavy legacy of having to build the state almost entirely from scratch. A functioning political system, government, ministries, civil service, police force, even a postal service – all had to be created out of nothing. Even the army, rendered little more than a symbolic body by Qaddafi, had to be set up from the remnants of what was left after the conflict. This was a task of gargantuan proportions.

Moreover, setting up these institutions was one thing; peopling them was something else. Another of the sad legacies of Qaddafi's four decades at the helm was that this promoter of the masses left a population utterly unprepared for life beyond him. The country was sorely lacking in trained or qualified personnel – not least because, whenever it needed expertise, the regime had simply bought it in from abroad. The thousands of functionaries who filled the country's huge and unwieldy state bodies regarded their employment there almost as a rite of passage. They were the unproductive, low-paid beneficiaries of an enormous distributive state: for many public sector employees, going to work was a chance to have a coffee and a chat with colleagues before heading off to drive a taxi or to engage in some other small-scale private or illegal business activity in the afternoon and evening. Qaddafi's Jamahiriyah was not a place that encouraged dynamism in the formal sector. It was not a place, either, where the middle class could flourish. The professional middle class was not totally absent, but it was small and completely emasculated by the state. Thus, whereas Tunisia's large and solid middle class was able to help drive the country through its transition, Libya had no such pool of skilled personnel to draw on.

This dearth of qualified personnel has come to pose particular challenges for post-Qaddafi Libya. Given that people want a clean break with the past, even filling posts in the country's interim ruling bodies has proved difficult. Libyans living in exile have had to be brought back to take up senior positions, including at ministerial level. This has generated some resentment among certain parts of the population, which are somewhat disgruntled at the privileges being bestowed upon these 'newcomers', who lived in relative ease abroad, while those left at home stuck it out for years under the old regime. Yet the country had little choice. Qaddafi left Libya a land without politicians, and the personalization of politics was so utterly overwhelming that there was no space for anything in the political arena other than the Colonel and his own hallowed image. The only exception was Saif Al-Islam, although even the Leader's son was limited in how far he could project his own ideas. Those figures who had the potential to become personas in their own right – such as Abdelsalam Jalloud or Omar Al-Meheishi – were simply pushed out of the way over the years, so starved of oxygen that they could not make any real contribution of their own. Qaddafi was a 'Messiah' who had little time for his disciples. Instead, he relied on technocrats, who tried their best to navigate their way through the endless layers of meaningless bureaucracy he had created.

Not only was Libya a land with no politicians, but it was also a country with no real political experience. Its experiment with democracy in the early years after independence had hardly been a resounding success, and in any case it was abruptly cut short by the revolution of 1969. Despite the fact that the Qaddafi years, and particularly the early decades, were a whirlwind of political experimentation, Libyans themselves were only ever the guinea pigs. Not only were political parties barred, but there was not even space for Libyans to be active in the realm of civil society. The weight of the Jamahiriyah was such that civil society organizations, trades unions and all independent bodies were strictly off limits.

While post-conflict Libya has seen the emergence of an array of non-governmental organizations and political parties, the long years of Qaddafism have taken their toll. Among whole swathes of the population there is still a lingering suspicion of the democratic process, of political parties and of liberalism more widely. These are viewed in some quarters as foreign inventions that have little to do with the country's inherent traditions. It is as if the country has been in stasis since the days of the monarchy, suspended in a bubble and isolated from the rest of the world. This is hardly astonishing: Qaddafi's years of half-baked experimentation left a population turned in on itself. As the Colonel dragged the country to hell and back, Libyans got used to keeping their heads below the parapet. In the face of his endless efforts to force them to play a part in his perpetual revolution and to become the masses he believed he was put on the planet to lead, the people took refuge in tradition and social conservatism. Many also took refuge in Islam. Qaddafi may have been able to take everything from them, but at least their pride, their traditions and their innermost faith could not be touched by the grubby and cruel hand of the Jamahiriyah.

Therefore, while the country's new leaders have been valiantly putting in place the steps to transform what was one of the world's quirkiest states into a modern, functioning democracy, the road ahead is hard and full of obstacles. Indeed, the Colonel put Libya through such an extreme experience that it came out the other side completely ill-equipped to deal with being a modern state.

Qaddafi also left behind a country steeped in corruption. His was a regime propped up by patronage, where the elite creamed money off the state like there was no tomorrow. Despite the Colonel's repeated complaints about corruption among state officials, who, he claimed, were perverting the course of his revolution, he knew that doing anything serious to tackle the problem would risk undermining his regime. Corruption was a key component of Qaddafi's tool kit, a way to buy loyalty from the very top to the very bottom – from the country's tribal elders to the henchmen who filled his thuggish security apparatus.

For all that Libyans hoped the Colonel's demise would bring an end to such goings on, old habits die hard. The country's new leaders soon found themselves accused of the very same dubious practices that they had vowed to get rid of. If corruption had been the domain of the elite under Qaddafi, it was fast becoming the province of an ever-widening circle in the new Libya: corruption was being democratized, and it was soiling the purity of the revolution and all it had stood for.

It is perhaps unfair to pin the blame for the corruption that has already seeped into the new Libya entirely on the Colonel. Corruption seems to be the curse of developing nations – particularly those that are oil rich. (Post-Saddam Iraq has seen an explosion in corruption that makes what went on under the former regime almost pale into insignificance.) However, Qaddafi's willingness not only to buy loyalty over the decades, but also to stand by as the country was turned into what was effectively a kleptocracy, a family business *par excellence*, left Libya with a heritage of corruption that will prove difficult to shake off.

Likewise, Qaddafi cannot be saddled with all the blame for the fact that the country has fractured along regional lines. Libya is still a product of its geography and its history. However, the assertion of the local that has characterized the post-Qaddafi era so forcefully is a direct response to the gaping chasm that opened up at the centre. Qaddafi's Jamahiriyah was so overwhelmingly centralized, and his personality so all-encompassing, that when he collapsed, the entire state collapsed with him. It is hardly surprising, therefore, that local power brokers – from militia chiefs, to local councils, to tribal heads – all moved in to fill the gap, pursuing their own interests with devastating consequences. To quote W.B. Yeats: 'Things fall apart; the centre cannot hold; mere anarchy is loosed upon the world.'[1]

Anarchy was certainly one word for it. The revolutionary brigades, which had come to act like militias, took the law into their own hands. In the absence of a police force or any meaningful state security force, the young fighters who swelled their ranks, and who were part of the enormous pool of disaffected and disenfranchised youth that Qaddafi had left in his wake, began acting with almost total impunity. Locals could only look on in dismay as these militias fought it out among themselves, vying for influence and power.

Yet the emergence of this localism and regionalism had another, deeper consequence: it played directly into the hands of the country's tribes. While tribes were certainly a feature of Qaddafi's Libya, the Colonel's skill was such that he reduced them to mere social institutions, making them function as mediators and tools of social control. With the demise of the centre, the country's tribes once again began to come to the fore and to seek out a place in the country's new political tapestry. Not that this point should be overplayed: the urbanization of the past half century and more has seen a decline in the importance of the tribe. However, for all that, the post-Qaddafi era has opened up a new space for the tribes to assert themselves politically.

The post-Qaddafi era has also seen a resurgence of the old antagonisms that traditionally divided east from west. While such divisions were cast aside as the country pulled together to oust Qaddafi, they soon re-emerged as Libya sought to define its new identity. Those in the east began to accuse the NTC of marginalizing them from the country's new power structures. Whether the concerns were real or imagined, some in Benghazi – where there was a strong sense of ownership of the revolution that had started there – believed they were being excluded once again. This got to the stage where there were growing calls in the east for Libya to adopt some sort of federal system. This is hardly unexpected: decades of distrust cannot simply be washed away overnight. Indeed, the Colonel sowed such bitterness in the east that healing these wounds will take generations.

Yet these are not the only wounds that need to heal. Years of frustration and anger had also been festering against those who had acted as bulwarks of the regime – those tribes and regions that had facilitated the repression, providing willing recruits to the security agencies and revolutionary bodies. With the lid of the regime lifted, some of this rage was unleashed. The country became host to brutal revenge attacks, as militias roamed through the streets of traditionally loyalist areas, such as Bani Walid and Sirte, engaging in the most horrific purges of those they accused of being 'Qaddafi's men'. The condemned had suddenly turned into executioners and appeared to be relishing their new role. Such actions, which seemed to be aimed at whole clans of tribes or areas, left entire sections of society feeling as though they were being systematically punished for the past. Indeed, Qaddafi had tarred them so heavily with his own brush that many were left feeling as though they had no place in the new Libya.

How Libya will navigate its way through this myriad of complexities remains to be seen. What is certain, however, is that the path will be long and difficult. Getting over a leader as all-encompassing as Qaddafi is not going to be easy. While he may have resembled other dictators, the Colonel was also utterly unique. He was a ruler like no other in the contemporary era. From his outspoken and bizarre world view, to his unstinting dedication to furthering his revolution, to his boundless self-confidence and his reckless fearlessness in dragging the country through one foreign policy exploit after another, there has been no one else quite like him. He was also a man who managed to make four decades of Libya's history read like his own biography.

Yet for all his eccentricities, as well as the ridicule he often inspired, underneath the showman was a shrewd leader who knew his people well. This simple Bedouin, who had come from nothing and who was inspired by the harsh beauty of the deserts he so loved, learned quickly how to manipulate the intricacies of Libya to his advantage. His ability to do so meant that for more than forty years this 'prophet' of the Jamahiriyah held the whole country in the palm of his hand. If it had not been for the outside intervention of NATO forces, Qaddafi would most likely still be in power today, or still in control of Tripoli, at least. The Qaddafi dynasty would have lived on.

In the end, however, the Brother Leader's worst fears were realized. He was destroyed by his own, with the help of the Western powers he had spent his life railing against. When it came, the end was brutal and inglorious. He left nothing in his wake; all that he had striven for was reduced to dust, his beloved Jamahiriyah relegated to the unforgiving rubbish heap of history. Worse, for all the years he had dedicated to the cause of pan-Arabism – his ultimate dream – it was only with his death that Libya felt it could finally take its rightful place in the Arab world. It is a sad legacy for a man who genuinely believed that he had the solution not only to the problems of Libya, but to the ills of all mankind.

Never were there more apt words than those of Percy Bysshe Shelley:

> I met a traveller from an antique land
> Who said: Two vast and trunkless legs of stone
> Stand in the desert. Near them, on the sand,
> Half sunk, a shattered visage lies, whose frown,
> And wrinkled lip, and sneer of cold command,
> Tell that its sculptor well those passions read
> Which yet survive, stamped on these lifeless things,
> The hand that mocked them, and the heart that fed;
> And on the pedestal these words appear:
> 'My name is Ozymandias, king of kings:
> Look on my works, ye Mighty, and despair!'
> Nothing beside remains. Round the decay
> Of that colossal wreck, boundless and bare
> The lone and level sands stretch far away.
>
> ('Ozymandias')

Endnotes

Introduction

1. Telephone interview with Mohamed Abdelmalik, European Representative of the Libyan Muslim Brotherhood, November 2011.
2. Yossi Melman, *The Master Terrorist: The true story behind Abu Nidal*, Mama Books, New York, 1986, p. 3.
3. Dictator Chic: Colonel Qaddafi – A life in fashion', *Vanity Fair*, 12 August 2009, available at: http://www.vanityfair.com/politics/features/2009/08/qaddafi-slideshow200908#

Chapter 1: Land of the Conquered

1. Angelo Piccioli, *The Magic Gate of the Sahara*, Dar Al-Fergani, Tripoli, undated, p. 1.
2. Education Division of the Leader's Comrades Forum, *Al-Qaddafi and the 4000-Day Journey of Secret Work*, unknown publisher, Benghazi, undated, p. 82.
3. Herodotus, *The Histories*, Book Four, 174, Oxford University Press, Oxford, 2008, p. 294.
4. ibid., 187, p. 298.
5. ibid.
6. Ali Abdullatif Ahmida, *The Making of Modern Libya: State formation, colonization and resistance, 1830–1932*, State University of New York Press, New York, 1994, p. 17.
7. ibid.
8. The Ottomans seized the port from the Knights of Malta, who had been given it as a present by the Spanish, who had invaded and occupied it five years earlier. Indeed, by this time the Tripoli coast was becoming prey to the European naval powers, which were extending their reach down into the southern Mediterranean.
9. Dirk Vandewalle, *A History of Modern Libya*, Cambridge University Press, New York, 2006, p. 16.
10. In 1850 even the main population centres were very sparsely populated. Tripoli city and Misarata had 12,000 inhabitants each, and Benghazi and Derna only 5,000 (Ahmida, *The Making of Modern Libya*, p. 15).

11. Edward E. Evans-Pritchard, *The Sanusi of Cyrenaica*, Oxford University Press, Oxford, 1954, p. 4.
12. Piccioli, pp. 50–51.
13. Evans-Pritchard, p. 4.
14. ibid.
15. The Order courted the most important Bedouin sheikhs of the area in order to get their permission to build a lodge, which required a community and land that could provide food, water and transportation. These lodges were not insignificant constructions. Among other things, they had to comprise a mosque, a school, residents' quarters and lodgings for guests. In order to convince the local tribesmen to host such a *zawiya* the Sanussi ensured that, once built, every *zawiya* became the public property of the tribe. In this way the *zawiya*s became centres for tribal unity – something that fostered greater loyalty to the Order (Mohamed Yousef Al-Magarief, *Libya Bayn Al-Madi Wal-Hadir: Safahat min Al-Tarikh Al-Siyasi* [Libya Past and Present: Chapters in political history], Part 1, Volume 1, Centre for Libyan Studies, Oxford, 2004, p. 68).
16. George Joffe, 'Qadhafi's Islam in local historical perspective' in Dirk Vandewalle (ed.), *Qadhafi's Libya, 1969–1994*, St Martin's Press, New York, 1995, p. 143.
17. Lisa Anderson, 'Nineteenth-century reform in Ottoman Libya', *International Journal of Middle East Studies*, 16:3 (1984), pp. 325–48.
18. Some of the locals welcomed this new commercial presence, seeing it as a refreshing alternative to the years of Ottoman domination. This included some wealthy merchants from Tripoli's Jewish community who dominated the import-export trade with Italy and who spoke Italian, as well as rich Libyan trading families, such as the Muntasirs, from Misarata. Most, however, were less enamoured with this Italian encroachment on their territory.
19. The Italians met with greater success in Tripolitania, where there was no such organized or unified force that could repel the foreign invaders. Although there was a resistance force in Tripoli (which in 1913 comprised some 15,000 fighters), these forces were weak and undermined by factionalism among urban notables, as well as by the continued collaboration of some wealthy locals with Italian forces. The situation in the Fezzan was complicated by the presence of French troops, which had tried to expand their presence in Africa up into Borku and Tibetsi, the area that straddles Chad and Libya. Moreover, the Italians struggled against the local tribes and, despite triumphing over the main oases in the south in 1913, were pushed out by the end of the following year.
20. Vandewalle, *A History of Modern Libya*, pp. 28–29.
21. John Wright, *Libya: A modern history*, Croom Helm, London and Canberra, 1981, p. 35.
22. Ahmida, *The Making of Modern Libya*, p. 42.
23. J. Wright, p. 37.
24. Quoted in ibid., p. 38.
25. William N. Connor, *The English at War*, Secker & Warburg, London, 1941, p. 45.
26. Freya Stark, *The Coast of Incense*, John Murray, London, 1953, p. 163.
27. In 1939 there were estimated to be some 14,000 Libyan exiles in Egypt, most of them semi-nomadic, impoverished and utterly miserable, who were desperate to return to their homeland (V. Peniakoff, *Popski's Private Army*, Jonathan Cape, London, 1950, p. 26).
28. K. S. Sandford, Lord Tweedsmuir, W. B. Fisher, H. J. Fleure, L. M. Kiral, St John Cook, A. M. Frood, 'Problems of Modern Libya: Discussion', *Geographical Journal*, 119: 2 (June 1953).
29. Quoted in Al-Magarief, *Libya Bayn Al-Madi Wal-Hadir*, p. 300.
30. Nina Epton, 'Libya on the eve', *Spectator*, 13 October 1950.
31. Jane P. C. Carey and Andrew G. Carey, 'Libya: No longer "Arid Nurse of Lions"', *Political Science Quarterly*, 76:1 (March 1961).

Chapter 2: Ripe for Revolution

1. The white crescent and star design on a black background was based on the banner of the Sanussi order, while the red strip represented Fezzan and the green represented Tripolitania.
2. Mohamed Yousef Al-Magarief, *Libya Bayn Al-Madi Wal-Hadir: Safahat min Al-Tarikh Al-Siyasi* [Libya Past and Present: Chapters in political history], Part 1, Volume 1, Centre for Libyan Studies, Oxford, 2004, p. 280.
3. Jane P. C. Carey and Andrew G. Carey, 'Libya: No longer "Arid Nurse of Lions" ', *Political Science Quarterly*, 76:1 (March 1961).
4. *Al-Wasat* magazine, Issue 194, 16 October 1995.
5. Alec Kirkbride, 'Libya – which way facing?', *African Affairs*, 56:22 (1957).
6. ibid.
7. Edward E. Evans-Pritchard, *The Sanusi of Cyrenaica*, Oxford University Press, Oxford, 1954, p. 155.
8. Al-Magarief, *Libya Bayn Al-Madi Wal-Hadir*, p. 244.
9. Alison Pargeter, 'Anglo-Libyan relations and the Suez Crisis', *Journal of North African Studies*, 5:2 (Summer 2000).
10. Dirk Vandewalle, *A History of Modern Libya*, Cambridge University Press, New York, 2006, p. 50.
11. Pargeter, 'Anglo-Libyan relations and the Suez Crisis'.
12. Evans-Pritchard, p. 156.
13. Ruth First, *Libya: The elusive revolution*, Penguin Books, Harmondsworth, 1974, p. 80.
14. The National Congress had expected to secure a landslide victory in the west of the country. However, when the results were announced the government had secured forty-four out of the fifty-five seats on offer, and while the party had done well in urban constituencies in the west, it had failed to win any real support in the Tripolitanian hinterlands. While this was most likely because the party's progressive political platform went way beyond the comprehension and aspiration of most rural folk, to whom the king's more traditional style of ruling was probably far more reassuring, the party cried 'foul' and took to the streets to protest.
15. Mustafa Ahmed Ben Halim, *Libya: The years of hope*, AAS Media Publishers, London, 1995, p. 61.
16. Vandewalle, *A History of Modern Libya*, p. 63.
17. ibid., p. 72.
18. Carey and Carey.
19. John Wright, *Libya: A modern history*, Croom Helm, London and Canberra, 1981, p. 100.
20. H. M. Bulugma, *Benghazi through the Ages*, unidentified publisher, 1972, p. 69.
21. Ali Abdullatif Ahmida, *The Making of Modern Libya: State formation, colonization and resistance, 1830–1932*, State University of New York Press, New York, 1994, p. 79.
22. PREM 11/1148, Tripoli to Foreign Office, 4 August 1956.
23. FO 371/126039, Report of Meeting between King Idris and Fletcher, January 1957.
24. Department of State, Central Files, POL LIBYA-US, Memorandum of Conversation/1/ Tobruk, 30 August 1967.
25. J. Wright, p. 103.
26. M. Bianco, *Gadafi: Voice from the desert*, Longman, New York, 1975, p. 43.
27. 'Thawrt Al Fateh Kma Yaraha Mustafa Ben Halim, H10 [The Fateh Revolution as seen by Ben Halim, Part 10]', undated, available at: http://www.aljazeera.net/programs/pages/bdbbd41b-d67f-48a7-8dd6-ea659576e1e1
28. Education Division of the Leader's Comrades Forum, *Al-Qaddafi and the 4000-Day Journey of Secret Work*, unknown publisher, Benghazi, undated, p. 44.

29. Department of State, Central Files, POL LIBYA-US, Memorandum of Conversation/1/ Tobruk, 30 August 1967.
30. First, p. 102.
31. ibid.
32. Bianco, p. 50.
33. Education Division of the Leader's Comrades Forum, p. 98.
34. First, p. 102.
35. Bianco, p. 48.
36. Education Division of the Leader's Comrades Forum, p. 19.
37. ibid., p. 10.
38. ibid., p. 185.
39. David Blundy and Andrew Lycett, *Qaddafi and the Libyan Revolution*, Weidenfeld and Nicolson, London, 1987, p. 56.
40. Education Division of the Leader's Comrades Forum, p. 27.
41. ibid., p. 37.
42. ibid., p. 237.
43. Blundy and Lycett, p. 56.
44. Muammar Qaddafi, *Qassat Al-thawra fi libya ... Asa'at Al-Ikhira* [The Story of the Revolution in Libya ... The Last Hours], formerly available in Arabic at: http://www. wata.cc/forums/showthread.php?t=48343 (accessed March 2009).
45. ibid.
46. Emhamed Magrayef was a member of Qaddafi's Revolutionary Command Council.
47. Abdelfatah Younis Al-Obeidi joined the 2011 revolution soon after the uprising in Benghazi. He became head of the rebels' military forces until he was killed in July 2011 by one of the Islamist brigades, who, it is believed, objected to the role he had played in Qaddafi's regime.
48. Qaddafi, *Qassat Al-thawra fi libya ...*
49. N. J. Dawood (trans.), *The Koran*, Penguin, Harmondsworth, 1968.
50. Qaddafi, *Qassat Al-thawra fi libya ...*
51. Bianco, p. 58.
52. ibid., p. 53.
53. Ben Halim, p. 54.
54. Pargeter, 'Anglo-Libyan relations and the Suez Crisis'.
55. Bianco, pp. 65–6.

Chapter 3: The Rise of the Jamahiriyah

1. The other young revolutionaries who, along with Qaddafi, made up the RCC were: Abdelsalam Jalloud, Mustafa Kharroubi, Bashir Hawadi, Mukhtar Abdullah Qarawi, Khweildi Al-Humaidi, Mohamed Najm, Ali Awad Hamza, Abu Bakr Younis Jaber, Abdelmonem Al-Houni, Mohamed Al-Magarief and Omar Abdullah Al-Meheishi. While some of these figures were to disappear from the political scene in the first few years of the revolution, others were to play a major role at the core of Qaddafi's regime until the end.
2. M. Bianco, *Gadafi: Voice from the desert*, Longman, New York, 1975, p. 4.
3. Khalifa Mohamed Al-Tilisi, *Ma'ajam Sukan Libya* [Encyclopaedia of Libya's Population], Dar Al-Raban, Libya, 1991, p. 302.
4. David Blundy and Andrew Lycett, *Qaddafi and the Libyan Revolution*, Weidenfeld and Nicolson, London, 1987, p. 34.
5. Education Division of the Leader's Comrades Forum, *Al-Qaddafi and the 4000-Day Journey of Secret Work*, unknown publisher, Benghazi, undated, p. 80.
6. Bianco, p. 4.

7. Quoted in Dr Mohamed Al-Magarief, 'Inqilab Biqiyadat Mukbur [Coup led by an informant]', Part 12, August 2008, available in Arabic at: http://www.libya-watanona.com/adab/mugariaf/mm12088a.htm
8. ibid.
9. Bianco, p. 4.
10. ibid., p. 8.
11. Quoted in Al-Magarief, 'Inqilab Biqiyadat Mukbur'.
12. Education Division of the Leader's Comrades Forum, p. 77.
13. Blundy and Lycett, p. 43.
14. ibid., p. 44.
15. Education Division of the Leader's Comrades Forum, p. 157.
16. Blundy and Lycett, p. 45.
17. Quoted in Michael Cockerell, 'Lieutenant Gaddafi in Swinging London', *Standpoint*, January/February 2012, available at: http://www.standpointmag.co.uk/node/4254
18. Blundy and Lycett, p. 46.
19. ibid.
20. Bianco, p. 25.
21. Quoted in Ruth First, *Libya: The elusive revolution*, Penguin Books, Harmondsworth, 1974, p. 121.
22. John K. Cooley, *Libyan Sandstorm: The complete account of Qaddafi's Sandstorm*, Sidgwick and Jackson, London, 1983, p. 12.
23. Blundy and Lycett, p. 62.
24. ibid., p. 70.
25. Omar I. El Fathaly and Monte Palmer, *Political Development and Social Change in Libya*, Lexington Books, Massachusetts, 1980, p. 130.
26. More than 300 high-ranking police officers were detained, as were over 250 army officers who held the rank of major or above (John Wright, *Libya: A Modern History*, Croom Helm, London and Canberra, 1981, p. 135).
27. 'Ghassan Sherbil interviews Abdelmonem Al-Houni, Part 3', *Al-Hayat*, 25 February 2011, available at: http://international.daralhayat.com/internationalarticle/237875
28. This was formalized in a constitutional proclamation issued on 11 December 1969, which named the RCC as the highest authority in the land and that gave it sovereign power to promulgate laws and to decide the state's general policies.
29. Quoted in J. Wright, p. 148.
30. Fathi Al-Deeb, *Abdul Nasser Wal Thawrat Libya* [Abdul Nasser and the Libyan Revolution], Dar Al-Mostaqbel Al-Arabi, Cairo, 1986, p. 253.
31. 'Ghassan Sherbil interviews Abdelmonem Al-Houni, Part 4', *Al-Hayat*, 26 February 2011, available at: http://international.daralhayat.com/internationalarticle/238228
32. Al-Deeb, p. 253.
33. 'Ghassan Sherbil interviews Abdelmonem Al-Houni, Part 2', *Al-Hayat*, 24 February 2011, available at: http://international.daralhayat.com/internationalarticle/237570
34. ibid.
35. Al-Deeb.
36. ibid.
37. First, p. 137.
38. Bianco, p. 91–92.
39. Al-Houni interview, Part 4.
40. ibid.
41. ibid.
42. Blundy and Lycett, p. 85.
43. ibid., p. 86.
44. J. Wright, p. 180.

45. Dirk Vandewalle, *A History of Modern Libya*, Cambridge University Press, New York, 2006, p. 85.
46. El Fathaly and Palmer, p. 122.
47. Mohamed Al-Magarief, 'Safahat min Tariq al-nidham al-inquilabi fi Libya [Pages from the History of the Coup Regime in Libya]', Libya Watanona Website, undated, available at: http://www.libya-watanona.com/adab/mugariaf/mm121010a.htm
48. Bianco, p. 112.
49. Blundy and Lycett, p. 86.
50. ibid., p. 87.
51. Interview with Libyan intellectual, London, June 2011.
52. Blundy and Lycett, p. 92.
53. Bianco, p. 114.
54. Blundy and Lycett, p. 95.
55. In July 1973, for example, the regime held a two-week conference for 350 Muslims from 103 countries, many of whom were left far from convinced by the Leader's thinking.
56. Blundy and Lycett, pp. 93–94.
57. Al-Magarief, 'Safahat min Tariq al-nidham al-inquilabi fi Libya'.
58. Deborah Davis (Linda Berg) with Bill Davis, *The Children of God: The inside story by the daughter of the founder, Moses David Berg*, Part 1, Chapter 9, 1984, available at: http://www.exfamily.org/art/exmem/debdavis/debdavis09.shtml
59. Al-Magarief, 'Safahat min Tariq al-nidham al-inquilabi fi Libya'.
60. ibid.
61. The Children of God were known for trying to lure men into conversion through what Moses David called 'flirty fishing', namely seduction by the group's young female members.
62. Davis.
63. Al-Magarief, 'Safahat min Tariq al-nidham al-inquilabi fi Libya'.
64. 'Gheddafi told Oriana "You massacre us" ', *Corriere della Sera*, 23 February 2011, available at: http://www.corriere.it/International/english/articoli/2011/02/23/oriana-fallaci-interview-gheddafi-1979.shtml
65. ibid.
66. Rajab Bou Debous commenting on Dr Mahadi Imberish's lecture, posted by Il Politico Libico, 25 January 2011, available at http://lyrcc.wordpress.com/2011/01/25/article-260/
67. Muammar Al-Qaddafi, *The Green Book*, World Centre for the Study and Research of the Green Book, Tripoli, 1984.
68. ibid.
69. ibid.
70. ibid.
71. ibid.
72. Muammar Gadaffi, *Escape to Hell and Other Stories*, Blake, London, 1999, p. 24.
73. ibid., p. 27.
74. The Belgians were totally bemused in April 2004, for example, when, on his historic trip to Europe following Libya's re-emergence from isolation, Qaddafi chose to erect his massive tent in the grounds of the Val Duchesse residence for visiting heads of state. Similarly, the tent caused major controversy during Qaddafi's September 2009 visit to New York, where he was attending a meeting of the United Nations. The Colonel first asked to pitch his tent in the five-acre estate that belongs to Libya in Englewood, New Jersey, but his request was turned down. He then asked to erect it in Manhattan's Central Park, something that was also denied him. He got as far as having one erected at a property belonging to US tycoon Donald Trump in a New York suburb, but had to take it down at the last minute, reportedly under pressure from Trump himself.

75. Al-Magarief, 'Safahat min Tariq al-nidham al-inquilabi fi Libya'.
76. ibid.

Chapter 4: Jamahiriyah in Practice:
A Revolutionary Decade

1. Those members of the now-moribund RCC who were still by Qaddafi's side – Abdelsalam Jalloud, Abu Bakr Younis Jaber, Khweildi Al-Humaidi and Mustafa Kharroubi – were also appointed to this body.
2. Hanspeter Mattes, 'The rise and fall of the revolutionary committees' in Dirk Wandewalle (ed.), *Qadhafi's Libya, 1969–1994*, St Martin's Press, New York, 1995, p. 91.
3. A report issued by the Accounts Office for the period 1973–76 greatly embarrassed Qaddafi, as it revealed not only the chaos that had been engendered by the economic policies of the early years, but also the widespread administrative and financial corruption that had taken hold.
4. Mohamed Al-Magarief, 'Al-Qaddafi Wal Lijan Al-Thawria ... Al-Asl Wa Sura [Qaddafi and the Revolutionary Committees ... Their Origin and their Image]', Libya Watanona Website, undated, available at http://www.libya-watanona.com/adab/mugariaf/mm210210a.htm
5. ibid.
6. By 1981 he had placed his cousin Sayyid Qaddaf Al-Dam as military commander in Tripoli, his brother-in-law Masoud Abdel Hafiz as military commander in Sebha in the south (a position he retained until the fall of the regime), and his cousin Hassan Ishkal as military commander in Benghazi (Claudia Wright, 'Libya's foreign strategy', *New Statesman*, 21 August 1981).
7. In April 1976, the Colonel went to Gar Younis University in Benghazi and announced that revolutionary committees would be set up in every college. In November 1977, the first revolutionary committee in Tripoli University was announced.
8. Mattes, p. 93.
9. ibid., p. 97.
10. Other figures included Ali Gaylani Qaddafi, and Ibrahim Abdelsalam Qaddafi.
11. David Blundy and Andrew Lycett, *Qaddafi and the Libyan Revolution*, Weidenfeld and Nicolson, London, 1987, p. 127.
12. 'Opinions are how the Colonel sees them', *Al-Majalla*, 17 June 2011, available at: http://www.majalla.com/ar/political_essay/article456457.ece?service=print
13. Bint Al-Mukhtar, 'Awraq Fatat Libeeya, 1 [Journal of a Libyan girl, 1]', 25 May 2010, Libyan Documentation Centre, available at: http://www.libya-watanona.com/news/ldc/ld250510a.htm
14. Bint Al-Mukhtar, 'Awraq Fatat Libeeya, 4 [Journal of a Libyan girl, 4]', 10 July 2010, Libyan Documentation Centre, available at: http://www.libya-watanona.com/news/ldc/ld110710a.htm
15. M. Z. Mogherbi, *Itijihad wa tatourat turkeybat an noghra al-siasiya fi Libya 1969–1999* [The Orientation and Development of the Political Elite in Libya 1969–1999], Gar Younis University, undated.
16. Bint Al-Mukhtar, 'Awraq Fatat Libeeya, 2 [Journal of a Libyan girl, 2]', 3 June 2010, Libyan Documentation Centre, available at: http://www.libya-watanona.com/news/ldc/ld030610a.htm
17. Footage of this trial is available at http://blog.witness.org/2011/08/execution-footage-found-in-libya-offers-glimpse-of-gaddafis-abuses-could-be-used-for-justice/
18. Al-Magarief, 'Al-Qaddafi Wal Lijan Al-Thawria ...'
19. Blundy and Lycett, p. 135.

20. Ali Al-Fazzan, 'Qaddafi ... Wa Alkhiar Shemshoni, 2 [Qaddafi and Samson Choice, 2]', available at: http://www.libya-watanona.com/adab/aalfazzani/af110310a.htm
21. ibid.
22. Blundy and Lycett, p. 138.
23. 'Interview with Musa Kusa', *The Times*, 11 June 1980.
24. Blundy and Lycett, p. 139.
25. Al-Magarief, 'Al-Qaddafi Wal Lijan Al-Thawria ...'
26. Mogherbi, *Itijihad wa tatourat turkeybat an noghra al-siasiya fi Libya*.
27. Al-Mukhtar, 'Awraq Fatat Libeeya, 4'.
28. Quoted in Lisa Anderson, 'Qadhafi and his opposition', *Middle East Journal*, 40:2 (Spring 1986).
29. ibid.
30. Sanussi Besikari, 'Khazkhaza Alqat Ala'am [Privatization of the public sector]', *Iqlam Online*, November–December 2006, available at: http://www.mafhoum.com/press10/291E14.htm
31. Anderson, 'Qadhafi and his opposition'.
32. Dirk Vandewalle, *Libya since Independence: Oil and state building*, I.B. Tauris, London, 1998, p. 112.
33. Anderson, 'Qadhafi and his opposition'.
34. Al-Fazzan, 'Qaddafi ... Wa Alkhiar Shemshoni, 2'.
35. *Middle East Economic Survey (MEES)*, 14 April 1985.
36. John Wright, *Libya: A modern history*, Croom Helm, London and Canberra, 1981, p. 202.
37. ibid., p. 201.
38. Women were not to be left out of this mass mobilization. Women were already involved in the Revolutionary Committees Movement and the Leader wanted them to play their part in defending the people's authority. In February 1979, Qaddafi set up a women's military college and, in the same year, opened a female military secondary school in Benghazi. In 1980, he set up the female revolutionary guards, often referred to as the Revolutionary Nuns, whom (famously) he came to rely upon as his bodyguards. Qaddafi once said of these women: 'If there is anyone who will enter paradise without being judged it will be the Muslim nun. Revolutionary nuns don't think of marriage, gold or silver. Rather they think of performing a historical task.' While Qaddafi may have revelled in his progressive take on women's role in society, the concept of revolutionary nuns did not go down well with much of Libyan society, which remained largely conservative. In her memoirs, one Libyan woman rather unkindly recounts: 'The girls who joined the military college were not from respected families. Rather they had no families or they were from revolutionary families. Most were ugly and they looked more like men than women' (Al-Mukhtar, 'Awraq Fatat Libeeya'). While this is a somewhat unfair assessment of the women who signed up for these colleges, it is reflective of how some of the more conservative parts of society viewed the women who joined these institutions.
39. For an excellent and comprehensive analysis of Libya's oil policy, see Vandewalle, *Libya since Independence*.
40. Ronald Bruce St John, *Libya and the United States: Two centuries of strife*, University of Pennsylvania Press, Philadelphia, 2002, p. 122.
41. From 1977 to 1978, for example, there were three separate ministries dealing with the economy: the Secretariat of Commerce, the Secretariat for the Budget and the Secretariat of Planning. From 1979 to 1981, the Secretariat for the Budget was changed to the Secretariat of Economy. From 1982 to 1984, the Secretariat of Economy was integrated with Light Industry. In 1985, planning and economy were amalgamated into one secretariat and a Secretariat for the Budget was established once again. Then, from 1986 to 1989, there were three separate secretariats again, one for economy and commerce, another for planning and a third for the budget (Mogherbi, *Itijihad wa*

tatourat turkeybat an noghra al-siasiya fi Libya). Although one could excuse these disruptions as the teething troubles of a new regime, these kinds of arbitrary changes characterized the administration throughout the following decades. Secretariats were set up, amalgamated and dissolved at whim, keeping the country's administration in a state of perpetual chaos.

42. Mogherbi, *Itijihad wa tatourat turkeybat an noghra al-siasiya fi Libya*.
43. Vandewalle, *Libya since Independence*, p. 107.
44. He once declared: 'I hold the Sharia for a positive law in the same way that I hold Roman law, the Napoleonic Code, and all the laws elaborated by lawyers in France, Italy, England and Muslim countries' (quoted in Francois Burget and William Dowell, *The Islamic Movement in North Africa*, Center for Middle Eastern Studies, University of Texas, Austin, 1983, p. 157).
45. 'Qaddafi Musaylimah Al-Aser [Qaddafi is the false prophet of this age]', no author, no date, available at: http://www.tawhed.ws/r1?i=3911&x=5n2xksni
46. Burget and Dowell, p. 155.
47. 'Communiqué from Hizb ut-Tahrir to Colonel Gadaffi', 9 September 1978, available at: http://www.khilafah.com/images/images/PDF/Books/gadaffi_extract.pdf
48. 'Qaddafi Musaylimah Al-Aser'.
49. YouTube clip of Al-Bishti interrogation, available at: http://www.youtube.com/watch?v=8teYuUEUAYc
50. Fathi Al-Fadhli, 'Harkat Masjid Alkasser, 2 [Movement of Alkasser Mosque, 2]', undated, available at: http://www.libya-nclo.com

Chapter 5: Foreign Adventurism

1. 'Ghassan Sherbil interviews Abdelsalam Jalloud, Part 1', *Al-Hayat*, 29 October 2011, available at: http://international.daralhayat.com/internationalarticle/323352
2. John Wright, *Libya: A modern history*, Croom Helm, London and Canberra, 1981, p. 158.
3. Mohamed Al-Magarief, 'Safahat min Tariq al-nidham al-inquilabi fi Libya [Pages from the history of the coup regime in Libya', Libya Watanona Website, undated, available at: http://www.libya-watanona.com/adab/mugariaf/mm121010a.htm
4. J. Wright, p. 165.
5. Needless to say, the uprising was not a success. France immediately jumped to the defence of her Mediterranean ally, sending military transport planes and helicopters to Tunisia, as well as stationing three warships in the Gulf of Gabès, as a warning to the Libyans. With the world in the grip of the Cold War, the US also sent military assistance to help staunchly Western-oriented Tunisia defend its border with Libya.
6. 'Ghassan Sherbil interviews Abdelmonem al-Houni, Part 4', *Al-Hayat*, 26 February 2011, available at: http://international.daralhayat.com/internationalarticle/238228
7. Jalloud interview, Part 1.
8. *Der Spiegel*, 17 December 1979.
9. Quoted in Ronald Bruce St John, *Libya and the United States: Two centuries of strife*, University of Pennsylvania Press, Philadelphia, 2002, p. 112.
10. J. Wright, p. 217.
11. ibid., p. 166.
12. ibid.
13. Ivan George Smith, *The Ghosts of Kampala: The rise and fall of Idi Amin*, Weidenfeld and Nicolson, London, 1980, p. 8.
14. Brian Titley, *Dark Age: The political odyssey of Emperor Bokassa*, McGill-Queen's University Press, Montreal, 2002, p. 129.
15. Jalloud interview, Part 1.

16. From 1973 the area was effectively run by a Libyan administration. The Libyan government began issuing identity cards and official Libyan family books, official documents containing details of one's personal details, to all the inhabitants of the strip, who were made part of the Merzaq People's Congress in the south.

17. Fathi Al-Fadhli, *A Book of the Chad War … Disaster … Disaster*, available in Arabic at: http://www.fathifadhli.com/art81.htm

18. ibid.

19. ibid.

20. David Blundy and Andrew Lycett, *Qaddafi and the Libyan Revolution*, Weidenfeld and Nicolson, London, 1987, p. 183.

21. ibid., p. 183.

22. J. Wright, p. 215.

23. St John, p. 110.

24. ibid., p. 122.

25. Qaddafi had always claimed that Libya had sovereignty over the entire bay of the Gulf of Sirte; the US challenged these claims and, in what Qaddafi deemed to be a gross act of provocation, its Mediterranean-based Sixth Fleet had taken to conducting air and naval exercises in the waters. This was too much for the proud Colonel, and he retaliated by sending Libyan fighter jets to try to intercept the US aircraft, some of them flying dangerously close to the American planes.

26. St John, p. 134.

27. ibid., p. 135.

28. 'US raid haunts Libya', *MERIP Middle East Report*, 141 (July–August 1986).

29. 'Ibn Al-Kaid Libyee yenshur majallat siasiya, yetahadith aan hayat [Libyan leader's son to publish political magazine, speaks about his life]', *Al-Sharq Al-Awsat*, 16 July 2002.

30. 'US raid haunts Libya'.

31. 'A week after raid: Qaddafi seems firmly in control', *New York Times*, 23 April 1986.

32. *Al-Hayat*, 31 October 2011, available at: http://international.daralhayat.com/internationalarticle/324036

33. Quoted in Blundy and Lycett, p. 214.

34. 'Speech to the Libyan General People's Congress', Tripoli TV, 2 March 1987.

Chapter 6: Jamahiriyah in Crisis

1. 'Ghassan Sherbil interviews Abdelsalam Jalloud, Part 3', *Al-Hayat*, 31 October 2011, available at: http://international.daralhayat.com/internationalarticle/324036

2. ibid.

3. Figures from InflationData.com. In March 1987, the outgoing secretary of the General People's Committee, Jadallah Azzuz Al-Talhi, acknowledged 'the circumstances resulting from the collapse in oil prices incomes necessary for financing the budgets adopted by the Basic People's Congresses for 1986 fell by the very large proportion of almost 40%. This resulted in real difficulties in facing up to the requirements of various budget expenditures' (Tripoli TV, 1 March 1987).

4. Dirk Vandewalle, *A History of Modern Libya*, Cambridge University Press, New York, 2006, p. 154.

5. 'US raid haunts Libya', *MERIP Middle East Report*, 141 (July–August 1986).

6. Dirk Vandewalle, *Libya since Independence: Oil and state building*, I.B. Tauris, London, 1998, p. 145.

7. David Hirst, 'Last days of the prophet', *Guardian*, 24 February 1992.

8. 'Qadhafi interviewed on release of prisoners and role of revolutionary committees', Tripoli TV, 3 May 1988 (BBC Monitoring Summary of World Broadcasts [henceforth SWB] ME/0144/A/1).

9. Interview with Mohamed Belqassim Zwai, London, 2004.
10. David Hirst, 'Dramatic gestures in Libya', *Guardian*, 10 July 1988.
11. ibid.
12. 'Speech on improving the Libyan economy', Tripoli TV, 26 March 1987 (SWB ME/8528/i).
13. The Colonel also took steps to shake up light industry, a sector he acknowledged was failing miserably, with production levels in decline or virtually non-existent. He concluded that the reason for this failure was that, while the factories were in public ownership, the workers were still effectively wage-workers and therefore not interested in production. Characteristically laying the blame for these failings on the people's inability to implement the Jamahiriyah properly, he bemoaned: 'Some [workers] pretend to be ill, others sign in and then leave; this proves that the system of partnership is not implemented and you are not capable of implementing it because you do not believe in it and have not got sufficient courage to take part in such an experiment' (ibid.). Qaddafi's solution was for factories to operate entirely outside the state sector: they would be handed over directly to the workers, who would share the profits between them. Within one year, some 140 medium and small-scale enterprises had been handed over to workers' management committees and no longer received state subsidies (Vandewalle, *Libya since Independence*, p. 152).
14. 'Speech on improving the Libyan economy'.
15. Qaddafi furthered these economic reforms in the early 1990s, introducing other measures to encourage the private market and foreign investment. In September 1992, a law was introduced that allowed for the establishment of more private companies and specifying that they could have access to credit from state and commercial banks, the latter of which were established in 1993.
16. 'Libyan leader addresses Revolutionary Committees' Movement on anniversary of the Great Fateh Revolution', Tripoli TV, 29 August 1988 (SWB ME/0244/A/3).
17. Vandewalle, *Libya since Independence*, p. 155.
18. 'Qaddafi scoffs at demands for bombing suspects', *New York Times*, 29 November 1991.
19. ibid.
20. See for example Jim Swire's website http://www.lockerbietruth.com/; and John Ashton and Ian Ferguson, *Cover-up of Convenience: The hidden scandal of Lockerbie*, Mainstream Publishing, Edinburgh, 2001. It has also been pointed out that it was highly convenient for the US and Britain to switch their attentions to Libya at this time, as they were trying to court both Syria and Iran for their support against Iraqi leader Saddam Hussein in the Gulf war of 1990–91.
21. 'Ghassan Sherbil interviews Abdelrahman Shalgam, part 3', *Al-Hayat*, 18 July 2011, available at: http://international.daralhayat.com/portalarticlendah/289104
22. 'US hunts Gaddafi – Libya PM', *Herald Sun*, 28 November 1991.
23. 'Qadhafi's address to Libyan General People's Congress', Libyan TV, 2 March 1992 (SWB ME/1319/i).
24. ibid.
25. For a full account of the twists and turns of Libyan diplomacy over the Lockerbie affair, see Tim Niblock, *'Pariah States' and Sanctions in the Middle East*, Lynne Rienner, London, 2001.
26. In an even more desperate gesture, in 1993 he sent a group of Libyan pilgrims to Jerusalem, in the hopes that this would soften the US stance. However, this gesture was deemed bizarre (to say the very least) by the Americans, who were not impressed when the pilgrims began shouting slogans calling on all Muslims to liberate Jerusalem in order for it to become the capital of the Palestinian state.
27. Niblock, p. 64.
28. ibid., p. 65.

29. 'Speech by Qadhafi to Awlad Abu Sayf meeting', Libyan TV, 21 September 1993 (SWB ME/1802/MED).
30. 'Libyan Television broadcasts further "confessions of spies"', Libyan TV, 9 March 1994, (SWB ME/1943/MED/12[23]).
31. Interview with Ashur Shamis, Libyan writer and commentator, UK, August 2011.
32. 'Amnesty International Report 1996 – Libya', available at: http://www.unhcr.org/refworld/publisher,AMNESTY,,LBY,3ae6aa0654,0.html
33. Faraj Boualesha, 'Alla kableen wajah ween [To the tribalists and regionalists]', undated, available at: http://www.libyanfsl.com/%D9%85%D9%82%D8%A7%D9%84%D8%A7%D8%AA/tabid/59/newsid417/3179/mid/417/language/en-US/Default.aspx
34. ibid.
35. 'Qadhafi on danger of foreign intervention, role of Social People's Commands', Libyan TV, 14 September 1994 (SWB ME/2103/MED).
36. 'Qadhafi addresses Zintan tribes: traitors must be eliminated', Libyan TV, 3 August 1994 (SWB ME/2067/MED).
37. Interview with former Libyan militant, London, 2008.
38. Interview with Noman Ben Otman, former member of the LIFG, London, January 2006.
39. Qaddafi launched many tirades against the *hijab*. On 8 December 1988, for example, in a speech before the Tunisian parliament, he provocatively declared: 'Eve wore no clothes at all. Do you understand more than God? Our God created her in that way right from the beginning. This is nature. If it wasn't for the devil there wouldn't be any fig leaf ... The hijab is the act of the devil because the hijab is an expression of the fig leaf. The fig leaf is the devil's act so that instead of becoming emancipated and forging ahead, women wear hijabs and sit at home' (http://www.tawhed.ws/r1?i=3911&x=5n2xksni).
40. Interview with former Libyan militant, London, 2008.
41. Although Islamist sources claim that the Ajdabia cell, the first to be uncovered, was discovered while its members were practising rifle shooting on a farm, Qaddafi described their unearthing as follows: 'In the past months some individuals came and said we saw a group of people whom we suspected. If someone approaches them, they open fire on him. Where? They said south of Ajdabiya. They have a car, they dug a hole. Anyone who passes by or searches ... they open fire on him ... Some security men went to them and said "Peace be upon you" and hardly had they finished saying this than fire was opened on them and it killed them. Another group came and encircled them. They exchanged fire. Some died and those remaining were arrested' ('Qadhafi's address to General People's Congress', Libyan TV, 7 October 1989 (SWB ME/0583/A/10)).
42. Interview with senior LIFG leader, Tripoli, June 2010.
43. 'Qadhafi's address to General People's Congress', 7 October 1989.
44. ibid.
45. Muammar Al-Qaddafi, 'A prayer for last Friday', in *The Village ... The Village ... The Earth ... The Earth and the Suicide of the Astronaut*, Ad-Dar Jamahiriya, Sirte, 1996.
46. Interview with Noman Ben Otman, former member of the LIFG, London, January 2006.
47. Interview by author with Noman Ben Otman, former member of the LIFG, London, January 2006.
48. For a more detailed account of the history of the Muslim Brotherhood in Libya, see Alison Pargeter, 'Libya and the Islamist opposition' in Dirk Vandewalle, *Libya Since 1969: Libya's revolution revisited*, Palgrave Macmillan, Basingstoke, 2008.
49. 'General People's Congress passes resolution on "collective punishment" ', Libyan TV, 9 March 1997 (SWB ME/D2866/MED).
50. Milton Vorst, 'The colonel in his labyrinth', *Foreign Affairs*, March/April (1999).
51. Niblock, p. 68.

52. Moncef Mahroug, 'La vie au temps de l'embargo', *Jeune Afrique*, 1840 (10–16 April 1996).
53. In 1997, monthly rations for an average family included a sack of sugar, a tin of vegetable oil, tea, milk, cheese, rice, soap and baby milk (Niblock, p. 76).
54. Mahroug.
55. Niblock, p. 78.
56. ibid., p. 34.
57. The number of pupils enrolled in secondary education in 1990/91 stood at 113,683, but by 1995/96 this had risen to 251,275 (Niblock, p. 79).
58. 'Qadhafi on oil wealth, defence, "cleanup committees", trade', Libyan TV, 29 December 1996 (SWB ME/2806/MED/12).
59. Saad Al-Bazzaz, ' "Take 20 sheep and shut up" – why Libyans are not impressed', *Mideast Mirror*, 7 March 1997.
60. 'Sanctions keep West off the road to Libya', *New York Times*, 28 June 1992.
61. Middle East Economic Digest (MEED), *Maghreb Quarterly Report*, 18 (June 1995), Part 2 of 4.

Chapter 7: The Chimera of Reform

1. With the sanctions in force, Libya found itself unable to keep up with the advances being made in oil technology. To make matters worse, the regime ignored maintenance, focusing its energies on trying to extract as much oil as possible to ensure that production did not flag. Exploration also suffered. Thus, while oil production was maintained, the country's energy infrastructure was gradually eroded and new discoveries were stymied by the lack of exploration.
2. They also proposed that, if found guilty, the men would serve their sentences in Scotland; if acquitted, they would not face any other charges arising from evidence revealed during the trial.
3. Yahia H. Zoubir, 'Libya in US foreign policy: From rogue state to good fellow?', *Third World Quarterly*, 23:1 (2002).
4. It also sought to satisfy the demands of the British victims' families, who, unlike the US families, were more willing to countenance the idea of a trial being held in a third country.
5. It has been said that Libya had little choice but to accept. US Secretary of State Madeleine Albright had made it clear that if Qaddafi did not accept the offer, the Clinton administration would push for additional sanctions on Libya, including an oil embargo. However, given the similarity of this proposal to the one put forward by Libya in 1994, it seems that Qaddafi would probably have accepted without the additional US pressure.
6. Tim Niblock, *'Pariah States' and Sanctions in the Middle East*, Lynne Rienner, London, 2001, p. 54.
7. The British also gave guarantees that the prisoners would not be interrogated by British security or police forces, nor by the forces of any other nation; that the prison would be open to inspection by international bodies and by Libyan diplomatic officials; that a Libyan consulate would be opened in Scotland to attend to the men's needs and those of their families; that the prisoners would be treated humanely; and, crucially, that they would not be extradited to the United States (Niblock, p. 57).
8. In January 1999, under the auspices of the UN, Mandela sent a delegation to Tripoli, along with Prince Bandar Bin Sultan of Saudi Arabia, which sought to reassure Qaddafi and to convince him to accept the American and British proposal.
9. Professor Robert Black, for example, who had first proposed the idea of a third-country trial, had argued that the case against the two defendants was based entirely on circumstantial evidence, and therefore convictions would be difficult to obtain (Menas Associates, *Focus on Libya*, February 2001).

10. ibid.
11. ibid.
12. 'Ghassan Sherbil interviews Abdelrahman Shalgam, Part 3', *Al-Hayat*, 18 July 2011, available at: http://international.daralhayat.com/portalarticlendah/289104
13. 'Libyan PM denies Lockerbie guilt', BBC News Online, 24 February 2004, available at: http://news.bbc.co.uk/1/hi/scotland/3515951.stm
14. Wyn Q. Bowen, *Libya and Nuclear Proliferation: Stepping back from the brink*, Adelphi Paper 380, Routledge, London, 2006, p. 26.
15. ibid., p. 60.
16. 'Brother Leader of the Revolution Moammar Ghadhafi presents an analysis about the actual crisis the world is passing through about terrorism', undated, formerly available at: http://www.algathafi.org/terrorism/terrorism.htm
17. Dirk Vandewalle, *A History of Modern Libya*, Cambridge University Press, New York, 2006, p. 180.
18. Shalgam interview, Part 3.
19. In fact, the Libyans had shown a potential willingness to engage over their WMD programmes as early as 1992, when they tried to reach out to the US to restore relations. This is hardly surprising. While the Libyans had succeeded in acquiring the equipment for a nuclear weapon, they were far from being in a position to actually build one. They were thus prepared to use their WMD programmes as a bargaining chip in their bid to get sanctions removed. However, the regime's approaches were rebuffed by the US, which wanted Tripoli to comply with UN resolutions before it engaged in dialogue.
20. Bruce St John, 'Libya is not Iraq: Preemptive strikes, WMD and diplomacy', *Middle East Journal*, 53:3 (Summer 2004), p. 394.
21. Bowen, p. 62.
22. Shalgam interview, Part 3.
23. The Libyans agreed to: Eliminate all elements of its chemical and nuclear weapons programs; Declare all nuclear activities to the International Atomic Energy Agency(IAEA); Eliminate ballistic missiles beyond a 300-kilometer (km) range with a payload of 500 kgs; Accept international inspections to ensure Libya's complete adherence to the Nuclear Nonproliferation Treaty (NPT), and sign the Additional Protocol; Eliminate all chemical weapons stocks and munitions and accede to the Chemical Weapons Convention (CWC); and Allow immediate inspections and monitoring to verify all of these actions. (The White House, Fact Sheet: The President's National Security Strategy to Combat WMD, Libya's Announcement, December 19, 2003).
24. Quoted in St John, p. 399.
25. 'Libya decided 10 years ago against developing WMD, Foreign Minister says', *Independent on Sunday*, 11 February 2004.
26. Shalgam interview, Part 3.
27. Thomas Omestad, 'Follow the Leader', *US News and World Report*, 7 June 2004.
28. Shalgam interview, Part 3.
29. 'Gaddafi invents "rocket car" ', BBC News Online, 6 September 1999, available at: http://news.bbc.co.uk/2/hi/middle_east/440161.stm
30. The General People's Committee returned shortly afterwards and continued its functions, although with fewer ministries.
31. Menas Associates, *Focus on Libya*, June 2001.
32. Menas Associates, *Focus on Libya*, March 2000.
33. Libya News and Views website, September 1999, available at: http://www.libyanet.com/9-99nwsc.htm
34. 'Libya – Moammar Mohammed Abdel Salam Abu Minyar Al Qadhafi', 29 July 2002, available at: http://www.allbusiness.com/periodicals/article/222869-1.html. At this conference Libya announced an economic development plan for 2000/01 to 2005/06 which would govern the expenditure of US$35 billion of investment in new assets. Some 30–40 per cent of this would, it hoped, come through direct private investment.

The regime made it clear that its priorities were in modernizing the telecoms and transport sectors and in power generation.

35. 'Libya – the economic base', *APS Review Downstream Trends*, 2 July 2007, available at: http://goliath.ecnext.com/coms2/gi_0199-6692384/LIBYA-The-Economic-Base.html
36. Dirk Vandewalle, 'The institutional restraints of reform in Libya: From Jamahiriyah to constitutional republic?', paper prepared for the Oxford Conference, 25–27 September 2009.
37. Quoted in Vandewalle, *A History of Modern Libya*, p. 189.
38. M. Z. Mogherbi, *Itijihad wa tatourat turkeybat an noghra al-siasiya fi Libya 1969–1999* [The Orientation and Development of the Political Elite in Libya], Gar Younis University, undated.
39. Figures taken from the Libyan National Office of Statistics.
40. 'Lika'at al-Doctor Shukri Ghanem Interviews: Dr Shukri Ghanem', *Libya Today*, 20 September 2005, formerly available at: www.libya-today.com (accessed 2005).
41. Illustrative of these pressures was the fact that, in the mid-2000s, some half a million state employees were drafted into the National Centre for Qualifications and Professional Development, which was supposed to retrain and redraft them into private sector jobs. However, as these private sector jobs failed to materialize, the state was forced to continue paying salaries to these individuals while they were not working. In fact, some continued to take their salaries from the state but spent their time working in the unofficial economy. As a result, the regime decided to return these employees to the public sector – something that necessitated the state's having to increase its 2009 wage bill by 14 per cent.
42. 'Al-Juz al-thani min mudakhalat Dr Shukri Ghanem howlalaotha al-iktisadiawalhayatia fi Libya[The second part of Dr Shukri Ghanem's response regarding the situation of living conditions in Libya]', General People's Committee Website, 4 March 2006, formerly available at: www.gpc.gov.ly (accessed 2006).
43. Interview with Abdullah Al-Badri, Head of NOC, Tripoli, June 2005.
44. Although private banks had been allowed to operate since the 1990s, the Central Bank continued to maintain a 50 per cent share in the privatized banks, ensuring that it could put a brake on any attempts by the private ventures to overstep the mark. In March 2005, the sector was opened up significantly, when a new banking law was passed, permitting foreign banks to open branches or offices in Libya. Three months later, plans to restructure and privatize five state banks were announced, with the promise that foreign banks would be able to buy shares in two of them. In 2007, these promises were realized, when BNP Paribas acquired a 19 per cent stake in Sahara Bank, the second largest commercial bank in the country, with the option to purchase up to 51 per cent by 2012. Early the following year, the Jordanian Arab Bank acquired a 19 per cent stake in Wahda Bank (with the same option to purchase up to 51 per cent at a later date). Yet despite this progress, the restructuring of the banking sector remained beset with difficulties, and Libya stayed largely a cash economy with an archaic banking system focused on trade financing (European Commission DG Trade, *Trade Sustainability Impact Assessment (SIA) of the EU-Libya Free Trade Agreement. Inception Report*, February 2009, available at: http://trade.ec.europa.eu/doclib/docs/2009/april/tradoc_142928.pdf).
45. 'Libya Al-Youmfi hewarkhassma'a Al-Doctour Fathi al-Ba'aja [Libya al-Youm has special interview with Dr Fathi al-Ba'aja]', 19 August 2007, formerly available in Arabic at: http://www.libya-alyoum.com/look/article.tpl?IdLanguage=17&IdPublication=1&NrArticle=9994&NrIssue=1&NrSection=14 (accessed 2007).
46. Interviews by author with Libyans in Tripoli between 2003 and 2010.
47. 'Ibn Al-Kaid Libyee yenshur majallat siasiya yetahadith aan hayat [Libyan leader's son to publish political magazine, speaks about his life]', *Al-Sharq Al-Awsat*, 16 July 2002.

48. Witness statement in the High Court of Justice, Queen's Bench Division, between Saif Al-Islam Gaddafi (Claimant) and Telegraph Group Ltd., available at: http://www. libya-watanona.com/news/n21aug2a.htm

49. In January 2006, the charity changed its name to the Gaddafi International Foundation for Development. The charities that came under this umbrella included the Fighting Drug Addiction Society, the Land Mine Fighting Society, the Underprivileged Society, the Human Rights Society and the Martyrs Society.

50. 'Interview with Saif al-Islam Gaddafi', London, November 2002, available to purchase from World Investment News at: http://www.winne.com/mena/libya/report/2004/to01inter.php

51. 'The good bad son', *New York Magazine*, 22 May 2011.

52. A number of victims came forward to register their complaints, yet not one case was followed up and no one was brought to justice. Interview with the head of the Libyan Human Rights Association, Tripoli, May 2005.

53. Ashur Shamis, 'Gaddafi and me', *Critical Muslim*, 1 (2011).

54. Al-Jahemi was released from prison in March 2004, having served time for publicly calling for a constitution, free speech and democracy, but he was re-arrested just weeks later after he conducted a telephone interview with the international media in which he called for democracy. Despite being the subject of major international human rights campaigns, Al-Jahemi remained in detention until he was transferred to Jordan in May 2009 on account of his seriously deteriorating health. He died there shortly afterwards. Similarly, Dr Idris Abufayed, a former exile who returned to the country from Europe was arrested in 2007 after he tried to organize a peaceful demonstration in Green Square in Tripoli. In June 2008, Dr Abufayed and a group of others who were arrested with him were given harsh prison terms, having been convicted on vague charges ranging from 'attempting to overthrow the political system' to 'spreading false rumours about the Libyan regime'.

55. Nowhere was this truer than for the families of the victims of the Abu Slim massacre. This atrocity had always been buried deep by the regime; Saif Al-Islam began talking publicly about the need to open the file. Heartened by his support, the families gathered the courage to start demanding that the security services provide them with details about how their loved ones had died. They even took to holding regular protests in Benghazi – something that would have been unthinkable in an earlier time.

56. It is noteworthy that the prisoners were not cleared of their crimes, having had their convictions upheld by the Supreme Court at the beginning of 2006. Rather their release was an 'act of clemency' on the part of the regime. They were also freed as individuals rather than as a group, effectively neutralizing the movement, which remained banned; and they were only given their freedom after they agreed not to engage in any political activity outside the framework of the Jamahiriyah.

57. Belhaj went on to head the Tripoli Revolutionary Council after the 2011 uprisings.

58. Interview with Mohamed Tarnish, Head of the Libyan Organization for Human Rights, Tripoli, June 2010.

59. While it may have made a nice scene, this initiative was not all about human rights. On one level, it was about the regime's age-old obsession with security: neutralizing some of its fiercest foes was a way of banging the final nail into the coffin of movements like the LIFG. The initiative served other purposes, too. Despite Qaddafi's having more or less wiped out his Islamist foes at the end of the 1990s, the regime feared a new generation of militants, inspired by Al-Qa'ida, and driven by its culture of martyrdom. Reports were already emerging in the east of the country about small cells of young men so desperate that they had blown themselves up to evade capture by the security services. Then there were the large numbers of young Libyans who had gone to join the jihad in Iraq. Not that the regime had anything against their youth fighting it out against US and British forces, but, with the Afghanistan experience in mind, it feared what havoc those returning from the battlefields might wreak. While arresting

those suspected of militancy remained the policy of choice for the regime, it hoped that the revisions and the freed prisoners, who had a strong standing in the eastern regions, would help dissuade the younger generation from violence.

However, the scheme was also a golden opportunity for Saif Al-Islam to show the outside world just how much Libya had changed; aware of the growing interest in de-radicalization in the West, the young Qaddafi went out of his way to court publicity, producing glossy literature about the revisions and inviting Western journalists (from outlets such as CNN) to Libya to make glowing reports on the scheme. The initiative also afforded Saif Al-Islam some popular mileage at home. The young 'reformer' held a series of public seminars inside Libya, to which he invited famous popular theologians, including from Saudi Arabia. At these the LIFG leaders were put through the humiliation of having to laud the revisions and pay tribute to the regime for their release.

60. 'Interview with Abdelmoutleb Al-Houni', *Al-Majalla*, 19 July 2011, available at: http://www.majalla.com/arb/2011/07/article1867
61. Interview with Mohamed Belqassim Zwai, Tripoli, 2006.
62. 'Interview with Dr Yousif Sawani, Part 1', *Al-Sharq Al-Awsat*, 8 October 2011, available at: http://www.aawsat.com/details.asp?section=4&article=644004&issueno=12002
63. ibid.
64. ibid.
65. 'Ibn Al-Kaid Libyee yenshur majallat siasiya yetahadith aan hayat [Libyan leader's son to publish political magazine, speaks about his life]', *Al-Sharq Al-Awsat*, 16 July 2002.
66. 'Moqabala Hasa: Al-Saadi Qaddafi [Special Interview: Saadi Qaddafi]', Al-Arabiya Television, 8 March 2011, available at: http://www.alarabiya.net/programs/2011/03/08/140605.html
67. 'Interview with Dr Yousif Sawani, Part 3', *Al-Sharq Al-Awsat*, 10 October 2011, available at: http://www.aawsat.com/details.asp?section=4&issueno=12004&article=644297&search=[??163]%20[??163]&state=true
68. 'Said Saif Al-Islam Muammar Qaddafi: al-Ifraj Aan Al-Meghrahi Munasaba Tariqiya Fi Hayat al-Libeen [Mr Saif Al-Islam Muammar Qaddafi: The release of Al-Meghrahi is a historic occasion for the Libyans]', *Oea*, 22 August 2009, available in Arabic at: http://www.oealibya.com/front-page/local-news/5266-2009-08-22-00-46-36
69. Eliza Griswold, 'The heir', *New Republic*, 20 July 2010.
70. 'Mohamed Zaidan: Kadnahtaj Dictator Akhar [Mohamed Zaidan: We may need another dictator]', *Al-Majalla*, 25 August 2011, available at: http://www.majalla.com/arb/2011/08/article3475
71. Alison Pargeter, *Reforming Libya: Chimera or reality*, Mediterranean Paper Series, October 2010, available at: http://www.iai.it/pdf/mediterraneo/GMF-IAI/Mediterranean-paper_08.pdf
72. 'Thakara Siasia: Abdelrahman Shalgam [The Political Memoirs: Abdelrahman Shalgam]', Al-Arabiya Television, 28 October 2011, available at: http://www.alarabiya.net/programs/2011/10/28/174240.html
73. ibid.
74. 'Ghassan Sherbil interviews Abdelrahman Shalgam, Part 4', *Al-Hayat*, 19 July 2011, available at: http://international.daralhayat.com/internationalarticle/289450
75. ibid.

Chapter 8: A New Dawn

1. For example, the Kawarsha project in Hay Al-Fatah in Benghazi, which comprised some eight hundred housing units, was broken into and occupied. In Al-Medina Jadida, near Tajoura, a 10,000-unit project was occupied, despite the fact that the buildings were still under construction and did not have electricity or water supply. A 608-flat

project in Badia that was run by Aisha Qaddafi's Watassimu charity was also occupied, as was one of Saif Al-Islam's projects in Derna.

2. Menas Associates, *Libya Focus*, January 2011.
3. ibid.
4. Video of interview available at: http://www.youtube.com/watch?v=nNQLbGVOnY8
5. However, Saadi had made time before he was trapped to offer serious financial rewards to members of security brigades in the east, to convince them to remain loyal to the regime. See 'Suttat Al-Libyea Tusabak Al-Zaman Li Ijhad Ghadhab Al-Khamis Al-Muqabel [The Libyan authorities in a race against time to abort next Thursday's anger]', *Libyan Politician*, 14 February 2011 available at: http://lyrcc.wordpress.com/2011/02/14/news-295/
6. The regime also replaced some personnel, such as the highly unpopular dean of Gar Younis University, who was pushed out of his job and replaced by someone chosen by university staff and students. In addition, a number of laptop computers were finally distributed under Saif Al-Islam's 'one million laptops for one million children' scheme, and some imams who had been banned from preaching for defying the authorities were reinstated. However these gestures were mere drops in the ocean, and for a population saturated with endless promises of change further talk of reform was the last thing they wanted to hear.
7. 'Mokabala Hassa: Fathi Terbil [Special interview: Fathi Terbil]', Al-Arabiya Television, 2 March 2011, available at: http://www.alarabiya.net/programs/2011/03/02/139882.html
8. Quoted in Menas Associates.
9. 'Libya protests: gunshots, screams and talk of revolution', *Guardian*, 20 February 2011, available at: http://www.guardian.co.uk/world/2011/feb/20/libya-gunshots-screams-revolution
10. ibid.
11. 'Ghassan Sherbil interviews Abdelsalam Jalloud, Part 4', *Al-Hayat*, 1 November 2011, available at: http://international.daralhayat.com/internationalarticle/324507
12. Middle East Economic Digest (MEED), *Maghreb Quarterly Report*, 14 (June 1994).
13. Interview with Noman Bin Othman, London, October 2011.
14. ibid.
15. 'Interview with Dr Yousif Sawani, Part 3', *Al-Sharq Al-Awsat*, 10 October 2011, available at: http://www.aawsat.com/details.asp?section=4&issueno=12004&article=644297&search=[??164]%20[??164]&state=true. Saif Al-Islam took a notably different line from that of his father on Tunisia, going so far as to congratulate Sheikh Rashid Ghannouchi, the leader of Tunisia's main Islamist opposition party En-Nahda, which went on to win the first round of elections in October 2011.
16. Jalloud interview, Part 4.
17. 'Mohamed Rachid Wallaqatahu Be Saif Al-Islam [Mohamed Rachid and his relations to Saif Al-Islam]', Al-Jazeera, 13 August 2011, available at: http://www.aljazeera.net/NR/exeres/7A05CF50-5F88-400A-8777-89055969D077.htm
18. Sawani interview, Part 3.
19. 'Interview with Abdelmoutleb Al-Houni', *Al-Majalla*, 19 July 2011, available at: http://almajalla.net/?p=1867
20. 'Saif Al-Islam Gadaffi addresses the nation', Libyan TV, 20 February 2011, available at: http://www.youtube.com/watch?v=eL6I5hktEs0&feature=related
21. Sawani interview, Part 3.
22. It was also this speech that opened the way for his being wanted by the International Criminal Court, along with his father and Abdullah Sanussi.
23. Interview with Noman Bin Othman, London, October 2011.
24. Menas Associates, *Libya Focus*, March 2011.
25. Email correspondence with Tripoli resident, November 2011.

26. They included figures such as Fathi Al-Baja, a political science professor at Gar Younis University, known for writing bold and highly critical articles in the semi-independent press, and lawyer Abdelhafed Abdelkader Ghoga, head of the Libyan Bar Association. Fathi Terbil was given responsibility for youth affairs.

27. 'Libyan rebels hampered by lack of weapons', *Washington Post*, 15 July 2011, available at: http://www.washingtonpost.com/world/middle-east/libyan-rebels-hampered-by-lack-of-weapons/2011/07/14/gIQAHIymFI_story.html

28. ibid.

29. Quoted in Menas Associates, *Libya Focus*, March 2011.

30. Menas Associates, *Libya Focus*, April 2011.

31. On 22 May the European Union's foreign policy chief, Catherine Ashton, opened an EU diplomatic office in the Tibesti Hotel in Benghazi.

32. Menas Associates, *Libya Focus*, June 2011.

33. He also encouraged Libyans to support the independence of Scotland from the UK, as well as the return of the Italian islands of Lampedusa and Pantelleria to Tunisia, and of the Spanish enclaves of Ceuta and Melilla to Morocco.

34. 'In his last days, Qaddafi wearied of fugitive's life', *New York Times*, 22 October 2011, available at: http://www.nytimes.com/2011/10/23/world/africa/in-his-last-days-qaddafi-wearied-of-fugitives-life.html?_r=1&pagewanted=all

35. Khamis had been killed at some point during the conflict, and Saif Al-Arab is believed to have been killed in a NATO airstrike in May 2011.

36. 'In Bani Walid, Kadhafi loyalists thirst for revenge', AFP, 31 October 2011, available at: http://www.google.com/hostednews/afp/article/ALeqM5i5UHw1HgdTKTMEkytk bgA4qRGaVw?docId=CNG.5d524819c48d9e64a04a1dad0fe0e767.5d1

37. 'In his last days, Qaddafi wearied of fugitive's life', *New York Times*, 22 October 2011.

38. ibid.

39. ' "I killed Gaddafi", claims Libyan rebel as most graphic video yet of dictator being beaten emerges', *Daily Mail*, 25 October 2011, available at: http://www.dailymail.co.uk/news/article-2052816/Gaddafi-death-video-I-shot-killed-says-Libyan-rebel.html

40. 'Gaddafi website publishes "last will" of Libyan ex-leader', BBC News Africa, 23 October 2011, available at: http://www.bbc.co.uk/news/world-africa-15420848

41. 'Gaddafi to be buried in secret desert grave: NTC', Reuters, 24 October 2011, available at: http://www.reuters.com/article/2011/10/24/us-libya-idUSTRE79F1FK20111024

Conclusion

1. W. B. Yeats, 'The Second Coming'.

Bibliography

Ahmida, Ali Abdullatif, *Forgotten Voice: Power and agency in colonial and postcolonial Libya*, Routledge, Abingdon, 2005
—, *The Making of Modern Libya: State formation, colonization and resistance, 1830–1932*, State University of New York Press, New York, 1994
Amnesty International, 'Amnesty International Report 1996 – Libya', available at: http://www.unhcr.org/refworld/publisher,AMNESTY,,LBY,3ae6aa0654,0.html
Anderson, Lisa, 'Nineteenth-century reform in Ottoman Libya', *International Journal of Middle East Studies*, 16:3 (1984), pp. 325–48
— 'Qadhafi and his opposition', *Middle East Journal*, 40:2 (Spring 1986)
Ashton, J. and I. Ferguson, *Cover-up of Convenience: The hidden scandal of Lockerbie*, Mainstream Publishing, Edinburgh, 2001
Ben Halim, Mustafa Ahmed, *Libya: The years of hope*, AAS Media Publishers, London, 1995
Besikari, Senussi, 'Khazkhaza Alqat Ala'am [Privatization of the public sector]', *Iqlam online*, November–December 2006, available at: http://www.mafhoum.com/press10/291E14.htm
Bianco, Mirella, *Gadafi: Voice from the desert*, Longman, New York, 1975
Blundy, David and Andrew Lycett, *Qaddafi and the Libyan Revolution*, Weidenfeld and Nicolson, London, 1987
Boualesha, Faraj, 'Alla kableen wa jahween [To the tribalists and regionalists]', undated, available at: http://www.libyanfsl.com/%D9%85%D9%82%D8%A7%D9%84%D8%A7%D8%AA/tabid/59/newsid417/3179/mid/417/language/en-US/Default.aspx
Bowen, Wyn Q., *Libya and Nuclear Proliferation: Stepping back from the brink*, Adelphi Paper 380, Routledge, London, 2006
Bulugma, Hadi M., *Benghazi through the Ages*, unidentified publisher, 1972
Burget, Francois and William Dowell, *The Islamic Movement in North Africa*, Center for Middle Eastern Studies, University of Texas, Austin, 1983
Carey, Jane P. C. and Andrew G. Carey, 'Libya: No longer "Arid Nurse of Lions"', *Political Science Quarterly*, 76:1 (March 1961)
Cockerell, Michael, 'Lieutenant Gaddafi in Swinging London', *Standpoint*, January/February 2012, available at: http://www.standpointmag.co.uk/node/4254
Connor, William N., *The English at War*, London, Secker & Warburg, 1941

Cooley, John K., *Libyan Sandstorm: The complete account of Qaddafi's Sandstorm*, Sidgwick and Jackson, London, 1983

Davis, Deborah (Linda Berg) with Bill Davis, *The Children of God: The inside story by the daughter of the founder, Moses David Berg*, Part 1, Chapter 9, 1984, available at: http://www.exfamily.org/art/exmem/debdavis/debdavis09.shtml

Dawood, N.J. (trans.), *The Koran*, Penguin, Harmondsworth, 1968

Al-Deeb, Fathi, *Abdul Nasser Wal Thawrat Libya* [Abdul Nasser and the Libyan Revolution], Dar Al-Mostaqbel Al-Arabi, Cairo, 1986

Education Division of the Leader's Comrades Forum, *Al-Qaddafi and the 4000-Day Journey of Secret Work*, unknown publisher, Benghazi, undated

El Fathaly, Omar I. and Monte Palmer, *Political Development and Social Change in Libya*, Lexington Books, Massachusetts, 1980

European Commission DG Trade, *Trade Sustainability Impact Assessment (SIA) of the EU-Libya Free Trade Agreement. Inception Report*, February 2009, available at: http://trade.ec.europa.eu/doclib/docs/2009/april/tradoc_142928.pdf

Evans-Pritchard, Edward E., *The Sanusi of Cyrenaica*, Oxford University Press, Oxford, 1954

Al-Fadhli, Fathi, *A Book of the Chad War ... Disaster ... Disaster*, available in Arabic at: http://www.fathifadhli.com/art81.htm

—, 'Harkat Masjid Alkasser, 2 [Movement of Alkasser Mosque, 2]', undated, available at: http://www.libya-nclo.com

Al-Fazzan, Ali, 'Qaddafi ... Wa Alkhiar Shemshoni, 2 [Qaddafi and Samson Choice, 2]', available at: http://www.libya-watanona.com/adab/aalfazzani/af110310a.htm

First, Ruth, *Libya: The elusive revolution*, Penguin Books, Harmondsworth, 1974

Gadaffi, Muammar, *Escape to Hell and Other Stories*, Blake, London, 1999

Herodotus, *The Histories*, Book Four, Oxford University Press, Oxford, 2008

Joffe, George, 'Qadhafi's Islam in local historical perspective' in Dirk Vandewalle (ed.), *Qadhafi's Libya, 1969–1994*, St Martin's Press, New York, 1995

Kirkbride, Alec, 'Libya – which way facing?', *African Affairs*, 56:22 (1957), pp. 49–55

Al-Magarief, Mohamed, 'Al-Qadhafi Wal Lijan Al-Thawria ... Al-Asl Wa Sura [Qaddafi and the Revolutionary Committees ... Their Origin and their Image]', Libya Watanona Website, undated, available at http://www.libya-watanona.com/adab/mugariaf/mm210210a.htm

— 'Inqilab Biqiyadat Mukbur [Coup led by an informant]', 12 August 2008, available in Arabic at: http://www.libya-watanona.com/adab/mugariaf/mm12088a.htm

— *Libya Bayn Al-Madi Wal-Hadir: Safahat min Al-Tarikh Al-Siyasi* [Libya Past and Present: Chapters in political history], Part 1, Volume 1, Centre for Libyan Studies, Oxford, 2004

— 'Safahat min Tariq al-nidham al-inquilabi fi Libya [Pages from the history of the coup regime in Libya]', Libya Watanona Website, undated, available at: http://www.libya-watanona.com/adab/mugariaf/mm121010a.htm

Mahroug, Moncef, 'La vie au temps de l'embargo', *Jeune Afrique*, 1840 (10–16 April 1996)

Mattes, Hanspeter, 'The rise and fall of the revolutionary committees' in Dirk Vandewalle (ed.), *Qadhafi's Libya, 1969–1994*, St Martin's Press, New York, 1995

Melman, Yossi, *The Master Terrorist: The true story behind Abu Nidal*, Mama Books, New York, 1986

Mogherbi, M. Z. *Itijihad wa tatourat turkeybat an noghra al-siasiya fi Libya 1969–1999* [The Orientation and Development of the Political Elite in Libya], Gar Younis University, undated

Al-Mukhtar, Bint, 'Awraq Fatat Libeeya [Journal of a Libyan Girl]', Libyan Documentation Centre, available at: http://www.libya-watanona.com/news/ldc/ld250510a.htm

Niblock, Tim, *'Pariah States' and Sanctions in the Middle East*, Lynne Rienner, London, 2001

Pargeter, Alison, 'Anglo-Libyan relations and the Suez Crisis', *Journal of North African Studies*, 5:2 (Summer 2000)

— 'Libya and the Islamist opposition' in Dirk Vandewalle, *Libya Since 1969: Libya's revolution revisited*, Palgrave Macmillan, Basingstoke, 2008

— *Reforming Libya: Chimera or Reality*, Mediterranean Paper Series, October 2010, available at: http://www.iai.it/pdf/mediterraneo/GMF-IAI/Mediterranean-paper_08.pdf

Peniakoff, Vladimir, *Popski's Private Army*, Jonathan Cape, London, 1950

Piccioli, Angelo, *The Magic Gate of the Sahara*, Dar Al-Fergani, Tripoli, undated

Al-Qaddafi, Muammar, *Qassat Al-thawra fi libya ... Asa'at Al-Ikhira* [The Story of the Revolution in Libya ... The Last Hours], undated, formerly available in Arabic at: http://www.wata.cc/forums/showthread.php?t=48343 (accessed March 2009)

— *The Green Book*, World Centre for the Study and Research of the Green Book, Tripoli, 1984

— *The Village ... The Village ... The Earth ... The Earth and the Suicide of the Astronaut*, Ad-Dar Jamahiriya, Sirte, 1996

St John, Ronald Bruce, *Libya and the United States: Two centuries of strife*, University of Pennsylvania Press, Philadelphia, 2002

— 'Libya is not Iraq: Preemptive strikes, WMD and diplomacy', *Middle East Journal*, 53:3 (Summer 2004), pp. 386–402

Sandford, K. S., Lord Tweedsmuir, W. B. Fisher, H. J. Fleure, L. M. Kiral, St John Cook, A. M. Frood, 'Problems of Modern Libya: Discussion', *Geographical Journal*, 119:2 (June 1953)

Shamis, Ashur, 'Gaddafi and me', *Critical Muslim*, 1 (2011)

Smith, Ivan George, *The Ghosts of Kampala: The rise and fall of Idi Amin*, Weidenfeld and Nicolson, London, 1980

Stark, Freya, *The Coast of Incense*, John Murray, London, 1953

Al-Tilisi, Khalifa Mohamed, *Ma'ajam Sukan Libya* [Encyclopaedia of Libya's Population], Dar Al-Raban, Libya, 1991

Titley, Brian, *Dark Age: The political odyssey of Emperor Bokassa*, McGill-Queen's University Press, Montreal, 2002

Vandewalle, Dirk, *A History of Modern Libya*, Cambridge University Press, New York, 2006

— *Libya since Independence: Oil and state building*, I.B. Tauris, London, 1998

— 'The institutional restraints of reform in Libya: From Jamahiriyah to constitutional republic?', paper prepared for the Oxford Conference, 25–27 September 2009

Vorst, Milton, 'The colonel in his labyrinth', *Foreign Affairs*, March/April (1999)

Wright, Claudia, 'Libya's foreign strategy', *New Statesman*, 21 August 1981

Wright, John, *Libya: A modern history*, Croom Helm, London and Canberra, 1981

Zoubir, Yahia H., 'Libya in US foreign policy: From rogue state to good fellow?', *Third World Quarterly*, 23:1 (2002)

Index